Study Guide to Accompany

THE LEGAL, ETHICAL AND REGULATORY ENVIRONMENT OF BUSINESS

FOURTH EDITION

D1482504

BRUCE D. FISHER
University of Tennessee

MICHAEL J. PHILLIPS
Indiana University, Bloomington

Prepared by
JOHN P. GEARY
Appalachian State University

West Publishing Company
St. Paul   New York   Los Angeles   San Francisco

Contents

Preface

This Study Guide represents a concentrated effort to assist you in comprehending the relationship of law and business developed in <u>The Legal, Ethical and Regulatory Environment of Business</u>, Fourth Edition, by Bruce D. Fisher and Michael J. Phillips.

Many students experience some bewilderment when first exposed to legal subject matter. This reaction is quite normal since many of you have never had any formal exposure to the legal system and the areas of law that comprise the legal environment of business. This Study Guide should help you in bringing order out of this initial confusion and provide a framework for structuring your efforts and energy. Your text is the primary source and it is assumed that you will read, study and become quite familiar with the materials contained therein.

You will find the following contained in this Study Guide:

1. Chapter Summary - Detailed and comprehensive review of legal rules and concepts presented in the respective chapters of the text.

2. Review Questions

   A. True-False - Provides a rapid self-test of terms and selected concepts from the text.

   B. Multiple Choice - A self-test of concepts, terms and selected statutes that vary in the degree of difficulty.

   C. Short Answer - Specially formulated to test your understanding of major rules, concepts and laws as set out and discussed in the text.

3. Answers to Review Questions - Answers for True/False, Multiple Choice and Short Answer questions are provided for quick reference.

4. Key Terms - Terms and selected concepts defined as they appear in each chapter of the text.

I want to thank my wife, Judith Geary, for her strong support and assistance in this project. Our children; Michael, James and Katherine should be mentioned since they had to contend with the unusual hours and pace that accompany a project of this type. A special note of thanks and appreciation to my typist, Mrs. Deborah Culler. Finally, I want to thank legal environment students for their interest, perseverance and good humor in approaching this interesting and important subject matter.

John P. Geary

LAW: LEGAL AND BUSINESS ETHICS

Chapter Summary

Ethics is what is right or good conduct in a set of circumstances. Most situations do offer individuals several choices of conduct. The prevailing view is that compliance with all forms of law constitutes ethical conduct. This emphasis on authority and sanction is the ethic known as positive law. Constitutional positive law is the ethic of our time. The difference in the two concepts is that constitutional positive law contains a moral element. An example of this morality characteristic is the U.S. Constitution's Bill of Rights.

There are other ethics or values that influence and challenge positive law.

1. The justice ethic defines law in terms of what is fair and just (natural law school). Professor Lon Fuller maintains that there is internal morality to positive law if certain tests are met. John Rawls, "the original position," and Immanuel Kant, the "categorical imperative," have made significant contributions to the natural law school. See <u>Ott</u> v. <u>Midland-Ross Corporation</u>, 523 F.2d 1367 (1975). Midland-Ross was not allowed to profit from its wrongdoing. The U.S. Court of Appeals exercised the estoppel principle to obtain a just and fair result.

2. The power ethic emphasizes strength and might. This is essential to positive law since a political superior must exist to apply sanctions. Advantages are order and stability; the disadvantage is abuse.

3. The custom ethic refers to the historical conduct of people. Positive law reflects these customs and traditions. The ethic of custom is deeply embedded in commercial law. Courts dislike to overturn

1

longstanding commercial rules and regulations. See <u>Geary</u> v. <u>U.S. Steel Corporation</u>, 319A.2d 174 (1974). The Pennsylvania Supreme Court refused to find an exception to the long-standing doctrine of employment at will. The court noted that the company had a legitimate interest in preserving internal order regardless of public policy considerations.

4. The norms of conduct ethic is similar to the custom ethic except the traditions are not as long-standing. An example would be norms or conduct accepted in a group.

5. The ethic of civilization influences positive law. Civilization in conjunction with legal rules attempts to prohibit certain types of harmful conduct. See <u>Reginia</u> v. <u>Dudley and Stephens</u>, L.R., Q.B. 61 (1884). The killing of a young boy in a life raft so that others may live is murder, not necessity. The court reasoned that separating law and morality in this case would be a mistake.

6. The ethic of realism emphasizes how law is applied. It takes into account the human factor in applying or not applying the rules of positive law. See <u>Delaware Tire Center</u> v. <u>Fox</u>, 411 A.2d 606 (1980). The Delaware Supreme Court decided a husband's suicide was job related and not willful.

7. The ethic of utilitarianism promotes the greatest good for the greatest number. This involves balancing alternatives to determine which produces the greatest good. In positive law it requires the choice of rules for the conduct of society. See <u>In the Matter of Baby M</u>, 537 A.2d 1227 (1988). The court invalidated a surrogacy contract involving a newborn because it violated the law and public policy of the state. The contract is degrading to women and illegal.

If other legal values and positive law obtain the same result, ethical unity is obtained. Positive law is society's ethical floor. Other legal ethics should not be used to justify conduct below this floor, but may be used to raise conduct. Positive law and legal ethics must be flexible to reflect changes in a society.

Business ethics are reflected in actions rather than words. The legal ethic of positive law is the ethical floor for business. This is not always the case, as pointed out in the Beech-Nut example.

Some objectives of the law are justice, speed, economy, flexibility, and knowability and stability.

Review Questions

True/False

_____ 1.   Jurisprudence deals with defining laws and values.

_____ 2.   Positive law includes sanctions for breaking the law.

_____ 3.   A corporate president makes positive law when issuing a procedural rule.

____ 4.   Natural law theorists define law in terms of balancing claims.

____ 5.   Equity courts show how the justice ethic influences positive law.

____ 6.   One of the disadvantages of the norm of conduct ethic is that conduct can be undesirable.

____ 7.   It has been observed that the ethic of civilization relates to the law because it frustrates instincts such as the desire to lie, cheat, and steal.

____ 8.   The concept of the regulation of private business interests is an application of the ethic of civilization.

____ 9.   The reality ethic reflects the fact that judges and juries do not always follow positive law.

____ 10.   Making a profit is one way that business can participate in ethical behavior.

Multiple Choice -- Please circle the best answer

1.   Positive law refers to
      a.   a private rule.
      b.   a public rule.
      c.   a government rule.
      d.   no rule.

2.   A weakness of positive law is
      a.   vagueness.
      b.   injustice.
      c.   lack of authority
      d.   a. and b.

3.   The natural law school defines law in terms of
      a.   custom.
      b.   justice.
      c.   history.
      d.   tradition.

4.   The reality ethic places great emphasis on
      a.   conflict of values.
      b.   history and tradition.
      c.   legal application.
      d.   rules and regulations.

5.   Society's ethical floor is
     a.   positive law.
     b.   natural law.
     c.   law enforcement.
     d.   history and tradition.

6.   Ethics refers to
     a.   right and wrong conduct.
     b.   classes of moral values.
     c.   choices in a given situation
     d.   all of the above.

7.   The statement, "If I obey the law, I am ethical" reflects what legal ethic?
     a.   positive law ethic.
     b.   justice ethic.
     c.   utility ethic.
     d.   reality law ethic.

8.   One disadvantage of the justice ethic is (the)
     a.   due process.
     b.   multiple-conscience problem.
     c.   equity courts.
     d.   punishment.

9.   According to Professor Lon Fuller, there is internal morality to positive law if
     a.   rules exist.
     b.   the rules are clear.
     c.   there is congruence between official conduct and rules.
     d.   all of the above.

10.   The power ethic maintains that
     a.   might does not make right.
     b.   a superior does not exist.
     c.   might makes right.
     d.   power is not essential.

11.   An advantage of the power ethic is
     a.   due process.
     b.   order.
     c.   abuse.
     d.   discrimination.

12.   The custom ethic refers to
     a.   long-standing conduct.

b.   individuals.
c.   short term conduct.
d.   prejudicial conduct.

13.   A form of utilitarian reasoning is
a.   congruence.
b.   power.
c.   balancing.
d.   disunity.

14.   One criticism of utilitarianism is
a.   that the decision maker has no power.
b.   that it lacks competing claims.
c.   that judges must enforce the rules.
d.   that it is amoral if not immoral.

15.   Reasons for studying law include
a.   knowledge.
b.   legalization.
c.   preventive law.
d.   all of the above.

Short Answer

1.   List the three requirements of positive law.

a.   _____

b.   _____

c.   _____

2.   List five theories of legal ethics discussed in this chapter.

a.   _____

b.   _____

c.   _____

d.   _____

e.   _____

3.   Why is the prohibition against murder an example of ethical unity?

_____

_____

_____

4.   "An unjust law is not law and should not be obeyed," is a statement reflecting which legal ethic.

_____

5.   List five positive ethical values that business can accomplish.

a.   _____

b.   _____

c.   _____

d.   _____

e.   _____

6.   Name the six objectives of law discussed in this chapter.

a.   _____

b.   _____

c.   _____

d.   _____

e.   _____

f.   _____

7.   Give three reasons why business students in particular should study law.

a.   _____

b.   _____

c. _____

8.   Explain the difference between norms and customs.

_____

_____

_____

9.   A jury decision that ignores existing law is an example of the influence of which ethic?

_____

10.   Explain the interaction of the positive law ethic and the reality ethic.

_____

_____

_____

Answers to Review Questions

True/False

1. T   6. T
2. T   7. T
3. F   8. T
4. F   9. T
5. T   10. T

Multiple Choice

1. c.   2. d.   3. b.   4. c.   5. a.   6. d.   7. a.
8. b.   9. d.   10. c.   11. b.   12. b.   13. c.   14. d.
15. d.

Short Answer

1.   a.   rule
      b.   form political superior to political inferior

       c.   sanctions if rule is broken

2.   a.   natural law (justice ethic)
       b.   custom ethic
       c.   norms of conduct ethic
       d.   civilization ethic
       e.   reality ethic

3.   It is just and represents longstanding custom. It is contrary to society's accepted norm of conduct, promotes civilization, and juries follow the law in murder cases--so positive law and realism do not conflict.

4.   justice ethic (natural law)

5.   a.   making a profit
       b.   delivering the best products and services
       c.   providing jobs
       d.   giving stockholders a good return on their investment
       e.   civic behavior

6.   a.   justice   d.   flexibility
       b.   speed   e.   stability
       c.   economy f.   knowability

7.   a.   Business persons need to know about legal system's mandates.
       b.   Business environment is becoming increasingly legalistic.
       c.   In order to practice preventive law, some knowledge of the law is required.

8.   They are similar except norms are not as longstanding as customs.

9.   reality ethic

10.   Some circumstances may justify not following positive law (see, e.g., <u>Delaware Tire</u>). On the other hand, with the reality ethic, prejudice may enter into the decision-making process in legal proceedings rather than a purely objective application of positive law.

Key Terms

<u>ethics</u>: right or good conduct in a given set of circumstances.

<u>positive law</u>: a rule from a political superior to a political inferior with sanctions for disobeying.

<u>jurisprudence</u>: "juris" = law; "prudence" = wisdom; study of defining law and values.

<u>natural law</u>: defines law in terms of justice and fairness.

<u>equity courts</u>: courts that originated in England as a reaction to the inflexibility of the law courts.

<u>custom ethic</u>: law that reflects longstanding custom and tradition.

<u>power ethic</u>: the will of the stronger.

<u>norms of conduct ethic</u>: law to create a civilized society.

<u>civilization ethic</u>: law to create a civilized society.

<u>utility ethic</u>: the greatest good for the greatest number.

CHAPTER 2

OVERVIEW AND FINDING LAW

Chapter Summary

Some of the most common forms of law are constitutions, statutes, federal regulations and ordinances.

1. Constitution - sets out the form and basic principles by which the government will operate.

2. Statutes - enactments by national and state legislatures. Ordinances are laws passed by city governments.

3. Federal Administrative Regulations - rules made by federal administrative agencies. Model uniform statutes have been adopted by many state legislatures.

Law can be classified in a number of ways.

1. Substantive law governs what people can do in society.

2. Procedural law are rules of legal administration.

3. Civil law governs the rights and duties between private individuals.

4. Criminal law consists of rules designed to protect society's interest with respect to individuals.

There are several differences between civil and criminal law. Civil Law is compensatory whereas criminal law in punitive. Compensatory and punitive damages may be awarded in a civil case. Punitive damages are designed to punish wrongdoers if the defendant's conduct is particularly reprehensible. See <u>Browning-Ferris Industries</u> v. <u>Kelco Disposal, Inc.</u>, 109 S.Ct. 3909 (1989). The Federal District Court awarded the plaintiff Kelco $6,066,082.74 in compensatory and punitive damages on a state-law claim. The Supreme Court held that the Eighth Amendment's Excessive Fines clause does not limit punitive damage awards between private parties in civil cases.

Nominal damages may be awarded when the plaintiff has suffered no actual damages. In addition to damage awards, the equitable remedies of specific performance and injunctions are available in specific cases.

The objectives of the criminal law are retribution, restraint, deterrence and rehabilitation. The plaintiff in a criminal case is a government represented by a prosecutor or district attorney. The burden of proof in a criminal case is beyond a reasonable doubt. The standard is lower in a civil case, by a preponderance of the evidence. Criminal and civil law may overlap, such as in drunk driving and Section 1 Sherman Act cases.

There are many sources where law may be found.

1. U.S. Code - contains federal statutes, the annotated version contains case interpretations.

2. State Code - contains state statutes, can come in annotated versions.

3. Code of Federal Regulations - regulations issued by federal regulatory agencies. When a regulation is first issued by an agency it is published in the Federal Register.

4. Common law or judge made law is found in written opinions of judges pursuant to settling a dispute. Federal and state appellant courts issue written opinions. Reporters (books) contains these written opinions.

5. Data bases now exist to assist in legal research (West Law and Lexis).

A judicial opinion or case can contain many issues, legal and factual. Cases are briefed in order to analyze them. A student analyzes a case by dividing it into five parts.

1. Case style

2. Facts

3. Legal issue

4. Holding, a yes or no answer

5. Reason for the holding

Review Questions

True/False

____ 1.   Substantive law provides the rules for legal administration.

____ 2.   Criminal law is concerned with the wrongs committed against society.

____ 3.   Constitutions at the state and federal levels create the branches of government and provide individual protections.

____ 4.   Statutes and ordinances are enactments of legislative bodies.

____ 5.   The United States Code Annotated contains federal legislative enactments along with the U.S. Constitution.

____ 6.   The Code of Federal Regulations contains federal legislative enactments along with the U.S. Constitution.

____ 7.   Grouping of codes by subject matter is accomplished through the use of sections.

____ 8.   A subject matter index is available for each code.

____ 9.   The Federal Reporter contains the opinions of the Federal District Courts.

____ 10.   Dicta refers to the holding in a case.

Multiple Choice -- Please circle the best answer.

1.   The statute of limitations is an example of
     a.   substantive law.
     b.   procedural law.
     c.   constitutional law.
     d.   criminal law.

2.   Punitive damages are designed to
     a.   compensate injured parties.
     b.   punish injured parties.
     c.   punish wrongdoers.
     d.   enhance criminal law.

3.   Courts of equity have jurisdiction to settle cases
   a.   when there is no adequate remedy at law.
   b.   when there is an adequate remedy at law.
   c.   when the parties do not settle their dispute.
   d.   when the law courts permit jurisdiction.

4.   In a civil trial, the plaintiff must prove the case
   a.   beyond a reasonable doubt.
   b.   to a moral certainty.
   c.   by a minority of the evidence.
   d.   by a preponderance of the evidence.

5.   Regulations first issued by an administrative agency can be found in the
   a.   U.S. Code.
   b.   General Statutes.
   c.   Code of Federal Regulations.
   d.   Federal Register.

6.   A court which would issue a written opinion is the
   a.   federal district court.
   b.   small claims court.
   c.   probate court.
   d.   trial court.

7.   Common law is
   a.   judge made law.
   b.   case law.
   c.   statutory law.
   d.   a. and b.

8.   The skeleton for a legal system is
   a.   federal regulation.
   b.   constitution.
   c.   statute.
   d.   code.

9.   Enactments by national or state legislatures is called a (an)
   a.   constitution.
   b.   regulation.
   c.   statute.
   d.   ordinance.

10.   The most significant model statute that has been passed is the
   a.   Uniform Partnership Act.

b.   Uniform Bills of Lading Act.
c.   Uniform Banking Act.
d.   Uniform Commercial Code.

11. Civil law refers to
a.   rights and duties of private individuals.
b.   rights and duties of the several states.
c.   rights and duties between a state and individual.
d.   rights and duties of a state and national government.

12. Damages that indicate little or no loss are called
a.   compensatory damages.
b.   punitive damages.
c.   nominal damages.
d.   negative damages.

13. A law that has not been passed by a state legislature is a
a.   statute.
b.   bill.
c.   regulation.
d.   code.

14. U.S. Supreme Court decisions are reported in the
a.   United States Reports.
b.   Supreme Court Reporter.
c.   Federal Register.
d.   a. and b.

15. A set of books that cover the different states' appellate courts
a.   reporter.
b.   code.
c.   Lexis.
d.   C. F. R.

Short Answer

1. In 383 U.S. 44, what does the 383 represent?

_____

The 44? _____

2. List five forms of law.

    a. _____

    b. _____

    c. _____

    d. _____

    e. _____

3.   List two sources for finding administrative regulations.

    a. _____

    b. _____

4.   List three sets of reporters where United States Supreme Court opinions can be found.

    a. _____

    b. _____

    c. _____

5.   Name and define two equitable remedies.

    a. _____

      _____

    b. _____

      _____

6.   Name the five parts of a case brief.

    a. _____

    b. _____

    c. _____

    d. _____

e. _____

7.   Remarks made by a judge in an opinion that are not essential to the resolution of a case are called:

_____

8.   List three differences between civil and criminal law.

a. _____

b. _____

c. _____

9.   List three types of damages available in a civil case.

a. _____

b. _____

c. _____

10. Name three branches of civil law.

a. _____

b. _____

c. _____

Answers to Review Questions

True/False

1.	F	6.	F
2.	T	7.	F
3.	T	8.	T
4.	T	9.	F
5.	T	10.	F

Multiple Choice

1.	b.	3.	a.	5.	d.	7.	d.	9.	c.	11.	a.
2.	c.	4.	d.	6.	a.	8.	b.	10.	d.	12.	c.
13.	b.	14.	d.	15.	a.						

Short Answer

1.   383 = volume, 44 = page

2.   a.   U.S. Constitution
     b.   state constitution
     c.   federal statutes
     d.   state statutes
     e.   municipal ordinances
     f.   federal administrative regulations
     g.   state administrative regulations
     h.   case law

3.   a.   Code of Federal Regulations
     b.   Federal Register

4.   a.   U.S. Reports
     b.   Supreme Court Reporter
     c.   Lawyer's Edition

5.   a.   injunction: order of a court to do or not do an act.
     b.   specific performance: a court order to perform what one has agreed by contract to do.

6.   a.   style
     b.   case facts
     c.   issue
     d.   holding
     e.   rationale

7.   dicta

8.   a.   civil law is compensatory; criminal law is punitive.
     b.   different plaintiffs: civil--individual; criminal--government
     c.   burdens of proof are different: civil--preponderance; criminal--reasonable doubt

9.   a.   compensatory
     b.   nominal
     c.   punitive

10.   a.   tort
      b.   insurance contract
      c.   property
           (or, any listed in Diagram 2.2)

Key Terms

constitution: supreme law of the area governed.

statute: written law enacted by a state or national legislature (usually at the state level.)

ordinances: written law passed by legislative bodies at the county or town level.

federal administrative regulations: rules made by federal administrative agencies.

executive orders: rules made by the President to interpret federal law.

procedural law: rules of legal administration.

substantive law: rules of law that govern the outcome of a case.

civil law: rights among private individuals.

criminal law: protection and vindication of society's interest.

compensatory damages: damages sustained as a result of the defendants wrong (civil.)

punitive damages: damages awarded in civil cases where defendant's conduct is reprehensible. (Can be awarded in addition to compensatory damages.)

tort: civil wrong committed against another.

nominal damages: nominal award for a wrong committed without actual harm.

equitable remedies: those afforded by a court of equity; injunctions; specific performance.

specific performance: remedy for obtaining actual performance under a contract.

injunctions: orders of equity courts stopping or ordering certain conduct.

retribution: one objective of the criminal law, imprisonment and fines.

restraint: conviction and imprisonment of criminals to prevent crime.

deterrence: imposing penalties that inhibit individuals from committing crimes.

rehabilitation: assisting convicted criminal through training to resist social pressures to commit crimes.

recidivism: tendency to relapse into criminal activity.

prosecutor: attorney representing governmental body in criminal prosecutions.

preponderance of the evidence: civil standard by which the plaintiff must prove a case.

beyond a reasonable doubt: criminal standard by which the government must prove a case.

bill: a proposed statute.

codes: law books containing public statutes or ordinances (state or federal.)

unannotated: adjective describing volumes containing only the language of a statute or ordinance.

annotated: adjective describing volumes containing the language of a statute or ordinance and summaries of related decisions and case interpretations.

Code of Federal Regulations (CFR): law books containing federal administrative regulations.

Federal Register: daily publication announcing proposed and recently adopted administrative regulations.

common law: law made by judges in deciding lawsuits.

opinions: written decisions of judges.

Reporters: set of books compiling court opinions.

brief: analysis of a case; facts, issue, holding, rationale.

case style: the parties suing, case cite and date of decision.

dicta (obiter dicta): remarks not essential to the case.

CHAPTER 3

SOURCES OF LAW: POLITICAL AND INSTITUTIONAL

Chapter Summary

This chapter discusses sources of law from a political and institutional perspective.

Political sources of law refer to the number of people who make law.

1. Monarchy is government by one person. This is an efficient system but limits are placed on personal rights and freedoms.

2. Oligarchy is government by a small group that lends continuity to the law making process.

3. Democracy is government by the governed. An effective democracy requires an educated population (body politic).

4. Anarchy exists when there is no legal authority (state of nature).

When individuals create a government a social contract is formed represented by a constitution. The U.S. has followed the Lockean idea of limited government. Federalism is an example of limited government and means that law making authority is divided between national and state government (dual sovereigns) in domestic matters.

Institutional sources of law refer to governmental bodies empowered to make law, such as courts and legislatures. Courts are a major source of law in our system. The U.S. has two court systems:

federal and state. State court systems vary from state to state. Lesser state courts (county, municipal, probate) are generally not courts of record. The basic trial level court is the superior or circuit court. The proceedings are recorded and civil and criminal cases can be heard before a jury. Appellate courts hear appeals from these lower courts when one party believes a legal error has been made. There are not witnesses or jurors in an appellate proceeding, only attorneys appear.

What happens if people take their cases to the wrong court? The case is dismissed for lack of jurisdiction. Jurisdiction has several aspects.

1. Subject matter jurisdiction refers to the court's power to hear a certain type of case. Some courts have limited subject matter jurisdiction (probate court).

2. In rem jurisdiction refers to the court's power over things. An Indiana court could hear a foreclosure action on property located in that state.

3. In personam jurisdiction refers to power over a person. This is based on the following: physical presence, state citizenship, consent, sufficient contacts with the state and commission of a tort within that state.

4. Quasi in rem jurisdiction refers to the court's power over things because an individual owns land or objects in the state. See Sofie v. Fibreboard Corp., 771 P 2d 711 (Wash. 1989). A state statute placed a limit on non-economic damages recoverable in a personal injury or wrongful death action. The jury returned a verdict of $1,154,592.00 in non-economic damages (pain and suffering and loss of consortium). This was reduced to $125,136.45 because of the prevailing statute. The Supreme Court of Washington ruled the statute unconstitutional. Awarding damages is within the province of the jury, hence the statute violates a right to a trial by jury.

Federal District courts are where most federal law suits begin and a jury trial is available. Their jurisdiction is limited to diversity and federal question cases. The U.S. Court of Appeals hears appeals from the District court and other special federal courts and administrative agencies. The U.S. Supreme Court consists of a Chief Justice and eight associate justices. Its authority to review cases comes from the U.S. Constitution and congressional statutes. The decision as to where to litigate in a Federal District Court, see Erie Railroad Co. v. Tompkins, 304 U.S. 64 (1938). Federal judges must follow state law when deciding diversity cases and a reserved power matters.

Legislatures are public bodies of elected officials who make law (congress - state legislatures). Most federal legislation begins as a bill and becomes an act or session law if passed by both houses and signed by the President. A joint resolution is similar to a bill. A concurrent resolution is usually not a law but deals with the operation of Congress. The courts act as gap fillers and interpret statutes. A number of rules of statutory construction have been developed by the courts such as giving words their ordinary meaning and examining legislative intent if the statute is unclear.

The differences in courts and legislatures are:

1. form - case law or statute

2. commutative vs. distribute justice

3. passive vs. self-animating law makers

4. greater procedural due process in courts

5. courts face legal issues - legislatures political issues.

Review Questions

True/False

____ 1.   An oligarchy is similar to a democracy.

____ 2.   The Hobbesian compact emphasizes individual rights.

____ 3.   The basic trial level courts in state court systems are courts of record.

____ 4.   Federalism means that lawmaking authority is divided between the federal government and the states

____ 5.   It is possible for a decision of the highest court in a state to be appealed to the U.S. Supreme Court.

____ 6.   Witnesses are generally called at the appellate level.

____ 7.   In rem jurisdiction is jurisdiction over the person.

____ 8.   Federal District Court is the general trial court in the federal system.

____ 9.   The Tenth Amendment permits states to form their own court system.

____ 10.   A concurrent resolution is a bill that becomes law after efforts from both houses of Congress.

Multiple Choice -- Please circle the best answer.

1.   In a democracy
    a.   no one makes legal rules.
    b.   a small group makes legal rules.

   c.   the ruled make the rules.
   d.   the person makes the rules.

2.   The document that comes closest to representing the social compact is
   a.   the U.S. Code.
   b.   the U.S. Constitution.
   c.   the Federal Register.
   d.   the body politic.

3.   Federalism means that law making authority is
   a.   divided between dual soverigns.
   b.   vested in the U.S. Government.
   c.   reserved to the states.
   d.   found in the enumerated powers.

4.   A court where a case begins is called a
   a.   court of secondary jurisdiction.
   b.   domestic relations court.
   c.   superior court.
   d.   court of original jurisdiction.

5.   Subject matter jurisdiction refers to the
   a.   court's power over things.
   b.   court's power over persons.
   c.   court's power over property.
   d.   court's power over the lawsuit.

6.   The court where a jury trial is available in the federal system is the
   a.   Federal District Court.
   b.   U.S. Courts of Appeals.
   c.   U.S. Claims Court.
   d.   Supreme Court.

7.   A federal judge hearing a diversity case involving a tort action would apply
   a.   federal law.
   b.   common law.
   c.   state law.
   d.   administrative law.

8.   The court that would hear an appeal challenging an administrative agency regulation is the
   a.   Federal District Court.
   b.   U.S. Court of Appeals.
   c.   U.S. Claims Court.
   d.   Supreme Court.

9.   A proposed statute is called a
      a.   resolution.
      b.   bill.
      c.   complaint.
      d.   principle.

10.   Revenue raising legislation must originate in the
      a.   House of Representatives.
      b.   U.S. Senate.
      c.   Office of the President.
      d.   U.S. Treasury.

Short Answer

1.   A Nevada resident is injured in a plane crash occurring in Pennsylvania while traveling on an airplane owned and operated by an airline incorporated in Delaware. The Nevada resident has well over $55,000 in medical expenses. The airline does business in Delaware, Pennsylvania, Massachusetts, New York, Virginia, West Virginia and New Jersey.

      a.   Which court will have subject matter jurisdiction? _____

      _____

      b.   Which law will apply? _____

      _____

      c.   Which court will have personam jurisdiction? _____

      _____

2.   List three different bases for personal jurisdiction (in personam.)

      a.   _____

      b.   _____

      c.   _____

3.   How many judges will generally hear a case at the court of appeals level?

      _____

4.   Name the federal court that will hear a dispute involving the classification of imported goods.

_____

5.   Name the three types of jurisdiction a court can have in terms of parties and things.

    a.   _____

    b.   _____

    c.   _____

6.   List the sections in the Constitution where the following are covered:

    a.   the U.S. Supreme Court _____

    b.   reservation of powers to the states _____

7.   List the two types of cases over which the federal district court has jurisdiction.

    a.   _____

    b.   _____

8.   List the forms a Congressional legislative proposal can take.

    _____

    _____

9.   List two different ways a representative democracy can create problems in a governmental system.

    a.   _____

    _____

    b.   _____

    _____

10.   List three differences between courts and legislatures.

    a.   _____

    _____

b. _____

_____

c. _____

_____

Answers to Review Questions

True/False

1.	F	3.	T	5.	T	7.	F	9.	T
2.	F	4.	T	6.	F	8.	T	10.	F

Multiple Choice

1.	c.	3.	a.	5.	d.	7.	c.	9.	b.
2.	b.	4.	d.	6.	a.	8.	b.	10.	a.

Short Answer

1. a. Federal district court -- diversity and greater than $10,000
    b. Citing <u>Tompkins</u>, Pennsylvania law
    c. Probably Pennsylvania since the airline has no contact with Nevada

2. a. physical presence in the state
    b. state citizenship
    c. consent to state's jurisdiction
    d. sufficient contacts with the state
    e. comission of a tort within the state

3. Three

4. U.S. Court of International Trade

5. a. in rem jurisdiction
    b. quasi in rem jurisdiction
    c. in personam jurisdiction

6   a. Article III

       b.   Tenth Amendment

7.   a.   federal question
      b.   diversity of citizenship and in excess of $10,000

8.   a.   bill
      b.   joint resolution
      c.   concurrent resolution
      d.   simple resolution

9.   a.   It gives rise to potential distortion of the popular will.
      b.   It may promote apathy regarding public matters.

10.   a.   Form--common law is judge-made; legislation in form of statutes or acts
      b.   commutative vs. distributive justice
      c.   passive vs. self-animating lawmakers
      d.   greater procedural due process protections in courts than legislatures
      e.   courts deal with legal issues and legislatures deal with political issues

Key Terms

monarchy: government by one ruler with absolute power.

oligarchy: government by a small group of individuals.

democracy: government by the governed.

body politic: citizens of a society make up the body politic.

representative democracy: government by representatives of the body politic.

anarchy: no legal authority.

states of nature: society before government.

social compact: agreement among people to form an organized society.

constitution: a government's social compact or framework.

federalism: law-making authority divided between dual sovereigns (state and federal government.)

sovereign: supreme law maker.

common law: judge-made law.

administrative agency: nonlegislative, nonjudicial law maker.

court of original jurisdiction: a court where a case begins.

domestic relations court: court dealing with divorce or delinquency.

probate court: court dealing with estate administration.

county, common pleas, district courts: courts handling small civil matters.

Justice of the Peace Courts: courts handling minor legal violations (civil and criminal.)

municipal courts: courts dealing with minor civil and criminal offenses.

courts of record: an official record is kept of the proceedings.

de novo: a trial anew.

superior or circuit courts: general trial courts of record.

equity courts (chancery): courts affording remedies other than money.

chancellor: judge in equity court.

law courts: courts providing money damages as remedies.

appellate courts: courts reviewing lower court decisions.

jurisdiction: power and authority of court to hear cases.

subject matter jurisdiction: jurisdiction over the type of lawsuit that is being brought before the court.

in rem jurisdiction: power over things.

in personam jurisdiction: jurisdiction over the parties involved in a law suit.

quasi in rem jurisdiction: "like in a thing," jurisdiction over property located in the state where the lawsuit is brought.

federal district court: trial court of the federal system where most lawsuits begin.

diversity of citizenship: jurisdictional requirement that parties reside in different states.

federal question: where a federal constitutional or statutory right is at issue.

U.S. Court of International Trade: federal court wilth exclusive jurisdiction over civil actions arising under U.S. tariff laws.

U.S. Court of Appeals for Federal Circuit: hears cases appealed from the U.S. Patent Office, U.S. Court of International Trade and the U.S. Claims Court.

U.S. Claims Court: trial court that hears lawsuits brought against the federal government.

U.S. Courts of Appeals: intermediate appellate court in the federal system.

en banc: all appellate court judges hear the case.

U.S. Supreme Court: highest court in the federal system.

bill: proposed legislation.

joint resolution: proposed legislation by members of both houses.

concurrent resolution: deals with operational details of Congress; cannot become a law.

simple resolution: resolution affecting running of only one house of Congress; not a law.

session law: an act or bill passed by Congress.

interstitial lawmaking: judicial interpretation of statutes (judicial gap-filling.)

statutes of limitations: laws setting maximum times for filing lawsuits.

legislative history: the vote, proceedings, debate, amendments and background of a statute.

commutative justice: justice as determined by judges when deciding lawsuits, corrects a past wrong between specific parties.

distributive justice: justice to remedy broad societal problems in the form of a statute enacted by a legislature; takes effect in the future.

passive lawmakers: judge may not rule on an issue until it is before the court in a lawsuit.

self-animating lawmakers: legislatures can pass laws that address present or future wrongs.

procedural due process: the constitutional requirement to notice and fair hearing.

CHAPTER 4

SETTLING LEGAL DISPUTES: ALTERNATIVE DISPUTE RESOLUTION, CIVIL LAWSUITS

Chapter Summary

Alternative dispute resolution (ADR) attempts to settle disputes outside the court system. There are several types of ADR: conciliation, mediation and arbitration. Advantages of ADR include speed, expense, privacy and lack of precedent. Disadvantages are no jury or attorneys, arbitration clauses, settlements can be challenged and surprise. ADR can be used to settle most types of disputes.

ADR is not new; the Federal Arbitration Act of 1925 required courts to enforce arbitration agreements. Stockbrokers used arbitration agreements to minimize customer claims. In the 1980s several U.S. Supreme Court cases upheld these provisions in contracts [Southland (1983) and Mitsubishi Motors (1985)--other than brokerage contracts]. The Shearson/American Express case upheld a predispute brokerage arbitration agreement regarding customer claims under the 1934 SEC Act. See Rodriguez de Quijos v. Shearson/American Exp., Inc. 109 S Ct. (1989). Petitioners signed a standard customer agreement that contained a binding arbitration clause. The investment lost money and suit was filed against Shearson and its broker agent under the 1933 SEC Act. The court reasoned that a party does not give up substantive rights granted by statute by agreeing to arbitrate a claim. This method of resolving disputes was strongly endorsed. The SEC, concerned about the fairness of predispute arbitration clauses, has adopted specific regulations governing their use. Conspicuous language must be included in the agreement that explains the effect of the arbitration clause to customers.

Attorneys advocate others' claims and assist the legal system in achieving justice, speed and economy. In civil cases, attorneys can be paid by fixed or contingent fees. A fixed fee is most appropriate in non-litigation matters and required for criminal cases. An attorney is paid a contingent fee only if successful in a suit or settlement for money.

Most civil lawsuits are settled before trial. This can result in the attorney getting a lower fee. A majority of states hold that the client should decide whether to accept the settlement offer. See P.A.D.D. v. Graystone Pines Homeowners, 789 P. 2d 52 (1990). The client entered into a contingency fee agreement that gave his attorney control over the settlement of the lawsuit. The client later refused a settlement offer as being too low. The attorney sued his client for breach of the fee agreement. The Utah court ruled that the settlement language was contrary to the Utah Code of Professional Responsibility governing attorneys and hence void. The case was sent back to the trial court to determine the validity of the entire contingency fee agreement.

Until recently state bar associations did not allow attorney advertising. Since Bates (1977) states cannot prevent truthful attorney advertising. See Shapero v. Kentucky Bar Association, 108 S. Ct. 1916 (1988). A majority of the Supreme Court concluded that the state may not prohibit attorneys from sending direct mail advertising (letters) to potential clients known to face specific legal problems. Such advertising is protected commercial speech which can be restricted only upon the showing of a substantial governmental interest.

Civil procedure is law designed to guide a civil dispute through the civil justice system. Standing is required before a plaintiff can proceed in civil case. Many individuals do not recognize a legal wrong. Class actions can bring a wrong to the attention of individuals if the statute of limitations has not run out. The plaintiff has the burden of proof and must prove all elements of a lawsuit by a preponderance of the evidence. The case must be filed in the proper court and in personam jurisdiction must be obtained over the defendant. Long arm statutes allow the state to get jurisdiction over out of state defendants for certain in-state wrongs.

The plaintiff must have a legal clause of action to proceed with a case. Steps in a civil lawsuit are as follows:

1. complaint - facts that give rise to the cause of action (must have service of process on the defendant)

2. answer - defendant's response to complaint (avoids a default judgement)

3. discovery - obtaining evidence

4. pretrial conference - attorneys meet with judge to narrow issues and expedite matters

5. motions - dismissal

6. trial and verdict - judgement entered

Parties have the right to have their case heard only once but an appeal can be taken to an appellate court.

If there is no appeal and the plaintiff has been awarded a money judgement, the plaintiff through a court order can seize property of the defendant. Writ of execution and garnishment can also be used by the judgement creditor (plaintiff). Prejudgment methods of seizing property can be dangerous and present constitutional problems. The Consumer Credit Protection Act places limitations on garnishment. Judgement debtors can avail themselves of the federal bankruptcy law. If a debtor transfers title to property to a third party, this can be attached as a fraudulent conveyance.

Review Questions

True/False

_____ 1.   Alternative dispute resolution refers to settling disputes outside the court system.

_____ 2.   Conciliation involves both parties to the dispute and a disinterested third party.

_____ 3.   ADR is used to settle international commercial disputes between multinational businesses.

_____ 4.   Fixed fees permit attorneys to be paid on an hourly basis.

_____ 5.   Arbitration is typically binding.

_____ 6.   Standing is required for every plaintiff in a civil law suit.

_____ 7.   The first step in a civil law suit is the filing of the answer.

_____ 8.   In civil cases the plaintiff has the burden of proof.

_____ 9.   Subject matter juris diction refers to the person.

_____ 10.   A writ of execution takes property being held by third parties.

Multiple Choice -- Please circle the best answer.

1.   Arbitration involves only
      a.   the two disputants.
      b.   the two parties and a judge.
      c.   the two parties and a nonjudicial third party.
      d.   the two parties and a six person jury.

2.   ADR is typically used to settle
      a.   contract disputes.
      b.   tort disputes.

    c.   divorce matters.

    d.   a. and c.

3. Customer complaints against a stock broker should be directed to the
    a.   FTC.
    b.   SEC.
    c.   EPA.
    d.   ICC.

4. These courts have been established to afford consumers with small dollar claims their day in court.
    a.   small claims courts.
    b.   superior courts.
    c.   federal courts.
    d.   appeals courts.

5. The statute of limitations
    a.   limits the number of defendants.
    b.   is an example of substantive law.
    c.   takes away the plaintiff's right to be restored.
    d.   requires certain documents to be in writing.

6. The burden of proof in a civil case is
    a.   beyond a reasonable doubt.
    b.   to a moral certainty.
    c.   established by jurisdictional requirements.
    d.   on the plaintiff.

7. One purpose for filing an answer is
    a.   to avoid a default judgment.
    b.   to gain in personam jurisdiction.
    c.   to challenge the merits of the plaintiff's claim.
    d.   to win the lawsuit.

8. The Fourth Amendment prohibits the government from
    a.   censoring the press.
    b.   prohibiting speech.
    c.   conducting unreasonable searches.
    d.   adopting a state religion.

9. An arrest may be made only when police have
    a.   a search warrant.
    b.   probable cause.
    c.   an arrest warrant.

     d.   booked a suspect.

10.   The purpose of the grand jury is
     a.   to weigh the prosecutor's evidence.
     b.   to find the accused guilty.
     c.   to determine the validity of the search warrant.
     d.   to allow the accused a day in court.

11.   Subject matter jurisdiction refers to the courts power to
     a.   dismiss a case.
     b.   hear a case.
     c.   confine the defendant.
     d.   serve a process.

12.   Which pleading begins the lawsuit?
     a.   answer.
     b.   complaint.
     c.   demurrer.
     d.   motion to proceed.

13.   If the jury returns a verdict completely at odds with the evidence, the other party can ask the court for a
     a.   judgement of dismissal.
     b.   directed verdict.
     c.   judgement notwithstanding the verdict.
     d.   res judicata.

14.   Appellate courts hear
     a.   issues of law.
     b.   issues of fact.
     c.   testimony from witnesses.
     d.   factual errors.

15.   All states exempt _____ to some extent.
     a.   welfare payments.
     b.   life insurance policies.
     c.   alimony and child support.
     d.   wages of the debtor.

Short Answer

1. List three disadvantages of ADR.

   a.   _____

   b.   _____

   c.   _____

2. List the proposed new rules governing securities arbitration issued by the SEC.

   _____

   _____

   _____

   _____

3. List two types of attorney fee arrangements.

   a.   _____

   b.   _____

4. Define standing.

   _____

   _____

5. How is the defendant informed of a civil suit?

   _____

   _____

6. What is the justification for class actions?

   _____

   _____

7. What type of writ is necessary for a judgment creditor to obtain the debtor's property?

   _____

8. What is a major difference between writs of execution and garnishment?

_____

_____

9. What constitutional problem exists with prejudgment attachment?

_____

_____

10. Name a requirement for a voluntary bankrupt.

_____

Answers to Review Questions

True/False

1. T	4. T	7. F	10. F
2. F	5. T	8. T	
3. T	6. T	9. F	

Multiple Choice

1. c	4. a	7. a	10. d	13. c
2. d	5. c	8. c	11. b	14. a
3. b	6. d	9. b	12. b	15. b

Short Answer

1. a. attack on the jury system
    b. substitutes amateurs for professionals
    c. agreements favor one of the parties
    d. can be challenged in court
    e. not knowingly entered into

2. a. independent public representatives on arbitration panel
    b. arbiters must undergo uniform training and updates
    c. better discovery to obtain relevant records

3.   a. fixed fee   b. contingent fee

4.   The plaintiff must have some legally recognized interest to lose.

5.   Through service of process -- a copy of the complaint and summons are served on the defendant.

6.   They make suits against social wrong doers economically feasible.

7.   writ of execution

8.   A writ of execution takes property directly from the judgement debtor whereas garnishments can reach property or money in hands of third parties that belong to the debtor.

9.   Procedural due process-defendant's property is taken without a trial or proceeding.

10.   Debts must be owed.

Key Terms

alternative dispute resolution: settling legal disputes without using courts.

conciliation: two parties resolve disputes.

mediation: third party hears both sides of the dispute and helps the parties compromise their claims -- nonbinding.

arbitration: formal submission of dispute to third person -- typically binding.

fixed fee: rate charged by attorney on an hourly or project basis.

contingent fee: attorney fee arrangement where attorney collects fee only upon winning a suit or securing an acceptable settlement.

judicare: plan to provide legal services for all segments of the population.

pro se litigant: party representing himself or herself in an action.

small claims court: courts that hear small dollar claims without high court costs.

standing: requirement that a party be directly and tangibly injured.

class action: suit by a large group of plaintiffs through a representative.

statute of limitations: time limit of filing suit for redress of a particular wrong.

plaintiff: party alleging violation of rights.

defendant: party alleged to have committed a wrong.

counterclaim: claim by defendant against plaintiff in same suit.

preponderance of the evidence: amount of proof plaintiff must present to win a civil lawsuit.

in personam: jurisdiction over persons.

long-arm statutes: statutes enabling state courts to obtain jurisdiction over out-of-state defendants for in-state wrongs.

cause of action: facts indicating a legal wrong and entitlement.

complaint: brief statement of the plaintiff's cause or causes of action.

answer: defendant's response to a complaint.

default judgment: judgment for plaintiff because of defendant's failure to answer.

pleading: complaint and answer.

discovery: process of discovering available evidence.

pretrial conference: meetings at which the opposing attorneys brief the judge on the issues of the case.

motion to dismiss: defendant's motion based on the idea that there is no legal claim or no jurisdiction.

demurrer: motion to dismiss because no cause of action is stated.

verdict: jury decision; from "vera dicta" -- say what is true.

judgment notwithstanding the verdict: reversal by trial court judge of jury verdict.

directed verdict: decision by court during the trial for judge to stop the proceedings and rule in favor of one of the parties.

res judicata: right to only one trial.

courts of record: trial courts in which transcripts of the proceedings are kept.

judgment creditor: one entitled to collect an awarded money judgment.

judgment debtor: one required to pay an awarded money judgment.

exemptions: property and wages exempt from judgment.

homestead exemption: protection of debtor's home from judgment execution.

writ of execution: document authorizing the taking of the judgment debtor's property.

garnishment: form of judgment authorizing the seizure of wages or accounts.

prejudgment attachment: attachment of property before judgment to debtor's default.

prejudgment garnishment: attachment of debtor's wages before judgment to insure payment.

perfected security interest: lien on property which has priority through public notification.

fraudulent conveyance: transfer of property by a debtor to avoid creditor collection.

criminal procedure: judicial steps in the trial of a criminal action.

procedural law: law governing conduct of litigation.
crime: a wrong committed against society.

search warrant: legal document authorizing the search of a place or object.

probable cause: sufficient reason to believe.

arrest: taking of criminal suspect into custody.

booking: record of arrest.

initial appearance: appearance of defendant for charges and bail.

preliminary hearing: hearing to determine if there is probable cause for trial.

misdemeanor: classification of crime generally carrying a lesser penalty.

felony: classification of crime carrying a higher penalty.

grand jury: panel of citizens reviewing evidence for probable cause determination

criminal complaint: indictment or "true bill."

indictment: document issued by grand jury charging criminal conduct.

information: document issued by court charging criminal conduct.

criminal prosecutor: party representing injured party in criminal action.

plea bargaining: deal on criminal charge negotiated between prosecutor and defendant.

arraignment: appearance by defendant to enter plea.

voir dire: process of questioning prospective jurors.

beyond a reasonable doubt: level of proof required for criminal conviction.

nolo contendere: plea of no contest; has effect of a guilty plea.

immunity from prosecution: prosecutor agrees not to bring charges, or to accept a lesser charge in exchange for information and testimony.

CHAPTER 5

BUSINESS AND THE CONSTITUTION: POWER TO REGULATE

Chapter Summary

Constitutions set up the basic structure of government and place limits on its power. The U.S. Constitution defines the powers of the federal government, the states and what happens when federal and state laws conflict. The Bill of Rights forbids certain types of government activity. An overview of the U.S. Constitution:

1. Article I sets out the legislative powers of Congress.

2. Article II places the executive power in the President and lists powers.

3. Article III deals with the judicial power of the federal government. It establishes the U.S. Supreme Court and gives Congress the power to create other federal courts.

4. Article IV sets out rules governing relationships between the states--"Full Faith and Credit Clause."

5. Article V sets out procedures for amending the constitution.

6. Article VI makes federal law supreme over state law if they clash (Supremacy Clause).

7. The Constitution contains twenty-six (26) amendments, the first ten (10) comprise the Bill of Rights. The Bill of Rights applies to federal and state government.

The Constitution is flexible and variable, the meaning of many of its provisions have changed over time. There are many reasons for this. The Constitution is a short and sketchy document and many of its key terms are vague. The most important factor contributing to flexibility is social change. It has been said that the Supreme Court follows the election returns.

The Supreme Court and other courts play a major role in determining the Constitution's meaning. The Constitution's brevity and open-endedness make interpretation necessary.   Under the doctrine of judicial review, the court can declare the action of other government bodies unconstitutional.

There are restraints placed on the courts. Language in the Constitution almost always has some meaning. Legal reasoning and education do not permit just any result to be reached. Finally, the courts and judges can be held accountable politically.

Chapters 5 and 6 discuss constitutional doctrines that permit government to regulate the economy. This consists of a two part analysis.

1. Did the government act pursuant to a constitutionally granted power?

2. Did the exercise of this power conflict with an independent constitutional check? (Chapter 6)

The Constitution limits congressional power by listing or enumerating the areas in which Congress can make law (Art. 1 sec. 8). In reality, congressional regulatory power far exceeds those enumerated in the Constitution. The Supreme Court has interpreted enumerated powers broadly. The main constitutional restrictions on federal regulation of the economy are independent of the enumerated powers. These independent checks create protected zones from government regulation.

The most important state regulatory power is the police power. This is a broad power to advance the public health, safety, morals and welfare. This power is restricted by independent constitutional checks.

The commerce clause (Art. 1, Sec. 8) is an enumerated power that gives Congress the power to regulate interstate commerce. The Supreme Court has greatly expanded the commerce clause and allowed regulation of intrastate matters that affect commerce. After 1937, the commerce clause was further expanded to include police power objectives. Today, the commerce clause is the most important source of power to regulate business. See Katzenback v. McClung, 379 U.S. 294 (1964). Ollie's Barbecue refused to serve Afro-Americans in violation of the public accommodations section of the 1964 Civil Rights Act. The Court ruled that this intrastate activity affected interstate commerce in violation of the act. This is an example of the commerce clause being used to achieve desirable ends (police power).

The taxing power (Art. 1 sec. 8) is used for regulatory purposes. The Supreme Court has placed some limits on the use of this power, tax versus penalty. However, today this power is a sweeping source of congressional regulatory authority.

The spending power (Art 1 sec. 8) gives Congress broad authority to spend for the public welfare. This power can be a powerful regulatory tool, conditional grants of money. The condition must be clearly stated and be reasonably related to the federal expenditure.

The takings clause is found in the Fifth Amendment to the U.S. Constitution and applies to the federal government and the states. The taking of private property by the government must be for a public use and the owner must receive just compensation. Government regulation can constitute a taking. There is no exact formula for determining this, factors include a means-end test and economic impact of the regulation. The courts have become increasingly aggressive in their use of the takings clause. See Hall v. City of Santa Barbara, 833 F. 2d 1270 (1987). Santa Barbara enacted an ordinance that required mobile home park owners to give their tenants' leases of unlimited duration with rent control provisions. The Court ruled that the right to occupy property in perpetuity comes under the takings clause. The case was remanded to the District Court for a full hearing consistent with the opinion.

Review Questions

True/False

____ 1.   Article I of the U.S. Constitution sets up the judicial branch.

____ 2.   There are twenty-six amendments to the U.S. Constitution.

____ 3.   Article II of the U.S. Constitution sets up the legislative branch.

____ 4.   Enumerated powers are those that apply to the states.

____ 5.   In early Commerce Clause decisions, "commerce" did not include "manufacture."

____ 6.   The states regulate economic matters by using the police power.

____ 7.   The Bill of Rights pertains to the federal government but not the states.

____ 8.   The U.S. Supreme Court distinguishes taxes from penalties in interpreting congressional taxing power.

____ 9.   Eminent domain gives Congress the power to tax.

____ 10.   The Fourteenth Amendment contains language that provides protection under both due process and equal protection guarantees.

Multiple Choice -- Circle the best answer

1.   The "Full Faith and Credit" clause deals with
       a.   financial institutions.
       b.   freedom of speech.
       c.   state relationships.
       d.   the Bill of Rights.

2.   A doctrine that gives the Supreme Court considerable power.
       a.   due process.
       b.   judicial review.
       c.   delegation doctrine .
       d.   rational basis test.

3.   Independent constitutional checks
       a.   allow extensive government regulation.
       b.   flow from the enumerated powers.
       c.   must be approved by Congress.
       d.   limit government regulation.

4.   Economic regulations are challenged under the
       a.   rational basis test.
       b.   strict scrutiny test.
       c.   police power test.
       d.   effects test.

5.   Regulation of the economy today is based on the
       a.   commerce clause.
       b.   full faith and credit clause.
       c.   First Amendment.
       d.   taxing power.

6.   The scope of the commerce clause has been expanded by application of the
       a.   state police power.
       b.   strict scrutiny test.
       c.   effects test.
       d.   rational basis test.

7.   The Constitution permits the federal government
       a.   to take private property without any compensation.
       b.   to take corporate property with compensation.
       c.   to issue government regulations if the business community receives compensation.
       d.   to take private property provided that the owner receives compensation.

8.   The takings clause is based on the
      a.   affects test.
      b.   power of eminent domain.
      c.   power to tax for the public welfare.
      d.   power to regulate for the general good.

9.   Article III of the Constitution establishes the
      a.   Court of Appeals.
      b.   Supreme Court.
      c.   Executive Branch.
      d.   District Court.

10.   Under the enumerated powers doctrine, Congress can
      a.   exercise any power it wishes.
      b.   declare acts of other government agencies unconstitutional.
      c.   exercise only those powers listed in the Constitution.
      d.   None of the above.

11.   The most important state regulatory power is the
      a.   commerce clause.
      b.   takings clause.
      c.   taxing power.
      d.   police power.

12.   Congress has used the commerce clause to regulate for
      a.   political purposes.
      b.   police power purposes.
      c.   state purposes.
      d.   spending purposes.

13.   What branch of government has the power "to pay debts and provide for the common Defense and general welfare of the United States."
      a.   executive.
      b.   legislative.
      c.   judicial.
      d.   states.

14.   The Fifth Amendment applies to
      a.   private property.
      b.   public property.
      c.   only the federal government.
      d.   none of the above.

15.   The takings clause can apply when the government

      a.   takes property.
      b.   issues a regulation.
      c.   occupies property.
      d.   all of the above.

Short Answer

1.   Name the two reasons for the Constitution's flexibility and uncertainty.

      a.   _____

      b.   _____

2.   Name three constraints on the Supreme Court interpretation of the Constitution.

      a.   _____

      b.   _____

      c.   _____

3.   List two tests employed by the Supreme Court in determining what type of commerce Congress could regulate.

      a.   _____

      b.   _____

4.   What is meant by the term enumerated powers?

      _____

      _____

5.   What is the standard used when applying the rational basis test to economic regulations?

      _____

      _____

6.   To determine whether a "taking" of property by government is constitutional, what two questions are raised?

a. _____

b. _____

7. What is the police power of a state?

_____

_____

8. Give an example of the use of the spending power to enhance federal authority.

_____

_____

9. What two broad purposes do constitutions have in the western world?

_____

_____

10. What is the "Full Faith and Credit" clause?

_____

Answers to Review Questions

True/False

1. F	3. F	5. T	7. F	9. F
2. T	4. F	6. T	8. T	10. T

Multiple Choice

1. c.	4. a.	7. d.	10. c.	13. b.
2. b.	5. a.	8. b.	11. d.	14. a.
3. d.	6. c.	9. b.	12. b.	15. d.

Short Answer

1. a. short and sketchy document
    b. key terms are not precise or defined
    c. social change

2. a. Decisions must reflect values and needs of society.
    b. Training of judges creates respect for past decisions.
    c. Language of Constitution provides restraints.
    d. Broad values of Constitution are easy to identify.

3. a. direct vs. indirect
    b. affecting commerce
    c. "police" power
    d. commerce vs. manufacture

4. Those powers that are specifically granted to Congress in the Constitution.

5. The regulations must be "rationally related to a valid governmental purpose."

6. a. whether there is a taking for public use
    b. whether there is just compensation

7. A broad state power to regulate for public health, safety, morals and general welfare.

8. The conditioning of federal appropriations on compliance with a specified course of behavior.

9. a. set up a basic structure of government.
    b. place limits on the power of government.

10. Each state must give "Full Faith and Credit" to the laws and legal proceedings of other states.

Key Terms

constitution: fundamental law of the society it governs.

enumerated powers: areas in the Constitution that specifically grant to Congress the power to legislate.

independent constitutional checks: sections in the Constitution that place limits on legislation flowing
    from the enumerated powers.

police power: power of a state to legislate for the public health, safety, morals and welfare.

commerce clause: Article I, Sec. 8, giving Congress the power to regulate commerce among the states.

interstate commerce: commerce between or among the states.

intrastate commerce: activities occurring within a particular state.

taxing power: Article I, Sec. 8, giving Congress the power to collect taxes.

spending power: Article I, Sec. 8, giving Congress the power to pay debts and provide for the welfare of the U.S.

takings clause: Fifth Amendment, government cannot take private property for public use without paying compensation.

eminent domain: power of government to condemn private property for public purposes.

BUSINESS AND THE CONSTITUTION: INDEPENDENT CONSTITUTIONAL CHECKS

Chapter Summary

Independent constitutional checks have assumed a greater role in blocking business regulation.

Certain constitutional checks apply to both the federal government and the states. Under the doctrine of incorporation, the Bill of Rights and the Fourteenth Amendment apply to both federal and state government. The means-end test is utilized to determine if a regulation "substantially" advances a legitimate government end. Three different varieties of mean-end scrutiny can be identified.

1. Full strict scrutiny--very tough, reserved for rights of special importance.

2. Intermediate scrutiny--fairly tough, must be substantially to an important government purpose (gender).

3. Rational Basis test--lenient, rationally related to a legitimate government purpose (business regulation).

Most of the Constitution's individual rights sections protect only against governmental action. This is described as government or state action. After World War II, the doctrine of state action was dramatically expanded. Since 1970, the Supreme Court has narrowed the state action doctrine. See Jackson v. Metropolitan Edison Co., 419 U.S. 345 (1974). Plaintiff sued the electrical utility for cutting off the electricity due to failure to pay electric bills, claimed there had been a deprivation of property without due process of law. The court ruled that a business subject to state regulation does not by itself convert acts into state action for Fourteenth Amendment purposes.

Corporations enjoy First Amendment protection for political speech (Bellotti). Commercial speech, such as advertising, did not receive First Amendment protection until the 1970s, but it receives less protection than political speech. Deceptive, fraudulent, misleading or advertising related to an illegal activity is not protected. One reason for protecting commercial speech is consumer education, such as advertising by professionals. See National Advertising Co. v. Town of Babylon, 900 F. 2d 551 (1990). National's proposed billboards were to carry both commercial and non-commercial messages. The signs were to contain off-premises advertising. Three towns had enacted ordinances that prohibited this type of billboard advertising. The Court applied the Central Hudson Gas test and concluded that the ordinances fail because they contained no statement of a substantial government interest and no extrinsic evidence of such an interest was introduced (such as traffic safety or aesthetics).

Due process of law is a basic constitutional right. The elements of a violation include deprivation of life, liberty or property, by government (state action) that lacks due process. Procedural due process requires a notice and fair hearing before government deprivation of life, liberty or property. After Roth, courts focus specifically on the words liberty or property when deciding if the government has deprived a person of either. See Board of Regents v. Roth, 408 U.S. 564 (1972). The Court ruled that an untenured assistant professor with a one year contract was not entitled to formal notice and hearing when not rehired. Roth was not charged with misconduct and he had no expectation of being rehired. Roth did not have a sufficient property interest to require Fourteenth Amendment protection.

Substantive due process looks at the reasonableness of a rule that governs social life. The analysis consists of including certain rights within a liberty or property interest and applying some kind of means-ends scrutiny. Economic substantive due process at the turn of the century included the freedom to contract. This is not an issue today as government has the freedom to regulate. Modern substantive due process is concerned with personal rights, the right of privacy (Roe v. Wade). Laws restricting nonfundamental liberty or property interests receive less protection. See Kelly v. Johnson, 425 U.S. 238 (1976). Suffolk County police department had a restriction on the length of police officer's hair. A patrolman challenged these grooming regulations. The Court applied the more lenient rational basis test and ruled that codes of this type made officers recognizable and promoted esprit de corps. Hence, there was a rational basis for the regulation.

The equal protection clause of the Fourteenth Amendment guarantees citizens' "equal protection of the laws." Not all individuals are treated equally by the law and equal protection sets the standards for these distinctions. These standards are tests that vary depending on the type of discrimination. Economic regulation is subject to the rational basis test. This test has been given liberal application and it is not an obstacle to regulation. See City of Dallas v. Stanglin, 109 S.Ct. 1591 (1989). The City of Dallas passed an ordinance that only those of 14-18 could be admitted to "Class E" dance halls. The ordinance did not apply to other places where teenagers congregate. The court applied the rational basis test and reasoned that the ordinance separated 14 to 18 year olds from the corrupting influences of other teenagers and young adults. This act was certainly within the boundaries of the test.

The courts now use more rigorous standards when examining certain classifications under the equal protection clause. These classifications include:

1. unequal enjoyment of certain fundamental rights (right to vote, travel interstate and procedural criminal protections).

2. discriminating on the basis of suspect classifications (race, national origin, sex, alien status and illegitimacy--these vary from each suspect classification).

The contract clause (Art. 1 sec. 10) is an independent constitutional check that applies only to the states. This clause was probably the most important check on state regulation of the economy in the nineteenth century. By the middle of this century the contract clause was a dead issue. In the 1970s the Supreme Court breathed new life into the clause ruling that state police power did not give the states authority to regulate contracts in all instances. The Court seems to have reverted to its passive pre-1970s stance in cases involving private contract impairments. See Exxon Corp. v. Eagerton, 462 U.S. 176 (1983). The State of Alabama raised a severance tax on oil and gas and prohibited producers from passing on the tax increase to purchasers. Exxon had contracts with customers that required reimbursement of these taxes. Exxon claimed that the state had impaired the obligations of these contracts. The court ruled that the state had a valid interest in protecting consumers from excessive prices and this was a valid exercise of its police power.

The commerce clause gives Congress the power to regulate interstate commerce. The states may regulate commerce if state law does not conflict with federal law. The test today balances state interest in regulating commerce with the burden placed on interstate commerce. Today, state laws almost always violate the commerce clause if they:

1. discriminate against interstate commerce

2. directly regulate interstate commerce

3. favor in-state economic interests over out-of-state interests.

Laws that regulate evenhandedly and have only an incidental effect on interstate commerce are constitutional if they serve legitimate state ends. See Kassel v. Consolidated Freightways Corp., 450 U.S. 622 (1981). Unlike all other states in the midwest, Iowa restricted the length of trucks (65 foot doubles) on its highways. The court ruled that the Iowa statute placed an undue burden on interstate commerce. Iowa could not prove by evidence that this was a valid exercise of state police power.

According to the supremacy clause, federal law defeats inconsistent state law. If state law does conflict and is declared unconstitutional, it is said to be preempted by federal law. These cases are decided on a case by case basis. Court will examine congressional intent, legislative purpose and history, and scope of the federal statute or regulation. See Ingersoll-Rand Co. v. McClendon, 111 S.Ct. 478 (1990). An employee was fired two months before pension fund rights vested (10 years of service required). Suit was filed in the Texas state court on a common law claim of wrongful discharge.

Ingersoll-Rand argues that the wrongful discharge claim is preempted by the Federal Employee Retirement Income Security Act (ERISA). The federal law was comprehensive, contained a broad preemption provision and a integrated civil enforcement scheme. The Supreme Court ruled that this federal statute preempted actions in state courts.

Review Questions

True/False

____ 1.   Debtor relief laws applying to existing contracts are unconstitutional.

____ 2.   The contract clause applies to public and private contracts.

____ 3.   A safety justification will always validate an otherwise extremely burdensome state regulation on interstate commerce.

____ 4.   In determining whether a state law is preempted, the applicable federal law must be examined first.

____ 5.   The Bill of Rights applies to the states but not the federal government

____ 6.   Public utilities regulated by the state but privately owned and operated are engaged in "state action."

____ 7.   State prohibitions on professional advertisements have been invalidated under the commercial speech protection of the First Amendment.

____ 8.   To invoke the procedural due process protections, state action must be involved.

____ 9.   Today, economic substantive due process is a tool utilized by business in fighting government regulation.

____ 10.   The rational basis test is applied in cases of suspect classifications.

Multiple Choice -- Please circle the best answer

1.   The Contract Clause has become subordinate to
      a.   the due process clause.
      b.   the preemption doctrine.
      c.   the states' police power.
      d.   the supremacy clause

2.   The Commerce Clause applies to the
    a.   federal government.
    b.   federal congress.
    c.   states.
    d.   all of the above.

3.   The Supremacy Clause defeats
    a.   consistent state law.
    b.   inconsistent state law.
    c.   silent state law.
    d.   most federal laws.

4.   The due process guarantee is an example of
    a.   national rights.
    b.   state rights.
    c.   arbitrary rights.
    d.   governmental interference.

5.   Infringement of personal rights by a private corporation does not violate
    a.   the First Amendment.
    b.   the due process clause.
    c.   the equal protection clause.
    d.   all of the above.

6.   The "public function doctrine" has been applied by the Supreme Court to
    a.   the federal government.
    b.   the states.
    c.   shopping centers.
    d.   oil companies.

7.   The Bellotti case involved
    a.   political speech.
    b.   commercial speech.
    c.   due process.
    d.   state action.

8.   Commercial speech would include
    a.   political statements.
    b.   advertisements.
    c.   disputes involving taxes.
    d.   all corporate statements.

9.   Procedural due process is concerned with
    a.   statutory interpretation.

    b.   notice and fair hearing.

    c.   most basic freedoms.

    d.   all property interests.

10.   In defining substantive due process, the courts have looked to

    a.   public policy.

    b.   state action.

    c.   government regulation.

    d.   procedural safeguards.

11.   The Fourteenth Amendment protects people from

    a.   private action.

    b.   state action.

    c.   corporate action.

    d.   none of the above.

12.   Certain forms of commercial speech do not receive First Amendment protection.

    a.   deceptive advertising.

    b.   professional advertising.

    c.   illegal advertising.

    d.   a. and c.

13.   The main reason for protecting commercial speech is

    a.   legal.

    b.   ethical.

    c.   economic.

    d.   political.

14.   The best known example of modern substantive due process is the

    a.   rational basis test.

    b.   right of privacy.

    c.   right of association.

    d.   strict scrutiny test.

15.   Gender based discrimination is judged under the _____ test.

    a.   strict scrutiny test.

    b.   rational basis test.

    c.   intermediate scrutiny test.

    d.   racial scrutiny test.

Short Answer

In each of the following five problems, determine which constitutional issues are involved and what tests should be applied:

1.   In 1854 and 1855, the U.S. government signed several treaties with Indian tribes in the state of Washington guaranteeing them a share of the salmon and trout run each year in Washington. A Washington state court issued a decision allocating fishing rights that reduced the Indian treaty rights. Can the state of Washington exercise such a right?

_____

_____

_____

2.   New York imposed a greater transfer tax on securities sold on out-of-state exchanges than the tax imposed on securities sold on the NYSE. The Boston stock exchange brought suit challenging the constitutionality of the law.

_____

_____

3.   What is meant by the doctrine of incorporation?

_____

_____

_____

4.   What are means-end tests?

_____

_____

_____

5.   Explain the concept of "state action."

_____

_____

_____

6.   What two factors contributed to the expansion of "state action" after World War II?

      a.   _____

      _____

      b.   _____

      _____

7.   List three factors considered in determining whether federal law preempts state law.

      a.   _____

      b.   _____

      c.   _____

8.   List three constitutional limitations applying to both state and federal government.

      a.   _____

      b.   _____

      c.   _____

9.   For due process standards to apply, what are three elements that are required?

      a.   _____

      b.   _____

      c.   _____

10.   What two tests are employed in determining whether the equal protection clause is violated?

      a.   _____

      b.   _____

Answers to Review Questions

True/False

1. T	3. F	5. F	7. T	9. F
2. T	4. T	6. F.	8. T	10. F

Multiple Choice

1. c.	4. a.	7. a.	10. b.	13. c.
2. d.	5. d.	8. b.	11. b.	14. b.
3. b.	6. c.	9. b.	12. d.	15. c.

Short Answers

1.   Supremacy clause is at issue. Test -- is there a preemption? Legislative intent? Purposes? History? Other Constitutional values? Since Indian tribes are primarily an exclusive federal matter, the Washington Court decision was invalid. See 443 U.S. 622 and 445 U.S. 253 for similar cases.

2.   Commerce clause, Article I, Section 8. State taxation -- Is the tax discriminatory? In this case, the tax favored in-state exchanges and imposed greater costs on out-of-state exchanges. Declared unconstitutional 429 U.S. 318 (1977) -- see also Armco, Inc. v. Hardesty.

3.   Provisions in the Bill of Rights have been incorporated into the due process clause of the Fourteenth Amendment and made applicable to the states.

4.   These tests are frequently used when laws are challenged under the Constitution's individual rights provisions. Since no constitutional right is absolute, such tests try to strike a balance between individual rights and the rights of society.

5.   Most of the Constitution is individual rights protections only protect people against governmental activity. This activity is described as government action or state action.

6.   a.   concern of the courts to protect personal rights
      b.   the blurring of the public-private division

7.   a.   Legislative intent
      b.   Legislative purpose
      c.   Constitutional factors

8.   a.   First Amendment
      b.   Fourteenth and Fifth Amendment -- due process of law
      c.   Fourteenth Amendment -- equal protection

9.   a.   taking of life. liberty, or property
        b.   by government (state action)
        c.   without due process of law

10.   a.   rational basis
        b.   strict scrutiny

Key Terms

contract clause: Article I, Section 10, of the U.S. Constitution, restricting governmental interference with existing contracts.

federal supremacy clause: Article VI of the U.S. Constitution makes federal law (Constitution, statutes and treaties) the supreme law.

federal preemption: doctrine that declares federal law exclusive in a field, even in the absence of a direct clash with state law.

state action: degree of government conduct necessary to invoke the Equal Protection Clause and other individual rights guarantees.

commercial speech: expression proposing a commercial transaction.

procedural due process: right to notice and fair hearing when rights of life, liberty, or property are affected by government action.

substantive due process: protects certain chosen freedoms, public policy, from unreasonable government regulation.

equal protection clause: a general check against arbitrary and unjustified governmental distinctions and classifications.

rational basis test: lenient equal protection standard applied to economic regulations. Requires that government classification have a rational relationship to a valid governmental objective.

strict scrutiny test: certain classifications that are subjected to a high degree of scrutiny, i.e., certain fundamental rights and suspect classifications.

fundamental rights: not completely clear, includes right to vote, interstate travel and certain criminal procedures.

suspect classifications: race, national origin, sex, alienage, and illegitimacy.

GOVERNMENT REGULATION: OVERVIEW

Chapter Summary

An administrative agency is any nonlegislative nonjudicial lawmaker. Agencies are usually created by statute called the agency's organic act. The organic act delegates legislative, judicial and executive authority to the agency. Congress creates most federal administrative agencies.

Reasons for the existence of administrative agencies:

1. expertise--courts and legislatures do not have the technical expertise

2. oversight of potential harm--air pollution

3. protect the weak--help the weak and poor fight corporate giants

4. speed and economy in running the government

5. circumvention of judicial and legislative roadblocks.

Some agencies have the power to issue legally binding regulations granted by enabling statutes. These are called substantive regulations.

The Federal Register Act passed in 1935 provides a way to get up-to-date information about an agency and its regulations. This is accomplished by the Federal Register System. The government manual contains the names and addresses of U.S. government agencies. The Federal Register is published daily and contains proposed and promulgated regulations. The third part of the system is the Code of Federal Regulations and contains all current federal agency regulations. Is the average person bound by what appears in the Federal Register? See Federal Crop Ins. Corp. v. Merrill, 332 U.S. 380 (1947). Merrill asked a government employee if his partially reseeded crop was insurable. The official said yes and Merrill purchased crop insurance. The agency refused to pay Merrill's claim because reseeded crops were not covered. Merrill claimed that he was told his crop was insurable. The Supreme Court ruled that Congress had conferred rule-making power upon the agency and Merrill was charged with knowledge of the regulation.

The Administrative Procedure Act (APA) regularized procedures for administrative agencies and sets requirements for rulemakings and adjudications. Among the more important APA amendments are:

1. Freedom of Information Act (FOIA)--This requires the disclosure of certain "tangible" pieces of information held by federal agencies. Making an FOIA request requires a reasonable description of records sought and compliance with the agency's request rules. There are numerous exemptions: national security, trade secrets, personnel matters, law enforcement investigations and privacy matters.

2. Federal Privacy Act of 1974--This protects individual privacy by preventing misuse of federal agency information. It requires prior written consent of the individual the record is about.

3. Government in the Sunshine Act--Requires that an agency headed by a collegial body (two or more individuals heading an agency) must meet in public.

Whistleblowers expose waste or fraud in an organization. Organizations retaliate against these individuals by demoting or firing them. Specific federal statutes protect whistleblowers. The Whistleblower Protection Act became law in 1989. It does the following to help federal employees:

1. gives whistleblowers a cause of action to pursue their own case

2. lessens the burden of proof in connection with a whistleblower being punished

3. restates the Office of Special Council's mission to protect whistleblowers.

Two major problems with the act are the many exemptions and "dual causation" problem. See Lockert v. U.S. Dept. of Labor, 867 F. 2d 513 (1989). Lockert worked as a Quality Control Inspector at a nuclear power plant. He reported a large number of safety problems and on several occasions left his work station to research these problems. Lockert was warned several times about leaving his work area. On December 14, 1983, Lockert left his work station for up to two hours to perform STPR (Steps to Prevent Recurrence), training and reinspection. He was discharged December 15, 1983 for absence from his work area. The Secretary of Labor supported the ALJ's finding that the witnesses against Lockert were credible and that the discharge was not motivated by retaliatory onimus. The court held that the discharge was supported by substantial evidence.

Ways have been developed to legally and economically control administrative agencies. Agency actions are reviewable by courts (APA). Courts can overturn agency actions for the following reasons:

1. Violation of the U.S. Constitution

2. acted beyond its statutory authority (ultra vires) 3. action was arbitrary, capricious or an abuse of discretion

4. did not follow legal procedures

5. adjudication not supported by substantial evidence.

Courts review questions of law and let agencies decide the facts. Agency fact decisions must be supported by the facts.

Sunset laws revoke the law that created the agency (rare) or require periodic renewal of the law creating the agency. Ombudsmen are utilized to see that the agency is acting properly. Federal civil rights actions can be brought against state or municipal agency employees for violating individual civil rights.

The U.S. Supreme Court invalidated the legislative veto that Congress used to control agency activity in certain areas. See INS v. Chadha, 462 U.S. 919 (1983).

The federal government and its agencies are protected from lawsuits by the sovereign immunity doctrine. This immunity has been waived by the Federal Torts Claims Act. There are important limits to the liability:

1. law of the state where wrong occurred controls

2. must be within scope of official duties

3. punitive damages not available

4. certain damages exempt, i.e., discretionary functions.

See Gaubert v. U.S., 885 F.2d 1284 (1989). Plaintiff Gaubert sued several administrative agencies of the federal government under the Federal Torts Claims Act for personal losses sustained in a savings and loan merger and daily operation of IASA. The Supreme Court ruled that advice and oversight rendered by federal officials in attempting to save several S&Ls fell within the discretionary function exemption to the Federal Torts Claims Act.

Review Questions

True/False

____ 1.   To be an administrative agency, the term ~~agency~~ must appear in the name.

____ 2.   Administrative agencies are created by statute.

____ 3.   The Code of Federal Regulations was established in the Administrative Procedures Act.

____ 4.   All persons dealing with an administrative agency are held accountable for knowledge of all pertinent regulations.

____ 5.   The Freedom of Information Act (FOIA) is an amendment to the Administrative Procedures Act.

____ 6.   Under the FOIA, agencies may not charge fees for compliance with requests.

____ 7.   The ICC was created to fight corporate grants.

____ 8.   Independent agencies are within the executive branch of the U.S. government.

____ 9.   The Federal Privacy Act only prohibits disclosure of written records.

____ 10.   The APA imposed uniform agency procedures.

____ 11.   Courts apply limited judicial review of agency actions.

____ 12.   The <u>Chadha</u> case invalidated the federal legislative veto under an interpretation of the First Amendment.

____ 13.   The Federal Torts Act increased the protection of sovereign immunity.

____ 14.   The Sunshine Ace is applicable only to federal agencies headed by collegial bodies.

____ 15.   Sunset laws can revoke the authority or budget of an administrative agency.

Multiple Choice -- Please circle the best answer

1.   Administrative law includes
      a.   statutes.
      b.   cases.
      c.   regulations.

    d.   all of the above.

2.   Agencies are created by
    a.   Congress.
    b.   courts.
    c.   enabling statutes.
    d.   regulations.

3.   Interpretative rules
    a.   have the force and effect of law.
    b.   do not have the force and effect of law.
    c.   are legally binding.
    d.   are found in enabling statutes.

4.   The Code of Federal Regulations
    a.   is published daily.
    b.   contains new and proposed regulations.
    c.   contains regulations indexed by agency.
    d.   contains the Government Manual.

5.   The Administrative Procedures Act
    a.   requires publication of the Federal Register.
    b.   regularizes agency procedures.
    c.   contains the Federal Privacy Act.
    d.   requires full disclosure.

6.   Courts can overturn agency actions for the following reason(s)
    a.   violation of the Constitution.
    b.   incorrect factual determination.
    c.   ultra vires acts.
    d.   a. and c.

7.   The substantial evidence test is used to review
    a.   informal rule making.
    b.   hybrid rule making.
    c.   arbitrary agency acts.
    d.   factual findings.

8.   The branch of government that has the veto power
    a.   legislative.
    b.   judicial.
    c.   executive.
    d.   administrative agency.

9.   The federal government is protected from lawsuits by the
    a.   doctrine of sovereign immunity.
    b.   delegation doctrine.
    c.   Federal Torts Claims Act.
    d.   arbitrary and capricious test.

10.   An agency would want its regulations judged under the
    a.   substantial evidence test.
    b.   arbitrary-unreasonable test.
    c.   Sunset Laws.
    d.   delegation doctrine.

11.   The Federal Register System includes the
    a.   Government manual.
    b.   Federal Register.
    c.   Code of Federal Regulations.
    d.   all of the above.

12.   A federal agency under the Federal Privacy Act of 1974 may not disclose any record in a system
    of records without
    a.   first checking to see if the information is true.
    b.   first clearing the request with the F.B.I.
    c.   the individuals prior written consent.
    d.   approval from the Office of Special Counsel.

13.   The whistleblowing protections in the Clean Water Act and OSHA protect
    a.   public sector employees.
    b.   private sector employees.
    c.   managerial employees.
    d.   a. and b.

14.   The Federal Torts Claims Act does not exempt
    a.   discretionary functions.
    b.   mandatory functions.
    c.   required functions.
    d.   any functions.

15.   A-An _____ agency is not attached to a branch of government.
    a.   dependent.
    b.   executive.
    c.   independent.
    d.   required.

Short Answer

1.   List the three components of the Federal Register System.

      a.   _____

      b.   _____

      c.   _____

2.   List three reasons for the existence of administrative agencies.

      a.   _____

      b.   _____

      c.   _____

3.   List the two types of administrative regulations.

      a.   _____

      b.   _____

4.   List two requirements for making an FOIA request.

      a.   _____

      b.   _____

5.   List three exemptions from an FOIA disclosure.

      a.   _____

      b.   _____

      c.   _____

6.   Why do administrative agencies exist?

      _____

      _____

7.   Do agencies have the power to make regulations?

_____

_____

8.   Why was the Administrative Procedures Act (APA) enacted?

_____

_____

9.   Name three protections for whistleblowers in the Whistleblower Protection Act.

a. _____

b. _____

10.   Describe the doctrine of sovereign immunity.

_____

_____

_____

Answers to Review Questions

True/False

1.	F	4.	T	7.	T	10.	T	13.	F
2.	T	5.	T	8.	F	11.	T	14.	T
3.	F	6.	F	9.	F	12.	F	15.	T

Multiple Choice

1.	d.	4.	c.	7.	b.	10.	b.	13.	d.
2.	a.	5.	b.	8.	c.	11.	d.	14.	b.
3.	b.	6.	d.	9.	a.	12.	c.	15.	c.

Short Answer

1. a.   Government Manual
    b.   Code of Federal Regulations
    c.   Federal Register

2. a.   expertise
    b.   oversight
    c.   protect the weak
    d.   speed & economy
    e.   court avoidance

3. a.   interpretive
    b.   substantive or legislative

4. a.   reasonable description of records
    b.   comply with agency rules on time, place, fees, and procedures

5. national defense or foreign policy
    internal personnel rules
    statutes permitting nondisclosure
    trade secrets and commercial or financial information
    interagency or intra-agency correspondence
    personnel, medical files (privacy)
    investigatory records for law enforcement
    financial institution reports
    geological maps

6. a.   expertise
    b.   ongoing supervision
    c.   protect the weak
    d.   speed and economy
    e.   class struggle

7. yes and no--only if the legislature gives them the power through enabling statutes.

8. Because of concern with the lack of regularized procedures for agency actions. Before the APA, some government agencies decided cases after hearing the government's evidence.

9. a.   gives an independent cause of action
    b.   lessens burden of proof whistleblower has to prove if punished
    c.   restates OSC's primary mission of protection of whistleblowers

10.   The federal government and its agencies are protected from lawsuits under this doctrine.

Key Terms

Administrative law: law of administrative agencies, including statutes, regulations, and court and agency interpretations.

administrative agency: nonjudicial, nonlegislative governmental lawmaker.

organic act: statute that creates agency.

enabling statute: statute passed by Congress delegating rule making authority to an agency.

regulations (regs) or rules: laws of administrative agencies.

substantive regulations: have the force and effect of law.

interpretive regulations: agency policy statements; do not have the effect of law.

Federal Register Act: created Federal Register system of update.

Government Manual: list of names and address of all federal agencies.

Federal Register: daily printed update of administrative agency regulations, proposals, and hearings.

Code of Federal Regulations (C.F.R.): multivolume set that arranges current effective agency regulations by agency.

Administrative Procedure Act: required uniform procedures for agency actions.

Freedom of Information Act: act permitting access to agency information.

Federal Privacy Act of 1974: regulation of information that can be disclosed by agencies.

Government in the Sunshine Act: federal open meeting law; notice requirements.

ultra vires: action beyond an agency's authority.

substantial evidence test: standard used by courts to review whether there is sufficient evidence to support agency action.

arbitrary, capricious and unreasonable test: standard used by courts to determine if there is sufficient evidence to support agency action.

sunset laws: laws terminating administrative agencies.

ombudspersons: agency employees who check on agency operation.

Federal Torts Claims Act: statute that allows suits against the federal government, its agencies and
      employees.

GOVERNMENT REGULATION: ANATOMY OF A REGULATION

Chapter Summary

An administrative agency has three basic functions:

1. executive--investigating and enforcing regulations

2. adjudications--hearings before ALJs

3. legislative--rulemaking (regulations).

Informal rulemaking involves notice in the Federal Register and comment. Formal rulemaking requires notice, a trial-type hearing and use of the substantial evidence test. Hybrid rulemaking is a cross between the two.

The life of a federal regulation-steps:

1. Society perceives a problem--individuals bring problems to the attention of legislators.

2. Congressional enabling act is passed creating the agency and authorizing regulations.

3. Agency studies the problem--the enabling act tells the agent to do something about the problem--studies conducted.

4. The agency issues a proposed regulation after studying the problem. The APA governs regulation making. Notice must be placed in the Federal Register with contents of the notice. Interpretive regulations and general policy statements need not be published. Another exception is when an agency for good cause finds that notice is not necessary. See Northwest Airlines, Inc. v. Goldschmidt, 645 F.2d 1309 (1981). The Secretary of Transportation proposed a regulation allocating 40 landing slots at national airports to avoid "chaos in the skies" during upcoming Thanksgiving-Christmas holidays. The regulation was published but only appear for seven days. The APA lets the proposing agency shorten or eliminate the comment period if there is good cause. The court ruled that avoiding disrupting airline service was good cause.

A federal agency must give notice of a proposed regulation by publishing it in the Federal Register. See National Tour Brokers Ass'n v. U.S., 591 F.2d 896 (1978). The ICC published a notice in the Federal Register but it was incomplete, it did not mention any regulation applying to tour brokers. The court ruled the publication of a general notice that did not set out the specific regulation was invalid under the APA.

5. The public comments--anyone can comment on a proposed regulation and the agency must give the public at least 30 days notice. The agency must consider the comments, that is all.

6. Agency promulgates, modifies, or withdraws the regulation--the agency must consider the comments and then take some action.

7. Court challenges to the regulation--the regulation can be challenged in a court of law. The regulation must not violate the U.S. Constitution. The arbitrary and capricious test governs informal rulemaking. This standard is more lenient than the substantial evidence test. See Motor Vehicle Mfgrs. Ass'n v. State Farm Mutual Auto. Ins. Co., 463 U.S. 29 (1983). A new Secretary of Transportation in 1981 proposed rescinding the passive restraint regulation because of a changed economy and problems in the auto industry. An auto insurer sued claiming the secretary's action was arbitrary, capricious and unreasonable. The court ruled against the secretary since there was no basis or explanation for rescinding the requirement. No modifications of the regulation were considered.

An agency must not make regulations beyond the authority (ultra vires) of the enabling act that creates the agency. If so, the courts will void the regulation. See Ernst & Ernst v. Hochfelder, 425 U.S. 185 (1976). The enabling act of the SEC Act of 1934, Section 10b, mandated the SEC to make regulations covering intentional fraud. The SEC promulgated rule 10b-5 which regulated negligent misrepresentations. The Supreme Court ruled that 10b-5 was partially invalid because the enabling act did not cover negligent representations. It was an ultra vires act rendering that part of the regulation invalid.

In 1980 Congress amended the APA (Regulatory Flexibility Act) to encourage agencies to publish proposed rules in trade and business journals.

8. Enforcement of a Reg through Investigation, Prosecution and Administration--an agency's executive job includes issuing permits and licenses. If a person or entity violates a permit or an administrative

regulation, the agency must prove the violation, innocent until proven guilty. Agencies must gather evidence to prove violations which may require an administrative search. Warrants are required for health and other administrative searches of homes and business. No warrant is necessary where business is pervasively regulated (liquor and firearms). See Marshall v. Barlows, 436 U.S. 307 (1978). The Supreme Court required an OSHA inspector to obtain an administrative search warrant since Mr. Barlows objected to the search. The Court ruled that the probable caused needed to obtain an administrative search warrant is less than that required to get a criminal warrant.

Agencies do not have the power to punish criminally although many regulatory statutes have criminal sanctions. The U.S. Justice Department would bring criminal charges. Agencies do have the power to assess civil penalties. See U.S. v. Ward, 448 U.S. 242 (1980). The Clean Water Act requires violations to be reported and punishes violators with civil penalties of up to $5000 per offense. Ward claims the fineis criminal in nature and his privilege against self-incrimination under the Fifth Amendment has been violated. The Supreme Court ruled that the fine was a civil penalty, hence the Fifth Amendment was not applicable.

9. Adjudicatory Hearings--agencies hold hearings similar to courtroom trials. The procedure is governed by the APA and there is no jury. The presiding official is an Administrative Law Judge (ALJ).

10. Appeal of an ALJs Decision--the appeal must be by one having standing (injured party) and must proceed through the agency's structure. Administrative procedure must be exhausted before an appeal can be taken to the courts, either the Federal District Court or the Court of Appeals (special statute). The Federal District Court holds a de novo proceeding while the Court of Appeals only reviews the evidence. The issues must be sufficiently developed (ripe) for court review. A reviewing court may declare agency action illegal and either force it to act or stop it from acting. See Wasson v. SEC, 558 F.2d. 879 (1977). Wasson, a broker, acted as his own attorney before an SEC hearing in which his brokers license was suspended for 45 days. Wasson argues on appeal that the ALJ did not inform him of his right to cross examine witnesses. The Court of Appeals ruled that the ALJ should have informed Wasson of his right to cross examine but concluded that failure to do so did not prejudice his case.

The 101st Congress enacted a statute that could have a significant impact on federal rulemaking. The law deals with negotiated rulemaking. A committee of interested parties is appointed by the agency to write a report and possible proposed regulation to submit to the agency.

Review Questions

True/False

_____ 1.   Informal rulemaking consists of a notice and comment process.

_____ 2.   The executive function of an administrative agency is rulemaking.

____ 3.   If a regulation's wording is changed after the time of original notice of rulemaking, the rulemaking must be reproposed.

____ 4.   An ultra vires regulation is one that goes beyond the agency's enabling act.

____ 5.   The substantial evidence test is more lenient than the arbitrary capricious standard.

____ 6.   In establishing violations of statutes or regulations, the charging administrative agency does not have the burden of proof.

____ 7.   A search made with the consent of the person being investigated still requires a warrant.

____ 8.   Administrative agencies have the power to assess civil penalties.

____ 9.   A hearing examiner is an administrative law judge.

____ 10.   The Fourteenth Amendment requires that defendants at administrative hearings have the right to confront and cross-examine witnesses.

Multiple Choice -- Please circle the best answer

1.   The legislative function of an administrative agency is
    a.   conducting investigations.
    b.   holding hearings.
    c.   issuing rules.
    d.   enforcement.

2.   The most common form of agency rulemaking is
    a.   informal.
    b.   formal.
    c.   hybrid.
    d.   requires testimony under oath.

3.   Independent agencies derive their rulemaking power from
    a.   the President.
    b.   Congress.
    c.   the Supreme Court.
    d.   the doctrine of inherent powers.

4.   The APA's regulation-making rule does not apply to
    a.   administrative law judges.
    b.   the Federal Trade Commission.
    c.   the U.S. Government.

   d.   foreign affairs functions.

5.   Notice of an agency regulation in the Federal Register is excused when
      a.   informal rulemaking is required.
      b.   wartime conditions exist.
      c.   the executive branch is involved.
      d.   parties are personally served.

6.   A federal agency must successfully give the public ___ in which to comment.
      a.   sixty days.
      b.   thirty days.
      c.   six months.
      d.   an indefinite time.

7.   The arbitrary-capricious standard controls
      a.   hybrid rulemaking.
      b.   informal rulemaking.
      c.   formal rulemaking.
      d.   all rulemaking.

8.   When an agency acts ultra vires, the courts discipline the agency by
      a.   suspending the regulation.
      b.   revising the regulation.
      c.   invalidating the regulation.
      d.   affirming the regulation.

9.   The Regulatory Flexibility Act strengthens:
      a.   search and seizure protection for small businesses.
      b.   the notice requirements of an agency.
      c.   the agency's power to act independently of Congress.
      d.   requirements of specific rules for large corporations.

10.   The court that a losing party would want to appeal from an adverse ruling of an administrative
      agency
      a.   District Court.
      b.   U.S. Court of Appeals.
      c.   Supreme Court.
      d.   Court of Claims.

11.   The executive function of an administrative agency involve
      a.   enforcement.
      b.   hearings.
      c.   rulemaking.
      d.   ALJs.

12.   The first step in the life of a federal regulation is
       a.   Congress passes an enabling act.
       b.   the agency studies the problem.
       c.   society perceives a problem.
       d.   a solution is proposed.

13.   The following need not be published in the Federal Register
       a.   interpretative regulations.
       b.   general policy statements.
       c.   rules of agency organization.
       d.   all of the above.

14.   Search warrants are not required before government inspectors can enter
       a.   commercial facilities.
       b.   a private home.
       c.   an apartment building.
       d.   stone quarries.

15.   Agencies have the power to assess
       a.   criminal penalties.
       b.   civil fines.
       c.   both a. and b.
       d.   none of the above.

Short Answer

1.   Describe the activities of the following three major roles of an administrative agency.

      executive _____

      _____

      legislative _____

      _____

      judicial _____

      _____

2.   List the ten possible steps in the life of a federal regulation.

      a.   _____

b. _____

c. _____

d. _____

e. _____

f. _____

g. _____

h. _____

i. _____

j. _____

3. Name the three theories on which court challenges to administrative agencies can be based.

a. _____

b. _____

c. _____

4. Describe the information that must be included in a <u>Federal Register</u> proposed rulemaking notice.

_____

_____

_____

5. After considering public comments, what three alternatives can an agency take on a proposed rule?

a. _____

b. _____

c. _____

6.   Who can comment during the public comment period?

_____

_____

7.   Name three exceptions to the Fourth Amendment warrant requirement.

a. _____

b. _____

c. _____

8.   What major difference in procedure exists when an agency decision is appealed to Federal District Court as opposed to the U.S. Court of Appeals.

_____

_____

_____

9.   Name the three instances in which the exhaustion doctrine need not be followed.

a. _____

b. _____

c. _____

Answers to Review Questions

True/False

1.	T	4.	T	7.	F	10.	T
2.	F	5.	F	8.	T		
3.	F	6.	F	9.	T		

Multiple Choice

1.	d.	4.	c.	7.	b.	10.	b.	13.	d.
2.	a.	5.	b.	8.	c.	11.	a.	14.	d.
3.	b.	6.	d.	9.	a.	12.	c.	15.	b.

Short Answer

1.   executive--law enforcement and administration
       legislative--rulemaking
       judicial--hearing before administrative law judges.

2.   a.   society perceives a problem
       b.   Congress passes an enabling act
       c.   agency studies the problem
       d.   agency proposes a regulation
       e.   public comment period
       f.   agency promulgates, withdraws or modifies the regulation.
       g.   possible court challenges
       h.   enforcement of valid regulations through investigation, prosecution, and administration.
       i.   agency adjudicatory hearing
       j.   appeal of administrative law judge's decision

3.   a.   the regulation is violation of the U.S. Constitution.
       b.   the regulation is arbitrary, capricious, or an abuse of discretion.
       c.   the regulation is an act ultra vires to the proposing agency.

4.   a.   time, place and nature of public rulemaking
       b.   the laws giving the agency authority to make the proposed rule
       c.   the provisions or substance of the proposed rule or a description of the subjects and issues involved.

5.   promulgate now
       modify and repropose
       withdraw

6.   anyone--public, private or governmental interests

7.   a.   consent searches
       b.   emergency situations
       c.   pervasively regulated industry

8.   Federal District Court will proceed de novo whereas the Court of Appeals will simply accept the evidence developed at the agency adjudicatory hearing.

9.   a.   irreparable harm would occur
       b.   agency exceeded its jurisdiction
       c.   futile effort

Key Terms

executive functions: enforcement and administration.

adjudication functions: hearing before administrative law judges.

legislative functions: promulgation of rules.

informal rulemaking: rules made by the notice and comment process.

formal rulemaking: rulemaking on the record (hearing).

hybrid rulemaking: combination of comments and hearings.

enabling act: statute that empowers administrative agency to issue regulations.

comment period: time in which anyone can submit comments to the agency proposing the regulation.

ultra vires: outside of an agency's power.

Regulatory Flexibility Act: requires publication of rule notices in trade and business journals.

permits, licenses: procedural process for obtaining permission to conduct certain activities.

prosecutions: bringing of action by government official for violation of an agency regulation.

Fourth Amendment: U.S. Constitutional Amendment protecting privacy and preventing warrantless searches.

administrative searches: searches for evidence by federal agencies requiring less probable cause than a criminal warrant.

adjudicatory hearing: agency held hearing with less due process safeguards.

administrative law judge: presiding official at the hearing, technically independent of the agency.

standing: having suffered sufficient harm to bring an action in adjudication.

exhaustion doctrine: requirement that matters proceed through an agency before going to court.

ripeness: requirement that a case be developed enough to sufficiently present the issues and interests.

CHAPTER 9

LAW IN INTERNATIONAL BUSINESS

Chapter Summary

International law can be defined as the treaties, conventions, and customs nations observe in dealing with each other. Treaties can be bilateral (two nations) or multilateral (more than two). The U.S. has learned that economic isolationism does not work. Isolationism or protectionism is accomplished by high tariffs, quotas, and trade barriers. Some say the Smoot-Hawley Act (Tariff Act of 1930) caused the Great Depression. Other acts dealing with U.S. tariffs include the Reciprocal Trade Agreements Act of 1934 (President has power to negotiate tariff), Trade Act of 1974 (President to negotiate reduction of non-tariff barriers, and the Trade Agreements Act of 1979 (countervailing duties, antidumping, and subsidies). Current U.S. policy favors international trade. There are some exceptions. The voluntary quota on Japanese automobiles and the decline of the U.S. dollar. Most favored nations (MFN) clauses in treaties give citizens of the contracting nation's privileges accorded by either party to those of the most favored nations.

There are many institutions and laws that affect international business.

1. General Agreement on Tariffs and Trade (GATT)--this took effect in 1947 and the main purpose is to reduce tariffs and trade restrictions.

2. United Nations Commission on International Trade Law (UNCITRAL)--meets one month per year and drafts model laws that promote international trade.

3. European Economic Community (EEC)--promotes tariff free trade among Common Market members

and common tariffs for outsiders. The idea is economically unified Europe by 1992.

4. Overseas Private Investor Corporation (OPIC)--this U.S. government agency provides insurance to individuals doing business abroad for a premium.

5. United States International Trade Commission (ITC)--provides studies, reports recommendations to the President, Congress and other governmental bodies regarding tariffs and other international trade issues. The Commission can also conduct investigations when requested by the President or Congress. Section 301 of the ITC develops strategies to protect intellectual property rights and gain market access for U.S. businesses. Special 301 requires identification of nations who deny "fair and equitable market access to U.S. persons who rely on intellectual property protection." Special 301 is permanent.

6. U.S. antitrust laws can apply to international business if overseas activities have some substantial effect within the U.S. Suit can be brought by U.S. or foreign governments. The Export Trading Company Act (1982) exempts certain business from U.S. antitrust laws that obtain a certificate of antitrust compliance from the Commerce and Justice Department. The EEC has several provisions that forbid anticompetitive business practices.

International business deals can present many problems. The Art-Ali contract presents many practical problems, including the following:

1. payment after shipment?

2. receive item or product after payment?

3. wrong goods sent--can deal be stopped? Art and Ali's mistrust problem is solved by a letter of credit and bill of lading (entrustment to third parties).

The Art-Ali contract using a Letter of Credit and a Bill of Lading:

1. contract entered into by parties

2. issuance of letter of credit to party--to make payment

3. utilization of a correspondent bank--issue letter of credit to seller

4. meeting of conditions by foreign seller to be able to draw on the letter of credit

5. seller writes draft on letter of credit

6. delivery of product or item to transport company

7. bill of lading provided to seller

8. bill of lading is provided to correspondent bank

9. bank pays seller

10. bill of lading is sent to bank of purchaser which checks over credit items

11. if bill of lading is in order, account of correspondent bank is credited

12. bank of purchaser charges purchaser for letter of credit and gives bill of lading to him

13. purchaser presents bill of lading at local office of transport company

14. transaction is complete.

Special considerations for a letter of credit:

1. independence principle--general rule that letters of credit are independent of the underlying contract; see GATX Leasing Corp. v. DBM Drilling Corp., 657 S.W.2d 178 (1983)

2. stopping payment due to forgery--knowingly submitting forged bill of lading allows stoppage of payment; see Prutscher v. Fidelity International Bank, 502 F. Supp. 535 (1980)

3. stopping payment on Irrevocable Letters of Credit due to fraud--buyer can stop issuer from paying on letter if fraud committed in the underlying contract; see Sztein v. J. Henry Schroder Banking Corp., 31 N.Y. S.2d 631 (1941).

Gray market goods refer to foreign made goods bearing a valid U.S. trademark that are imported into the U.S. without the consent of the U.S. trademark holder. There are three scenarios:

1. U.S. firm buys from an independent foreign firm rights to sell the foreign made goods in the U.S. and the right to register the foreign firm's trademark in the U.S. Gray market arises if after selling its trademark, the foreign manufacturer imports and sells its goods in the U.S.--itrabrand competition.

2. U.S. firm registers the U.S. trademark for goods made abroad by an affiliated manufacturer. Gray market arises when a third party (K Mart) purchases these goods abroad and sells them in the U.S. Estimated that 98% of gray market goods enter the U.S. under this arrangement.

3. U.S. firm holding U.S. trademark authorizes independent foreign manufacturer the exclusive right to use the trademark in a particular foreign location, but goods are not to be imported into the U.S. Agreement violated and goods imported into the U.S.--gray market; see K Mart Corporation v. Cartier Inc., 108 S. Ct. 1811 (1988), holding scenarios 1 and 3 illegal, 2 legal.

The Foreign Corrupt Practices Act prohibits bribes by domestic concerns to foreign officials. It covers businesses required to register their securities under the 1934 SEC Act. The FCPA prohibits the use of the mails or interstate commerce to commit a foreign corrupt practice by any domestic concern (covers nonissuers). Persons covered include issuer's shareholders, shareholders, officers and directors.   FCPA does not cover small bribes (grease payments), bribes to private foreigners and extortion payments.

The act of state doctrine says that U.S. courts should accept foreign governments' official acts at face value. This rule generally applies to a government's official act within its territory. This keeps U.S. courts out of foreign affairs. State securities law exception; see <u>Riedel</u> v. <u>Bancum, S.A.</u>, 792 F.2d 587 (1986). Mr. Riedel, an Ohio resident, had a CD in a Mexican bank payable in U.S. dollars instead of pesos which were declining in value. Mexico issued currency regulations forcing Mexican banks to pay back depositors only in pesos. Riedel suffered a substantial loss. None of the certificates were registered with either the SEC or the Ohio Division of Securities. The court ruled that the act of state doctrine does not bar the Ohio securities law claim. The claim is based on Bancum's failure to register the CD with the Ohio Division of Securities and not on Bancum's failure to repay dollars.

There are several ways of settling international business disputes.

1. private settlement--this is quick and inexpensive but the parties must be reasonable.

2. arbitration--the provision should be in the contract. This is slower and costs more than a private settlement.

3. lawsuit--this is expensive and slow and finding a court to handle the problem is difficult.

There are two problems associated with lawsuits by and against foreign countries.

1. Sovereign immunity doctrine states that foreign nations may not generally be sued in the U.S. The Foreign Sovereign Immunities Act (FSIA) gives two exceptions, waiver and commercial activity in the U.S.

2. Forum non conveniens presents the problem of where to sue. It is within the discretion of the trial judge when there is more than one court in which a lawsuit could be brought to tell the litigants, "Go to another court; it is more convenient." See <u>In re Union Carbide Corp. Gas Plant Disaster</u>, 809 F.2d 195 (1987). The U.S. Court of Appeals sent the case back to India on the grounds of forum non conveniens. U.S. courts will enforce foreign judgements when procedures are fair and the court has jurisdiction over the defendant.

There are two remaining legal problems:

1. expropriation--U.S. company has plant in a foreign country, seizure, inadequate payment

2. repatriation--are there limits on taking profits back to the U.S.

Review Questions

True/False

____ 1.   A person originally obtains a bill of lading from a bank.

____ 2.   Under the general rule, if a seller sends different colored versions of a product the purchaser sought, the letter of credit must be honored.

____ 3.   In cases dealing with forgery of a bill of lading that is within the knowledge of the seller, the buyer can stop payment on the letter of credit.

____ 4.   Even in cases of fraud, the Independence Principle demands that letters of credit must be honored.

____ 5.   A shareholder of an issuer who violated the Foreign Corrupt Practices Act by assisting in the bribery is subject to a federal misdemeanor.

____ 6.   Extortion payments of all kinds are considered corrupt practices under the FCPA.

____ 7.   The Act of State Doctrine only applies to a government's official acts within its territory.

____ 8.   It is illegal to put an arbitration agreement provision in a contract that has international implications.

____ 9.   The main factor in the forum non conveniens doctrine is convenience.

____ 10.   Expropriation cases may result in a seizing of business assets and a giving of less than fair value or even nothing at all.

Multiple Choice -- Please circle the best answer

1.   International law consists of
    a.   treaties.
    b.   conventions.
    c.   customs.
    d.   all of the above.

2.   This legislation protects U.S. exporters from U.S. antitrust liability.
    a.   Export Trading Company Act.
    b.   European Economic Act.
    c.   General Agreement on Tariffs and Trade.
    d.   Reciprocal Trade Agreements Act.

3   The European Economic Community (Common Market)
       a.   promotes free trade for all countries.
       b.   prohibits all forms of protectionism.
       c.   promotes free trade and tariffs.
       d.   promotes tariffs among its members.

4.   U.S. antitrust laws apply
       a.   to anticompetitive behavior in Ireland.
       b.   to anticompetitive behavior outside the U.S.
       c.   to anticompetitive behavior within the U.S.
       d.   to none of the above.

5.   The Foreign Corrupt Practices Act covers
       a.   bribes to private foreigners.
       b.   nonissuers of securities.
       c.   bribes that are requested by foreign officials.
       d.   all bribes.

6.   The sovereign immunity doctrine
       a.   prohibits foreign governments from using U.S. courts.
       b.   prohibits the U.S. from using foreign courts.
       c.   may be waived as a defense.
       d.   applies to all foreign governments doing business in the U.S.

7.   The concept of repatriation allows
       a.   U.S. assets to be seized in a foreign country.
       b.   foreign profits made by U.S. firms to be brought into the U.S.
       c.   foreign countries to prohibit exporting goods produced by foreign businesses.
       d.   none of the above.

8.   Current U.S. policy favors
       a.   international trade.
       b.   tariffs.
       c.   OPEC.
       d.   quotas.

9.   Gatt's main purpose is to
       a.   promote tariffs and trade restrictions.
       b.   reduce tariffs and trade restrictions.
       c.   promote the unification of international law.
       d.   draft model laws.

10.   A major purpose of "Special 301" is
       a.   to promote international trade.

b.   to provide reports to the President and House Ways and Means Committee.

c.   to protect intellectual property rights.

d.   to protect U.S. industry from dumping.

11.   U.S. antitrust laws apply if
   a.   anticompetitive activities outside the U.S. have a substantial effect within the U.S.
   b.   anticompetitive activities outside the U.S. have a substantial effect outside the U.S.
   c.   all parties are citizens of another country.
   d.   one party is a citizen of the U.S. and the other party is a citizen of France.

12.   The Act of State Doctrine says that U.S. courts should accept
   a.   foreign governments' official acts only if they comply with the U.S. Constitution.
   b.   foreign courts' official acts.
   c.   foreign governments' official acts at face value.
   d.   no foreign governments' act at face value.

13.   This doctrine says that when there is more than one court in which a lawsuit could be brought, the trial judge can tell the litigants to go to another court.
   a.   Act of State Doctrine.
   b.   Letter of Credit Doctrine.
   c.   Sovereign Immunity Doctrine.
   d.   Forum non Conveniens Doctrine.

14.   What ethic rules in the area of international law?
   a.   justice ethic.
   b.   power ethic.
   c.   positive law ethic.
   d.   custom ethic.

15.   If included in a treaty, the U.S. must give the foreign country the lowest tariff rate on a particular good that it gives to any nation.
   a.   most favored nation clause.
   b.   lowest tariff clause.
   c.   GATT clause.
   d.   UNCITRAL clause.

Short Answer

1.   What are the three things a bill of lading shows?

   a.   _____

   b.   _____

c. _____

2.   State the general rule that is called the Independence Principle.

_____

_____

3.   Explain the concept of a correspondent bank.

_____

_____

_____

4.   If a letter of credit requires the seller to submit a bill of lading to get paid, the buyer can stop payment on the letter for forgery if the seller submits:

_____

and_____

5.   The Foreign Corrupt Practices Act covers businesses required to register their securities under the 1934 SEA. List four kinds of businesses that might be covered under the Act.

a. _____

b. _____

c. _____

d. _____

6.   The main reason for the Act of State Doctrine is:

_____

_____

7.   What three means for dealing with problems that occur in international business transactions were discussed in the chapter? Provide some characteristics of each.

a. _____

b. _____

c. _____

8.   Explain the difference between expropriation and repatriation.

_____

_____

_____

9.   Define what a letter of credit is and why it is used.

_____

_____

_____

10.   List what punishments and penalties are available for violations of the Foreign Corrupt Practices Act.

a. _____

b. _____

c. _____

Answers to Review Questions

True/False

1. F	3. T	5. F	7. T	9. T
2. T	4. F	6. F	8. F	10. T

Multiple Choice

1. d.	4. c.	7. b.	10. c.	13. d.
2. a.	5. b.	8. a.	11. a.	14. b.
3. c.	6. c.	9. b.	12. c.	15. a.

Short Answer

1.   a.   receipt for goods
      b.   contract to transport goods
      c.   title to ownership of goods

2.   Letters of credit are independent of the underlying contract.

3.   A correspondent bank is a bank that another bank does business in a different city, state or country. This concept is utilized to provide entrustment in cases of letters of credit and bills of lading.

4.   a forged bill of lading
      has knowledge of it

5.   a.   corporations
      b.   partnerships
      c.   limited partnerships
      d.   business trusts
      e.   unincorporated organizations

6.   to keep U.S. courts out of foreign affairs

7.   a.   private settlement--quick and inexpensive, parties must be flexible and reasonable
      b.   arbitration--slower and more costly than private settlement, but faster and less costly than suing in court--binding decision
      c.   lawsuit--expensive and slow, filled with uncertainty, may destroy business's goodwill, difficult to find a court to handle the issue

8.   Expropriation refers to a foreign government's seizure of a business's assets in that country and giving less than fair value (or nothing) in return. Repatriation means the bringing back to the U.S. of income and investments that U.S. businesses have earned or made in foreign countries. This limitation is something U.S. businesses should ask about before they set up operations in a country.

9.   A letter of credit is a bank's commitment to pay a definite amount of money or extend credit to a third party. They are used to provide a "trust" element in transactions that cannot realistically guarantee performance and payment in all cases.

10.   a.   federal felonies
      b.   punishments for individuals include five years in prison or a $10,000 fine or both.
      c.   covered business issuers violating the Act can be fined up to $1 million

Key Terms

letter of credit: a bank's commitment to pay a definite amount of money or extend a certain amount of credit to a third party called a beneficiary.

bill of lading: document(s) that a transport company provides to a person to show (1) receipt of goods, (2) a contract to transport the goods, and (3) title to ownership of the goods.

correspondent bank: bank that another bank does business with in a different city, state, or country (physically issues a letter of credit.)

forgery: making of a false document or the altering of a real one with the intent to commit fraud.

Independent Principle: a general rule that letters of credit are independent of the underlying contract.

beneficiary: a third party who gains payment or property through the benefit of a contractual agreement between two other parties.

account party: a customer who makes payment to a bank so credit can be extended to a third party called a beneficiary.

gray market goods: foreign made goods bearing a valid U.S. trademark that are imported into the U.S. without the consent of the U.S. trademark holder.

Foreign Corrupt Practices Act: 1977 Act passed by Congress which prohibits foreign corrupt practices by domestic concerns and mainly addresses bribes to foreign officials to influence official acts.

bribery: offering, giving, soliciting or receiving of a thing of value to influence actions or decisions.

Act of State Doctrine: doctrine whereby U.S. courts accept foreign governments' official acts at face value so as to keep the courts out of foreign affairs.

private settlements: parties work out their problems themselves.

arbitration: procedure where dispute is formally submitted to a neutral third party whose decision is binding.

sovereign immunity doctrine: foreign governments are immune from suit in U.S.

forum non conveniens doctrine: where there is more than one court in which a lawsuit can be brought, the trial judge has the discretion to order the parties to go to another court that is more convenient.

expropriation: a foreign government's seizing of a business's assets in that country and giving less than fair value or nothing in return.

repatriation: the bringing back to the U.S. of income and investments that U.S. businesses earned or made in foreign countries.

CHAPTER 10

TORTS: NEGLIGENCE, STRICT LIABILITY AND INTENTIONAL TORTS

Chapter Summary

A tort is a breach of a noncontractual duty sometimes referred to as a civil wrong. Tort law is mainly state law made by state courts. Torts and crimes do overlap in some instances (striking another--both a tort and a crime). Torts and crimes differ in several ways:

1. duties owed

2. type of enforcer

3. objectives sought.

Tort law is a legal laboratory. There is a growing judicial trend to recognize new kinds of wrongs. Torts can be classified as follows:

1. type of victim--property/person

2. type of wrong.

Negligence involves carelessness that injures others. Negligence has four parts:

1. Duty--this arises by operation of law. Everyone is under a duty to drive carefully. Occasionally, the duty of care can arise by contract, malpractice cases being an example. Third parties can sue for

negligence who are not parties to the professional-client contract. See First Florida Bank v. Max Mitchell & Co., 558 So. 2d 9 (Fla. 1990). Mitchell, a CPA, negotiated a loan on behalf of his client and personally delivered the financial statements to the bank with knowledge that the bank would rely upon them. The bank discovered that Mitchell's client had overstated assets and not reported a large loan. Subsequently the client defaulted on the loan and the bank sues Mitchell for negligence.   The Florida Supreme Court rejected the Ultramares doctrine and adopted the Restatement rule. This rule limits an accountant's liability to those persons whom and accountant "knows" will rely on his opinion. Since Mitchell knew the bank would rely, he is liable to the third party bank.

2.   Standard of Care--is what the ordinary and reasonable prudent person would do in the same situation. If a defendant violates a statute this is negligence per se (doctrine). See Munford, Inc. v. Peterson, 368 So. 2d 213 (1979). The Mississippi Supreme Court ruled that the selling of alcoholic beverages to minors violated a Mississippi statute, hence the corporation owner and salesperson violated the negligence standard of care.

The doctrine of res ipsa loquitur helps a negligence plaintiff prove the defendant broke the standard of care.

3. Damage--the breach of duty must damage the plaintiff's person or property.

4. Proximate cause--plaintiff must prove that the defendant's carelessness in fact caused plaintiff's damage. The doctrine of foreseeability limits a defendant's negligence liability.

If a defendant can prove an affirmative defense, this defeats a negligence claim. Contributory negligence means that plaintiff's own carelessness contributed to the loss. This defense prevents recovery. Many states have adopted the doctrine of comparative fault which allows partial recovery. A refined version of comparative fault is damage apportionment. How much did plaintiff's negligence contribute to his or her damages? See Halvorson v. Voeller, 336 N.W.2d 118 (1983). Plaintiff suffered severe injuries, brain damage, when involved in an automobile accident with the defendant. Plaintiff was not wearing a motorcycle helmet at the time of the accident and defendant tried to show that this fact contributed to the severity of the injuries. The North Dakota court ruled that evidence of failure to wear a protective helmet while traveling on a motorcycle is admissible to reduce damages.

Strict liability means that a person is liable for harm even though no fault is shown. Some examples include blasting, fumigation, flying airplanes and keeping wild animals. Social value outweighs prohibiting these activities but strict liability for harm. Assumption of risk is a defense, contributory negligence is generally not a defense. See Indiana Harbor Belt Railroad Co. v. American Cyanamid Co., 517 F. Supp. 314 (1981). Does a chemical spill constitute an ultra-hazardous activity under the Illinois absolute liability doctrine? The court ruled that in order to apportion loss Illinois doctrine applies to spill.

Intentional torts are similar to and different from crimes. Compared with crimes:

1. similarities:

a. based upon intent usually
b. can be same act
c. justification for punishing

2. differences:
   a. victims are different
   b. punishment much harsher for crimes

Compared with negligence

1. differences:
   a. wrong in negligence is carelessness; in intentional tort, it is intent
   b. punitive damages awarded in intentional torts; not in simple negligence cases

2. similarities:
   a. both are civil wrongs
   b. victims are individuals--not society
   c. can recover both compensatory and nominal damages for both

Compared with contracts

1. similarities:
   a. both areas of civil law
   b. can recover both compensatory and nominal damages

2. differences:
   a. must be a broken contract before recovery in contracts; not so for tort
   b. intentional tort victim can recover punitive; normally not for broken contract.

The legal remedies for intentional torts include nominal, compensatory and punitive damages. Equitable remedies are injunctions, specific performance and accountings.

Types of intentional torts:

1. Fraud--one of the most frequently committed business torts. The elements of fraud are intent to defraud, either buyer or seller can commit fraud, misrepresentation of a fact (not opinion) and can occur by concealment--seller has a duty to disclose material facts not readily ascertainable. See Kinsey v. Scott, 463 N.E.2d 1359 (1984). Scott owned an apartment building that he later modified (fifth apartment) without getting a building permit. Scott sold the building to Kinsey, plaintiff, and in response to a question stated that the building complied with the building codes. The city "red tagged" the fifth apartment for non-compliance with the building code. Kinsey sued Scott for fraud. The court ruled that Scott had a duty to speak and that his concealment showed an intention to deceive. There was no reason for the plaintiff to suspect that the basement apartment was not validly constructed.

2. False imprisonment--this occurs when one person totally restrains another for an "appreciable period of time." There need not be physical harm but the person must be aware of the restraint. One of the main defenses is the "shopkeeper's privilege." This allows a merchant to detain a customer for investigation if there is reasonable cause.

3. Invasion of privacy--this tort covers four loosely related but separate wrongs:
    1. intrusion upon a plaintiff's seclusion or private affairs
    2. public disclosure of private facts
    3. unauthorized appropriation of a person's name or likeness
    4. holding up a person in a false light.

Defenses to the tort are public interest, privilege under libel or slander laws and consent. See Harkey v. Abate, 346 N.W. 2d 74 (1983). Defendant installed see-through panels in the ceiling of the women's restroom. There was no proof that the defendant actually viewed the plaintiff. The court ruled that installation alone interferes with privacy which a reasonable person would find highly offensive. There was also an Illinois criminal statute that classified the act as a felony.

5.   Conversion--is the unauthorized and unjustified interference with the dominion and control of another's personal property. Things other than land and buildings can be converted. Modern courts hold that intangible personal property can be converted.
6. Abuse of process--this tort involves misuse of civil or criminal procedures. Generally, malice is not required.

7. Wrongful interference with contractual relations--the elements are:
    1. a valid and enforceable contract
    2. which a third person has knowledge of
    3. and intentionally induces one of the parties to break. The defendant need not have malice or bad faith. Defenses include lack of a part of the definition of the tort and justification. See Texaco Inc. v. Pennzoil, Co., 729 S.W.2d 768 (1987). The issue is whether there is a binding contract between the Getty entities and Pennzoil. After bargaining back and forth, the museum's board voted to accept the Pennzoil offer. Pennzoil accepted the offer. That evening Getty Oil and the Museum drafted a press release describing the transaction between Getty Oil and Pennzoil. The terms were included on the Memorandum of Agreement. Texaco's board met the day after the announcement and made an offer. On January 6, Texaco and Getty entered into an agreement. Under New York law, parties can obligate themselves informally. The jury determined that Getty intended to be bound when the boards voted in favor of Pennzoil on January 3.

8. Intentional infliction of mental distress--this tort places liability for causing severe emotional distress that goes beyond reasonable decency. Recovery is allowed without physical harm.

9. Defamation--the elements are:
    1. statement must be made by someone by another person
    2. must hold up to ridicule, contempt or scorn
    3. must be published.

Compelled self--publication of defamation can occur when an employee repeats defamatory remarks to a prospective employer made by a previous employer. See Elmore v. Shell Oil Co., 733 F. Supp. 544 (E.D.N.Y. 1988). The plaintiff was discharged by Shell Oil Co. for allegedly accepting large cash gifts from dealers. The trial court dismissed plaintiff's case. The appellate court ruled that the plaintiff would be under strong compulsion to reveal why he was terminated and Shell Oil Co. should know this. The case was allowed to proceed.

The defenses to defamation (libel and slander) include truth, lack of an element and privilege (absolute and qualified).

Review Questions

True/False

_____ 1.   Res Ipsa Loquitur (R.I.L.) is a legal concept that assists the defendant in defending a negligence action.

_____ 2.   If a defendant owes a duty of care to a plaintiff and breaks that duty, the plaintiff will recover.

_____ 3.   Contributory negligence is generally a defense in strict liability cases.

_____ 4.   The same act can be both an intentional tort and a crime.

_____ 5.   Injunctions are court orders that can be both orders to do something or not to do something.

_____ 6.   Gates is a car salesman. He states to Stone, a prospective buyer, "That car is the best on the lot and will go forever." If the car fails to run after 75,000 miles, Gates has committed fraud.

_____ 7.   False imprisonment can occur even if someone is restrained only for a few minutes.

_____ 8.   Modern courts find that even intangible forms of personal property can be converted.

_____ 9.   Truth is a defense to defamation in all cases but those which involve public figures.

_____ 10.   Intervening factors can negate the effect of the original carelessness of a defendant so as to shift the proximate cause to another defendant.

Multiple Choice -- Please circle the best answer

1.   One of the objectives of tort law is
      a.   to punish the wrongdoer.
      b.   to compensate the victim.
      c.   to take revenge in the name of society.
      d.   to make an example of the victim.

2.   The negligence per se doctrine requires
      a.   that a crime be committed.
      b.   that plaintiffs be careless.
      c.   that a statute be violated.
      d.   that a statute designate the act as negligent.

3.   A negligence action requires
      a.   duty.
      b.   breach of duty.
      c.   damages.
      d.   all of the above.

4.   The doctrine of comparative fault requires
      a.   negligence on the part of the plaintiff.
      b.   negligence on the part of the defendant.
      c.   a. and b.
      d.   negligence only on the part of the defendant.

5.   A possible defense to a strict liability action is
      a.   assumption of risk.
      b.   contributory negligence.
      c.   comparative fault.
      d.   last clear chance.

6.   Legal remedies include
      a.   injunctions.
      b.   accountings.
      c.   specific performance.
      d.   compensatory damages.

7.   Fraud would include the element of
      a.   negligent misrepresentation.
      b.   intentional misrepresentation.
      c.   reckless misrepresentation.
      d.   innocent misrepresentation.

8.   A merchant who restrains a suspected shoplifter may commit the tort of
   a.   conversion.
   b.   negligence.
   c.   false imprisonment.
   d.   trespass.

9.   A merchant who calls a debtor at midnight to collect an overdue bill may commit the tort of
   a.   abuse of process.
   b.   invasion of privacy.
   c.   infliction of mental distress.
   d.   b and c.

10.   In order to commit the tort of wrongful interference with contractual relations, the third person
   a.   must act with malice.
   b.   must comply with good public policy.
   c.   must know both parties.
   d.   must have knowledge of the contract.

11.   Torts and crimes are similar in that
   a.   the both try to stop wrongful conduct.
   b.   they both require duties to individuals.
   c.   the district attorney represents the victim.
   d.   they both punish wrongdoers.

12.   The doctrine of _____ limits the defendant's liability for all injuries that s/he causes.
   a.   contributory negligence.
   b.   res ipsa loquitur.
   c.   foreseeability.
   d.   negligence per se.

13.   Compensatory damages in torts
   a.   punish the defendant.
   b.   make the victim whole.
   c.   award small amounts for slight injuries.
   d.   order the defendant to perform an act.

14.   Invasion of privacy would not include
   a.   placing see-through panels in restrooms.
   b.   holding a person up in a false light.
   c.   public disclosure of private facts.
   d.   an article about Roy Rogers.

15.   An element of conversion is
   a.   negligence.

       b.   intent.

       c.   a crime.

       d.   harm.

Short Answer

1.   Name three different areas in which torts differ from crimes.

     a.   _____

     b.   _____

     c.   _____

2.   Name four different elements that are included in negligence.

     a.   _____

     b.   _____

     c.   _____

     d.   _____

3.   Explain the concept of proximate cause and how it operates.

     _____

     _____

     _____

     _____

4.   Name two affirmative defenses to negligence.

     a.   _____

     b.   _____

5.   What are three different kinds of operations that might be considered "ultrahazardous activities."

     a.   _____

b. _____

c. _____

6.   What are five different forms of intentional torts covered in the chapter?

a. _____

b. _____

c. _____

d. _____

e. _____

7.   Describe the "shopkeeper's privilege" and how it relates to false imprisonment.

_____

_____

_____

8.   Name the three defenses to invasion of privacy.

a. _____

b. _____

c. _____

9.   Name two different forms of "process" that relate to the tort of abuse of process.

a. _____

b. _____

10.   List three possible problems that can result from allowing recovery for mental injury where there is no physical harm in an infliction of mental distress case.

a. _____

b. _____

c.   _____

Answers to Review Questions

True/False

1. F	3. F	5. T	7. T	9. F
2. T	4. T	6. F	8. T	10. T

Multiple Choice

1. d.	4. c.	7. b.	10. c.	13. b.
2. a.	5. b.	8. c.	11. a.	14. d.
3. c.	6. c.	9. b.	12. c.	15. b.

Short Answer

1. a.   to whom duty is owed (individuals vs. society in general)
    b.   enforcers (individuals vs. government's representatives)
    c.   objectives (compensatory vs. punishment)

2. a.   duty
    b.   breaking of the standard of care
    c.   proximate causation
    d.   damages

3. Proximate cause means that a defendant's carelessness in fact caused a plaintiff's damage or injury. The carelessness must be close in both time and space for a defendant to be liable and is judged by "forseeability." The issue of intervening factors may have a great effect of what may be the proximate cause in a case.

4. a.   contributory negligence
    b.   assumption of risk

5. a.   dynamiting
    b.   fumigating
    c.   aviation
    d.   keeping wild animals

6. a.   fraud
    b.   false imprisonment

      c.   invasion of privacy

      d.   conversion

      e.   abuse of process

      f.   wrongful interference with business

      g.   intentional infliction of mental distress

      h.   defamation

7.   When one person restrains another against his will for an appreciable amount of time, it is false imprisonment. The "shopkeeper's privilege" allows a merchant with reasonable cause to detain a customer suspected of shoplifting for investigation which must be conducted in a reasonable manner and time.

8.   a.   matter published of public or general interest

         b.   matter is privileged under liable and slander laws

         c.   individual claiming privacy consents to publication

9.   a.   arrest warrants

         b.   service of summons and complaint

10.   a.   fake claims for mental suffering

         b.   flood of cases in court

         c.   encouragement of "cry babies" who cannot withstand stress

         d.   way for angry employees to "get even" with employers

Key Terms

tort: a breach of a noncontractual civil duty where the duty did not come from a contract.

negligence: carelessness that injures others which includes a duty; a breaking of a standard of care that proximately causes damage.

ORP person: ordinary, reasonable, prudent person--objective standard that is utilized to determine liability in negligence cases.

negligence per se doctrine: violation of a relevant statute that sets a level of care constitutes negligence.

Res Ipsa Loquitur (R.I.L.): "the thing speaks for itself"--allows an inference of negligence, meaning that a plaintiff has proven negligence unless a defendant has some defense.

proximate cause: defendant's carelessness in fact caused a plaintiff's damage and must be close in both time and space.

intervening causes: factors which have the effect of breaking the chain of causation between carelessness and ultimate damage caused.

contributory negligence: a plaintiff's own carelessness partly caused the loss or injury.

assumption of risk: plaintiff's own exposure to known dangers undertaken in a manner which negates the ability to collect damages.

strict liability: liability for harm proximately caused even though no fault is shown.

ultrahazardous activities: activities such as dynamiting, fumigation, flying airplanes, keeping wild animals, and other risky activities which generally carry strict liability implications.

intentional torts: torts which include an element of intent.

legal remedies: remedies at law that refer to the collection of money by those who have been harmed.

nominal damages: legal remedy whereby a small amount of money (usually one dollar) is collected for the interference with a right, but where no substantial harm occurs.

compensatory damages: legal remedy whereby money is gained to "make the victim whole."

punitive damages: legal remedy to punish wrongdoers when their conduct is particularly outrageous and to act as a deterrent to others.

equitable remedies: remedies that may be recovered only when remedies at law would be inadequate.

injunction: equitable remedy where a court orders someone or some entity to do or to stop doing an activity.

specific performance: an equitable contract remedy which orders a person or entity breaking a contract to perform that obligation.

accounting: an equitable remedy which orders that someone, such as an agent, presents income and expense records to someone else.

fraud: a misrepresentation of a material fact which the defrauding person knows about; that includes an intent to defraud, reliance, and the realization of damages.

false imprisonment: occurs when one person totally restrains another for an appreciable period of time (can be just a few minutes.)

shopkeeper's privilege: privilege which allows a merchant with reasonable cause to detain a customer suspected of shoplifting for investigation; must be conducted in a reasonable manner and time.

invasion of privacy: intrusion upon a plaintiff's solitude or seclusion or into his or her affairs; public disclosure of private facts; unauthorized appropriation of a person's name or likeness.

conversion: unauthorized and unjustified interference with the domination and control of another's personal property.

abuse of process: an ulterior purpose and willful act that results in the use of the legal process not proper in the regular conduct of proceedings.

wrongful interference with contractual relations: the knowing interference with the existing contractual relation of others so as to attempt to induce a breach between them.

intention infliction of mental distress: the placing of liability on a person for intentionally causing severe emotional distress in situations where the actor's conduct goes beyond reasonable decency.

defamation: injury caused to a person's character or reputation by false statements that are published to third parties.

privilege: defense to otherwise defamatory statements due to a superior public policy of free expression.

CHAPTER 11

NATURE, DEFINITION, AND CLASSIFICATION OF CONTRACTS

Chapter Summary

Contracts are the basis for the market economy. In the mid- and late-twentieth century, two trends have emerged in contract law. The first trend has been toward long term contracts and the second is a trend concentration of economic power. The law governing contracts is generally state law. Article 2 of the U.C.C. governs contracts dealing with goods. Real estate, services and insurance contracts are controlled by common law and other state statutes. The Restatement, Second, Contracts define a contract as "a promise or set of promises for the breach of which the law gives a remedy, or the performance of which the law in some way recognizes as a duty." The objective theory of contracts means that contracts are determined by what people appear to have done (objective), not what they think they have done (subjective).

Contract classifications:

1. bilateral contracts--two people exchange promises--one promise for another.

2. unilateral contract--a person makes a promise and asks for an act in return. See Davis v. Jacoby, 34 P.2d 1026 (1934). Mr. Whitehead became ill and wrote to Caro and Frank Davis asking them to come to California and care for the Whiteheads until they die and in return they would receive everything under his will. The Davises cared for Mrs. Whitehead until she died. Mr. Whitehead died while they were en route. The will did not give the Davises everything. The estate argued that the offer was unilateral and since the act was not performed before Mr. Whitehead died there was no contract. The court ruled that the offer was ambiguous. In this case, the Restatement presumes that

111

the offer to enter into a contract is bilateral. The reasoning is that the rights and duties of the parties come into existence and both parties are protected. Mr. Whitehead was very ill and what he wanted was a promise from the parties.

3. express contract--contracts that are either oral or written.

4. implied contract--a contract that can be inferred from the parties' conduct.

5. valid contract--one that is enforceable under virtually all circumstances.

6. voidable contract--a contract that contains a defect that could make it unenforceable. One of the parties may escape liability by noting the defect (minors-fraud).

7. void contract--there was no contract at all. Examples would be illegal contracts, contracts against public policy and persons adjudged legally insane to contract.

8. executory contract--contracts that are only partly performed by the parties. If fully performed, the contract is executed.

9. Quasi-contracts are not contracts but a legal doctrine that creates a contract to prevent unjust enrichment. At times the court will not allow the quasi-contract concept. If the persons receiving the benefits do not have an opportunity to reject the benefits, quasi-contract is not allowed. For an example of a quasi-contract, see Matter of Estate of Milborn, 461 N.E.2d 1075 (1984). The Campbells cared and fed the decedent and handled her financial affairs. The decedent was ill for some time and would or could not care for herself. The Campbells expected compensation and filed a claim of $5,000. The executor disallowed the claim and argued that the Campbells failed to prove that the decedent requested or expected to pay for these services. The court ruled the deceased needed assistance and the services were not rendered on a gratuitous basis. The parties were not related. The claim of $5,000 was allowed as a reasonable value for services rendered.

The first step in making a contract is for one person to make an offer to another. The offer indicates what the offeror will do and what is expected in return. Objective intent is used to decide whether an offer is made. If an offer clearly is made as a joke or excited utterance, it is not enforceable. Social offers are not enforceable. Agreements to agree have no present effect and are not contracts. Some media ads can be offers if definite, complete, certain and limited to specific terms. The general rule is that offers must be definite and certain. Offers must be communicated before they are effective.

Offers can end in other ways than acceptance.

1. The offer will remain open for as long as the offer states. If not stated, for a reasonable time.

2. Revocation takes effect when communicated to the offeree. An earlier offer that contained a provision that it would remain open for a stated period of time can be revoked if not a firm offer (UCC)

or an option contract.

3. A offeror cannot revoke an option contract if offeror receives consideration.

4. A firm offer under the UCC is a written offer made by a merchant for the sale of goods and assurance is made that the offer will stay open for a stated period of time (three month maximum). Does not apply to realty or services.

5. A unilateral contract expects an act. If revocation attempted before completion of the act, most courts allow offeree a reasonable time to complete the contract.

6. A rejection ends the offer if it is unequivocal. Mere questions do not end the offer.

7. Changing or adding to terms in the original offer is a counteroffer and this ends the offer under the common law. The UCC treats this area differently and allows changes in contract formation. See Gibbs v. American Sav. and Loan Ass'n, 266 Cal. Rptr. 517 (1990). The acceptance was given to the mail clerk in the office of Mrs. Gibbs before 10:00 a.m. on June 6. At 11:00 a.m., a representative of the Savings and Loan withdrew the counteroffer. The envelope containing the acceptance was postmarked June 7. The court ruled that the acceptance had to be placed out of the control of the accepting party in order to be considered "in the course of transmission." The revocation therefore took place before the acceptance--no contract.

8. The death or insanity of either the offeror or offeree ends the offer.

9. The destruction of essential subject matter of the offer ends the offer.

10. An intervening or subsequent illegality ends the offer.

An acceptance is an assent by the offeree to the offeror's terms. This can occur by word or act. The offeree does not have to use the word accept, can communicate intent to accept. See Glover v. Jewish War Veterans of the United States, 68 A.2d 233 (1949). Can an individual collect a reward when they had no knowledge when information was given. The court ruled in the case of private rewards the claimant must know of the offer of the reward and act with the intention of accepting it.

The acceptance must be done in the manner requested by the offeror. See Champage Chrysler-Plymouth Inc. v. Giles, 388 So.2d 1343 (1980). Giles attempted to accept an offer that appeared on tv February 17. Giles in mid-February bowled a perfect game and claims he had accepted the offer. The court ruled that if the offer was a unilateral contract, it would not have been necessary to revoke it. These offers would expire by their own terms. The summary judgement in favor of Giles was reversed and the case sent back for trial.

Only the offeree can accept. Generally silence is not acceptance. The Federal Postal Reorganization Act of 1970 permits those receiving unordered goods to keep, used, discard, or dispose of them in any manner without obligation. If the offer is for realty or services, the acceptance must "mirror" the offer in all respects. If not, the acceptance is treated as a counteroffer voiding the original offer. The UCC rejects the "Mirror image rule" and treats additional terms as proposals which the offeror can accept or reject. If the offeror clearly states that the acceptance is effective when received, it is only valid upon receipt. If the offer is silent, a mailed acceptance is effective on the date it is sent. This rule applies even if the letter of acceptance never reaches the offeror. A telegraphed acceptance is effective when given to the telegraph office official, unless specified otherwise by the offeror. The telephone can also be used for acceptance. At an auction, an auctioneer makes invitations to negotiate and the audience's bids are offers. If the auction is "with reserve," the auctioneer may withdraw an item if bids are too low. If "without reserve," the item goes to the highest bidder.

Review Questions

True/False

____ 1.   The objective theory of contracts means that contracts are determined by what people think they have done.

____ 2.   "I'll pay you $100 if you take my sister to the football game," is an example of an offer contemplating a unilateral contract.

____ 3.   Even though a person receiving benefits does not have a reasonable opportunity to reject those benefits, the court will still allow recovery by the person supplying the benefit under a quasi-contract.

____ 4.   Offers can be made both expressly or by implication.

____ 5.   Although jokes or excited utterances are not normally enforceable, a person who makes such supposed offers must go to court to negate this obligation.

____ 6.   Offers must be communicated before they are effective, but if a potential offeree secretly learns of an offer before it is actually communicated -- an acceptance given at that time will mean a valid contract has been formed.

____ 7.   An express contract can be either oral or written.

____ 8.   Silence is valid as an acceptance if the offer explicitly agrees to it in the offer.

____ 9.   The UCC rule on additional or varying terms in acceptance is less flexible than the "mirror image" rule of the common law.

____ 10.   If an auction is "with reserve," the auctioneer may not withdraw an item if bids are too low and the highest bidder's offer (even if unsatisfactory) must be accepted.

Multiple Choice

1.   The libertarian idea as applied to the law of contracts is best described as follows:
      a.   each individual determines the greatest good for him or herself.
      b.   people are free to choose from many alternatives.
      c.   a command from the government with sanctions if broken.
      d.   ethics must be the deciding factor in all contracts.

2.   The law governing contracts is generally
      a.   federal law.
      b.   commercial law.
      c.   state law.
      d.   tort law.

3.   A bilateral contract contemplates
      a.   a promise for an act.
      b.   two promises on one side of the contract.
      c.   an unenforceable promise.
      d.   a promise for a promise.

4.   An example of a voidable contract is
      a.   a contract that contains fraud.
      b.   a contract required to be in writing.
      c.   an oral contract.
      d.   a quasi-contract.

5.   An unenforceable contract would be a contract
      a.   in which one party is a minor.
      b.   that has been executed on both sides.
      c.   that falls within the statute of frauds.
      d.   that is against public policy.

6.   The first step in making a contract is for one person to make
      a.   an invitation for another to make an offer.
      b.   an offer.
      c.   a counteroffer.
      d.   a statement of intention.

7.   If Robert asks Terry for a date and Terry agrees, they have entered into a(n)
      a.   agreement
      b.   contract
      c.   sham transaction
      d.   excited utterance

8.   A requirements contract exits when
    a.   one person agrees to purchase something and pay another's costs.
    b.   an offer covers an indefinite period of time.
    c.   a price is understood in the trade.
    d.   one company agrees to buy all of its needs from another.

9.   A revocation is effective when
    a.   sent.
    b.   received.
    c.   lost.
    d.   postmarked.

10.   For an option to stop the offeror from revoking during the stated option period, there must be
    a.   an agreement.
    b.   an oral understanding.
    c.   consideration.
    d.   revocation.

11.   Article 2 of the UCC covers contracts dealing with
    a.   realty.
    b.   goods.
    c.   land.
    d.   services.

12.   Harry has a charge account at the local grocery store. He enters the store, picks up a loaf of bread, waves it at the clerk, the clerk nods, and Harry walks out. This contract can be classified as
    a.   an express contract.
    b.   implied in law.
    c.   implied in fact.
    d.   voidable.

13.   A valid contract is
    a.   voidable at the option of one party.
    b.   unenforceable at the option of one party.
    c.   one that does not meet all the elements.
    d.   enforceable under all circumstances.

14.   An advertisement for apples at 49¢ a pound in the Boone Journal is
    a.   an invitation to make an offer.
    b.   an enforceable offer.
    c.   a voidable offer.
    d.   an executed offer.

15.   A rejection by the offeree is effective when
      a.   sent by the offeree.
      b.   received by the offeror.
      c.   placed in the mail.
      d.   postmarked by the post office.

Short Answer

1.   According to the Restatement, Second, Contracts of the ALI, what is the definition for a "contract?"

      _____

      _____

      _____

      _____

2.   What is the objective theory of contracts?

      _____

      _____

      _____

3.   What are four different contract classification groupings discussed in the chapter?

      a.   _____

      b.   _____

      c.   _____

      d.   _____

4.   Describe the difference between an implied-in-fact and implied-in-law contract.

      _____

      _____

_____

5.   Explain the respective roles of the offeror and the offeree in a contract.

_____

_____

6.   Name four exceptions to the rule that offers must generally be definite.

a.   _____

b.   _____

c.   _____

d.   _____

7.   Name five different ways that an offer ends other than acceptance.

a.   _____

b.   _____

c.   _____

d.   _____

e.   _____

8.   Explain what a "firm offer" is under the UCC.

_____

_____

_____

9.   Explain the effect of the Federal Postal Reorganization Act of 1970 on unordered goods in the mail transactions.

_____

_____

10.   Describe what the "mailbox rule" means to acceptances that are placed in the mail.

Answers to Review Questions

True/False

1. F   3. F   5. F   7. T   9. F
2. T   4. T   6. F   8. F   10. F

Multiple Choice

1. c.   4. a.   7. d.   10. c.   13. d.
2. b.   5. b.   8. c.   11. b.   14. a.
3. b.   6. a.   9. a.   12. c.   15. b.

Short Answer

1.   A contract is a promise or set of promises for the breach of which the law gives a remedy, or the performance of which the law in some way recognizes as a duty.

2.   It means that contracts are determined by what people appear to have done (objective) and not what they think they have done (subjective.) This theory forces judges to point to evidence people can see to decide if a contract exists, if at all possible.

3.   a.   bilateral and unilateral
       b.   express and implied
       c.   valid, voidable, void and unenforceable
       d.   executed and executory
       e.   quasi-contracts

4.   Implied-in-fact contracts are formed when nothing is said and yet the parties' conduct shows they intended to make a contract. Implied-in-law contracts are a legal idea that lets judges force a contract on parties even though they did not have one and exist to prevent unjust enrichment.

They apply in situations where a benefit is conferred, no gift is intended, and compensation for reasonable value of the benefit should be paid.

5.   The offeror is the person making the offer and the offeree is the person to whom the offer is directed in a contract.

6.   Any of the following:
      a.   trade custom   e.   contracts of indefinite length
      b.   previous dealings   f.   cost-plus contracts
      c.   implicit terms   g.   requirement and output contracts
      d.   open terms in sale of   h.   retainer contracts
            goods contracts   i.   incorporation of another writing

7.   Any of the following:
      a.   time lapse   e.   death or insanity of the offeror or offeree
      b.   revocation   f.   destruction of essential subject matter
      c.   counter-offer   g.   intervening or subsequent illegality
      d.   rejection

8.   A firm offer is a written offer made by a merchant for the sale or purchase of goods, assuring that the offer will be irrevocable for the period of time stated in the offer (up to a three month maximum, which is renewable.)

9.   The act permits people receiving unordered goods in the mail from businesses to keep, use, discard or dispose of the goods in any manner without obligation.

10.   Where the offeror fails to say anything about an acceptance's effective date, a mailed acceptance is effective under common law on the date it was sent (deposited) with correct postage and address. The rule applies even if the letter of acceptance never reaches the offeror.

Key Terms

contracts: agreements between all types of persons and entities that set up a legal relationship that is enforceable by the parties.

objective theory of contracts: contracts are determined by what people appear to have done and not by what they think they have done.

bilateral contract: the exchange of promises whereby one promise is made for the other.

unilateral contract: an agreement that consists of a promise for an act.

express contracts: those contracts having terms completely stated in words; can be oral or written.

implied contracts: contracts that are determined from the parties' conduct even though nothing is said or written.

valid contract: a contract with no legal flaws that is enforceable under virtually all circumstances.

voidable contract: a contract that allows a party to escape liability, if he or she so chooses, due to certain defects that may exist.

void contract: there has been no contract at all--ever--because it contains fatal flaws in its legality.

unenforceable contracts: contracts which fail to meet procedural or formal requirements.

executory contracts: partly performed or totally unperformed.

quasi-contract: an "implied-in-law" concept that allows a judge to force a contract on parties to avoid unjust enrichment.

offer: when the offeror in some way that meets legal requirements tells the offeree that the offeror wants to enter a contract with the offeree.

offeror: the person or entity making the offer.

offeree: the person or entity to whom the offer is made.

sham transactions: things that appear to be contracts in form but in fact are not contracts in substance.

revocation: the recalling or calling back of an offer.

options: offers that stop the offeror from revoking the offer during the stated period or until a certain date.

firm offer: special UCC provision that makes a written offer by a merchant for the sale of goods an assurance that the offer will be irrevocable for the period stated (up to three months maximum, which is renewable.)

rejection: offeree's unequivocal refusal of an offer that is communicated to the offeror.

counter-offer: statements by the offeree to the offeror changing terms in the original offer which under common law end offers.

acceptance: assent by the offeree to the offer's terms which can occur by word or act.

Section 3009 of the Federal postal Reorganization Act of 1970: section that permits people receiving unordered goods in the mail from businesses to keep, use, discard or dispose of the goods in any manner without obligation whatsoever to the sender.

mailbox rule: common law rule that applies when an offeror fails to say anything about an acceptance's effective date and means that a mailed acceptance is effective on the date it was sent (deposited) with correct postage and address.

12 PROPERTY

Chapter Summary

Property is the rights one person has regarding other people with respect to something. Property law is governed by state law, 50 states, 50 different laws. Some federal laws regulate property, the Fifth and Fourteenth Amendments. The Interstate Land Sales Full Disclosure Act regulates the sale of undeveloped land by giving the buyer a three (3) day cooling-off period. Title is ownership. Title documents, deeds for land and titles for cars and trucks, is a piece of paper saying who owns the object.

Property is classified as follows:

1. Personal property refers to movables.

2. Real property refers to land and buildings. Realty also includes air rights and subsurface rights.

3. A fixture is personal property that is permanently attached to land. Trade fixtures are items used for the conduct of business and remain personal property.

4. Tangible property can be seen; intangible property cannot be seen.

5. Private property belongs to one person and public belongs to the government.

There are several types of real property estates or interests in land.

1. A fee simple absolute is the highest interest in land. The owner may sell, give or devise the realty.

2. A life estate is an interest for one's lifetime. Upon death, the realty goes to someone else.

3. A leasehold is the lease of another's realty. This gives the "tenant" a temporary right in the realty. This right may be for a fixed period or run from period to period.

4. An easement is a nonpossessory right to use someone else's realty.

5. Profits are a right to enter someone else's realty to remove something (minerals, crops, water).

6. A license is not a real property interest but a right to use another's realty (theatre seat).

      Property can be owned by more than one person.

1. Tenants in common have a right to the whole realty. They can give, sell or devise their interest.

2. Joint tenants own the realty together with the right of survivorship. They cannot convey their interest by will-except for the last joint tenant. If an interest is conveyed by one of the joint tenants, the transferee becomes a tenant in common for that share. This tenancy is not presumed, it must be specified.

3. Tenancy by the entirety is a specialized form of joint tenancy. The joint tenants must be spouses. There is a right of survivorship.

4. Tenancy in partnership occurs when business partners own property; realty, personalty, or fixtures. It has a survivorship feature.

5. Real estate syndications arise when several persons own property. It can be a partnership, limited partnership or corporation.

6. Community property is a way married couples own property. When one spouse acquires property, half of it belongs to the other.

7. A condominium is a way individuals can own the space between the walls of their unit.

      Property can be acquired in a number of ways.

1. A thief cannot pass legal title. The original owner can reclaim the property even from a good faith purchaser.

2. If title is obtained by fraud or duress (voidable title), the property can be passed on to a good faith purchaser.

3. UCC 2-403(2)--In some instances, merchants who deal in goods of like kind can pass on title to a buyer in the ordinary course of business. This concept protects the marketplace.

4. Title can be obtained by adverse possession. The property must be held openly, adversely and continuously and owned by another. Property must be held for the statutory period of time (10-20 years). See Pieper v. Pontiff, 513 So.2d 591 (1987). Land can mistakenly be held and still be adverse. Once title ripened in Mrs. Reynolds by adverse possession and once she conveyed it to her daughter Mrs. Pontiff, Mr. Pieper could not defeat the claim.

5. Property can be transferred by making a gift. The elements of a gift are intent, delivery and acceptance.

6. Capture is a way to acquire title to animals in the wild.

7. The finder of lost property has superior title except as to the true owner. If the property is abandoned, title goes to the first one who takes possession.

8. Deceased persons' estates may transfer property (inheritance) either by the statute of descent or by will.

9. One can acquire property as a trustee or as a trust beneficiary.

10. A person may acquire ownership of property by manufacturing it from materials s/he owns.

11. Title to property may arise from use of fungible goods. Fungible goods are those which are uniform in size, shape or nature.

12. Purchase is the most common means of acquiring property. Personalty or realty can be acquired by a contract.

One basic right a property owner has is to use the rights in the property. Often an owner of personalty will want to lend their property to some friend. This is called a bailment. The law recognizes three types of bailments: bailment for the sole benefit of the bailor; bailment for the sole benefit of the bailee; and mutual benefit bailment. The owner of real estate could let others use his or her realty. A license is the right to enter another's realty for a limited time and purpose. An easement is also a non-possessory interest in someone else's realty. A lease is a limited right to possess and use someone else's realty for a limited time. This is frequently refereed to as landlord-tenant law and is state law. About one-third of the states have passed the Uniform Residential Landlord Tenant Act (URL&A). This law only covers residential leases. URL&A addresses deposits, subleasing, habitability, landlord right of access, landlord rules governing tenants, general duties and unconscionability. See National Corp. for Housing Partnership v. Liberty State Bank, 836 F.2d 433 (1988). The bank had no right to the proceeds of the CDs since the landlord did not own the tenant's deposits but was merely a bailee of them.

Several devices protect ideas including copyrights, trademarks, and patents. Copyrights protect artistic, literary or musical works. Ideas cannot be copyrighted but expression of ideas can. Owners have the exclusive right for their lifetime plus 50 years (if copyrighted after January 1, 1978). This is federal law and failure to obtain permission amounts to infringement. The fair use doctrine allows copying of copyrighted material for instruction, research and criticism. Under some circumstances, a custom computer program can be copyrighted. See Whelan Associates, Inc. v. Jaslow Dental Laboratory, Inc., 797 F.2d 1222 (1986). Trademarks refer to any word, letter, number, design, picture, or combination to designate someone's goods. There are federal statutory trademarks, common law and state trademarks. The Lanham Act creates federal statutory trademarks and provides for a registration system. The mark is protected for 20 years. Services can be given a service mark. Common law trademarks are created by use over a period of time. Only goods can be trademarked. See Mutual of Omaha Ins. Co. v. Novak, 836 F.2d 397 (1987). The court ruled that the use of a mark similar to that of Mutual of Omaha's created a "likelihood of confusion" and hence constituted an infringement. A patent is a legal monopoly that entitles the patentee to make, use and sell the patented item for 17 years. This is exclusively federal law and protection is limited to the U.S. These rights are assignable or inheritable and unauthorized use can constitute an infringement. See Diamond v. Diehr, 450 U.S. 175 (1981). When a claim containing a mathematical formula implements or applies the formula in a structure or process which, when considered as a whole, is performing a function which the patent laws were designed to protect, then the claim can be patented.

Property rights can be limited by various forms of government regulation.

1. A public nuisance can be a tort or a crime. A private nuisance injures some private right not common to the public.

2. Local, state and federal governments have the power to tax property.

3. The power of eminent domain comes from the Fifth Amendment. Government can take private land for public use if it gives just compensation. The term "use" has been expanded to mean purpose. See Hawaii Housing Authority v. Midkiff, 467 U.S. 229 (1984). It is not a taking to confer a private benefit on a particular private party. The Hawaii Legislature enacted the Land Reform Act to attack certain perceived evils of concentrated property ownership in Hawaii ... a legitimate public purpose.

Review Questions

True/False

_____ 1.   Realty refers to land and buildings.

_____ 2.   A trade fixture attached to a building becomes a permanent part of the realty.

_____ 3.   A fee simple absolute is the highest interest that can be owned in realty.

____ 4.   An easement in gross benefits an adjacent piece of land.

____ 5.   Joint tenancy is an inheritable estate.

____ 6.   A deed is not necessary in order to convey realty by gift.

____ 7.   A person may acquire title to mislaid property by taking possession of it.

____ 8.   A trust interest must vest within a life in being at the time the trust becomes effective plus 21 years.

____ 9.   A bailee must exercise ordinary care in a bailment for the sole benefit of the bailee.

____ 10.   Ideas cannot be copyrighted.

Multiple Choice -- Circle the correct answer

1.   Fructus industriales includes
      a.   trees.
      b.   grass.
      c.   crops.
      d.   weeds.

2.   Whether personalty becomes a fixture depends on the
      a.   time of attachment.
      b.   intent of the owner.
      c.   type of business.
      d.   type of ownership.

3.   An easement is
      a.   a possessory interest in land.
      b.   a non-possessory interest in land.
      c.   a right to enter someone else's land.
      d.   not a real property interest.

4.   Tenants in common may
      a.   sell their interest.
      b.   not sell their interest.
      c.   not be a husband and wife.
      d.   have survivorship rights.

5.   A thief has
      a.   voidable title.

   b.   void title.
   c.   good title and can give valid title to a good faith purchaser.
   d.   voidable title but can pass good title to a merchant who deals in goods of like kind.

6.   Adverse possession applies to
   a.   realty.
   b.   personalty.
   c.   only named individuals in the deed.
   d.   the true owner of the land.

7.   The court that has jurisdiction over wills is the
   a.   district court.
   b.   superior court.
   c.   municipal court.
   d.   probate court.

8.   Wills take effect when the
   a.   testator executes the will.
   b.   bequests are made.
   c.   testator dies.
   d.   testator so states in the will.

9.   A beneficiary of a trust
   a.   equitable title to the res.
   b.   legal title to the res.
   c.   a mere expectancy and nothing more.
   d.   no title to the res.

10.   The Lanham Act protects registered trademarks for
   a.   17 years.
   b.   50 years.
   c.   20 years.
   d.   10 years.

11.   A life estate
   a.   may be transferred by will.
   b.   may not be transferred by will.
   c.   is the highest form of ownership.
   d.   is an interest for life plus 21 years.

12.   If a joint tenant conveys her/his interest while alive, the joint tenancy becomes a
   a.   tenancy by the entirety.
   b.   community property.
   c.   tenancy in common.

     d.   survivorship interest.

13.   The capture doctrine is a way to acquire title to animals
     a.   in the wild.
     b.   in captivity.
     c.   who are lost.
     d.   that are abandoned.

14.   Mislaid property becomes the property of the
     a.   state.
     b.   one who parted with it but forgot it.
     c.   the finder.
     d.   first one to take possession.

15.   If the bailment is for the benefit of the bailor, the bailee has
     a.   a high standard of care.
     b.   the duty of ordinary care.
     c.   no duty of care.
     d.   a slight duty of care.

Short Answer

1.   Name two legal philosophies reflected in property law.

     a.   _____

     b.   _____

2.   What is the difference between title and title documents?

     _____

     _____

3.   Name four elements used to determine if personalty has become a fixture.

     a.   _____

     b.   _____

     c.   _____

     d.   _____

4.   Name three types of joint realty ownership.

   a.   _____

   b.   _____

   c.   _____

5.   Explain the entrustment provision found in section 2-403(2) of the U.C.C. What does this provision protect?

   _____

   _____

   _____

6.   Name three elements of inter vivos gift.

   a.   _____

   b.   _____

   c.   _____

7.   What is the difference between lost and mislaid property?

   _____

   _____

   _____

8.   Name the formal requirements of a will.

   a.   _____

   b.   _____

   c.   _____

   d.   _____

9.   Name two duties of a trustee.

    a.   _____

    b.   _____

10.   What is the power of eminent domain?

    _____

    _____

Answers to Review Questions

True/False

1. T	3. T	5. F	7. T	9. F
2. F	4. F	6. F	8. T	10. T

Multiple Choice

1.	c.	4.	a.	7.	d.	10.	c.	13.	a.
2.	b.	5.	b.	8.	c.	11.	b.	14.	b.
3.	b.	6.	a.	9.	a.	12.	c.	15.	d.

Short Answer

1.   a.   positive law
    b.   historical jurisprudence
    c.   natural law
    d.   sociological school

2.   title refers to actual ownership whereas a title document is a piece of paper telling who owns the object

3.   a.   intent of the owner
    b.   who attached the item
    c.   how securely is the item attached
    d.   function of the personalty to the realty

4.   a.   tenants in common

b.   joint tenants
c.   tenancy by the entirety
d.   tenancy in partnership
e.   real estate syndication
f.   community property
g.   condominiums

5.   any entrusting by the owner of goods to a merchant who deals in goods of that kind gives the merchant the power to transfer all rights in the goods to a buyer in the ordinary course of business. This protects commerce or the marketplace.

6.   a.   donative intent
b.   delivery
c.   acceptance

7.   lost property was unintentionally parted with whereas mislaid property was intentionally parted with

8.   a.   declaration
b.   witnesses
c.   attestation
d.   age

9.   a.   duty to manage according to terms of the instrument
b.   duty not to act negligently
c.   highest duty of good faith and loyalty (fiduciary duty)
d.   duty to account

10.   government may take any private property if it gives just compensation and there is public use or purpose.

Key Terms

property: the rights people or a person has to something (not the object).

eminent domain: the right of the government to take private property, if it gives just compensation and there is public use.

title: refers to ownership.

title document: piece of paper saying who owns the object (deeds-titles).

deed: title document that conveys realty.

personalty (personal property): refers to movables.

realty (real property): refers to land and buildings.

fructus naturales: grow naturally on the land without help of humankind.

fructus industriales: crops arising from vegetation grown partly by human effort.

fixture: personal property that is permanently attached to realty.

trade fixture: such items as signs and counters, firmly attached to the realty, yet remain the tenants' personal property.

tangible: property that can be seen.

intangible: property that cannot be seen.

private property: belongs to one person.

person: legal entity--can be a partnership or corporation.

public property: owned by a government.

interest: right of use or ownership.

estate: an interest in realty.

fee simple absolute: the highest interest one can have in realty.

life estate: an interest in realty for one's life but no longer.

life tenants: persons who have life estates.

leasehold: a temporary interest in another's realty.

tenant: a person with a leasehold.

easement: a nonpossessory right to use another's realty for some purpose.

servient estate: property subject to the easement.

dominant estate: property enjoying the benefit of the easement.

easements appurtenant: benefit another piece of land.

easement in gross: benefit a certain person or business.

affirmative easement: one is given the right to use another person's land.

negative easement: prevents one from doing something on one's land.

profits: right to enter another's real estate to remove something.

licenses: right to use another's realty (not a real property interest.)

tenants in common: two or more people have title to an interest in realty.

joint tenants: own realty together but with a right of survivorship.

tenancy by the entirety: a specialized form of joint tenancy in which the tenants must be spouses --
    survivorship.

tenancy in partnership: joint ownership of property by business partners with survivorship.

community property: joint ownership by married couples; when one spouse acquires property, half
    belongs to the other spouse.

condominiums: method by which individuals can own the space between the walls of a unit and have
    equal interests in the common areas of the unit.

theft: the act of stealing.

voidable title: title gotten by duress or fraud can be voided; however, clear title can be passed to a
    good faith purchaser for value.

adverse possession: claim to ownership by openly, adversely and continuously using property owned
    by another.

gift: voluntary transfer of title to property where the transferor receives nothing in return.

donor: giver of the gift.

donee: person receiving the gift.

intervivos gifts: gifts between living persons.

gift causa mortis: gift in contemplation of death.

capture: a way to acquire title to animals in the wild.

lost property: personalty that has been unintentionally, involuntarily parted with by the owner.

finder: one who locates lost property.

mislaid property: personalty one intentionally parts with, but cannot recall parting with.

abandoned property: personalty that has been intentionally and permanently parted with by leaving it in another's custody.

statute of descent: a will made by a state legislature for individuals who die intestate (without a will.)

will: document in which a testator (maker of the will) indicates who is to have property.

holographic will: handwritten will.

formal requirements: procedural requirements for a will.

ambulatory: will can be changed before testator dies.

executor: person named in the will to manage and wind up the estate.

administrator: person named by the court to manage and wind up the estate.

bequest: personal property given by a will.

devise: realty given by a will.

trust: legal relationship consisting of a settlor, a res, a trustee, and a beneficiary.

settlor: person who sets up a trust.

res: subject matter of the trust.

trustee: person having legal title who manages the res.

beneficiary: person who receives trust benefits and holds beneficial title.

rule against perpetuities: sets a time limit in which all interests in a trust must vest.

vest: to take effect and become the property rights of someone.

inter vivos trust: trust that takes effect during the settlor's life.

testamentary trust: trust that takes effect at the settlor's death.

fiduciary duty: highest duty of good faith and loyalty.

bailment: separation of title and possession of personal property.

bailor: owner of bailed property.

bailee: borrower of bailed property.

tenancy at sufferance: person who has overstayed lawful time.

tenancy at will: for no definite length of time.

periodic tenancy: for discrete periods of time, e.g., a week or month.

tenancy for years: leases beginning and ending at definite times.

copyright: federal law that protects artistic, literary or musical works.

trademark: refers to any word, letter, number, design, picture or combination to designate someone's goods.

patent: legal monopoly conferred by the federal government that grants exclusive rights for the patented item to the patentee.

public nuisance: unreasonable or unlawful use of property producing material annoyance or hurt.

private nuisance: unreasonable use of property or personalty to obstruct, annoy or hurt some private right not common to the public.

EMPLOYER-EMPLOYEE RELATIONS: COMMON LAW RULES

Chapter Summary

This chapter governs common law rules governing employers' relations with individual employees. The legal classifications of this relationship are as follows:

1. A master-servant relationship arises when one person employs another to perform physical tasks that do not involve making contracts.

2. A principal-agent relationship arises where one person employs another to enter into business relationships with third parties (contracts).

3. An employer-independent contractor relationship is when the employer does not have the right to control the means by which the independent contractor does the work.

One who has the mental capacity to act in one's behalf may be a principal. Minors can be principals but can later avoid the contract. One may be an agent, servant or independent contractor as long as one has the mental and physical capability to perform. Minors, corporations and partnerships may be agents.

An employer has greater liability if the employee is classified as a servant or agent. The doctrine of respondent superior applies to servants or agents; it generally does not apply to independent contractors. See <u>Fruit</u> v. <u>Schriener</u>, 502 P.2d 133 (1972). The court upheld a jury verdict that an employee traveling to the convention headquarters where he was attending meetings as part of his employment was acting for his employer, Equitable Assurance. Equitable is therefore liable for the negligent acts of its employee-agent.

There are several types of agents.

1. A general agent has broad authority for various transactions.

2. A del credere agent is similar to a guarantor.

3. A special agent is one who is employed to accomplish a particular task.

A principal must give actual notice to those who have dealt with a general agent, not so if a special agent, upon termination. A principal or an employer is generally not liable for the acts of an independent contractor. Social security and worker's compensation taxes do not have to be paid on an independent contractor. See Toyota Motor Sales v. Superior Court, 269 Cal. Rptr. 647 (1990). The issue is whether a pizza deliveryperson is an employee or an independent contractor for liability purposes. The most significant factor in determining the relationship is the right to control the manner and means of accomplishing the result. The Court of Appeals held that the deliveryperson was an agent or servant, not an independent contractor.

Employees can obtain authority to do their work in at least four ways.

1. express authority is given orally or in writing.

2. Implied authority is inferred from express authority. It can arise from emergency or necessity.

3. Apparent authority is created by words or conduct of a principal leading third persons to believe that the agent has authority. See Northington v. Dairyland Ins. Co., 445 So. 2d 283 (1984). The court found that Dairyland Ins. Co. did nothing to lead Ms. Northington to believe that Mr. Wills had authority to act for the company in the manner in which he acted. Apparent authority must be based on conduct of the principal and not of the agent.

4. The unauthorized act of an agent can be later ratified by the principal. This can be accomplished by accepting the benefits and burdens of the unauthorized act of the agent.

The duties that masters owe servants is to provide a safe work place, to provide proper tools and to pay reasonable value for services. See Overstreet v. Norman, 314 S.W. 2d 47 (1957). The court, in rejecting standard defenses, held the employer liable for failing to maintain a safe workplace by not having a proper step from the truck to the ground. The duties principles owe agents are payment, reimbursement for ordinary and necessary expenses and to indemnify for losses and liabilities in performance of agency duties. Agents owe principals the duty to account; to use proper care and skill; to follow instructions and to act with great faith, loyalty and accountability (fiduciary duty).

An agent or servant is always personally liable for her/his torts. The doctrine of respondent superior is applicable to both principal/agent and master/servant. This doctrine makes the principal or master liable for acts of the agent/servant if done within the line and scope of employment. Agents may be subjected to liability to third persons with respect to contracts in three ways: on the contract, for the tort of fraud and for breach of warranty of authority. An agent is liable where there is a non-existent principal.

An agent is always personally liable for a crime. Employers can be liable if they ordered the conduct. Corporate employers can also be held liable. A corporation can be held liable under the doctrine of respondent superior for crimes committed by employees in the course of employment or for the corporation's benefit. See U.S. v. Gibson Products Co., Inc., 426 F. Supp. 768 (1976). The court found beyond a reasonable doubt that the employee (Alvarado) acted within the scope of his employment, and with intent to benefit the corporation, when he made the illegal entries. The defendant corporation is guilty of criminal acts.

A number of regulatory statutes (Clean Water Act) impose strict criminal liability even though there is no criminal intent. Both employees and corporations are liable. Officers and directors of the corporation are liable only if they did not use due diligence in supervising employees.

An agency may be terminated in many ways.

1. Voluntarily or ended by one party. The other party may have an action for breach of contract.

2. End of work.

3. Insanity or death by either principal or agent.

4. Bankruptcy of principal and sometimes of agent.

5. The employment at will relationship favors employers. Lawsuits based on wrongful dismissal have become common in most states. See McDonald v. Mobil Coal Producing, Inc., 789 P.2d 866 (1990). Mobil placed a disclaimer in its employee handbook stating that it was not a contract. Three out of five of the justices found for the employee; two applied the doctrine of promissory estoppel and the other the disclaimer was not conspicuous. Case returned for a new trial.

Actual notice must be given by the principal to those who have dealt with the agent in the past. Constructive notice (newspaper ad) must be given to others. No notice is required for a special agent.

Review Questions

True/False

_____ 1.   Respondeat superior does not apply to master-servant relationships.

_____ 2.   A del credere agent is one employed to accomplish a particular task.

_____ 3.   Employers of independent contractors need not pay as many taxes for employees.

_____ 4.   Express authority may be given orally or in writing.

_____ 5.   An agency can exist only when there is some express authority.

_____ 6.   Implied authority can arise from an emergency.

_____ 7.   Valid ratification requires knowledge of all material circumstances by the principal.

_____ 8.   An agent acting for both parties in a transaction is still entitled to compensation.

_____ 9.   An agent is always liable for torts committed against third parties.

_____ 10.   The death of either the agent or the principal terminates the agency.

Multiple Choice -- Please circle the best answer

1.   In an independent contractor relationship, the employer retains
        a.   the right of supervision.
        b.   the right to control the behavior of the employees.
        c.   the right to control the object of the work.
        d.   the right of physical control.

2.   Minors who are principals retain the right of
        a.   avoidance.
        b.   ratification.
        c.   a and b.
        d.   none of the above.

3.   The doctrine of respondeat superior does not apply for
        a.   master-servant relationships.
        b.   employer-independent contractor relationships.
        c.   principal agents.
        d.   gratuitous agents.

4.   An agent who is also a guarantor is know as a
        a.   special agent.
        b.   gratuitous agent.
        c.   general agent.
        d.   del credere agent.

5.   What type of authority is created when a principal and an agent enter into a written contract?
    a.   implied authority
    b.   express authority
    c.   apparent authority
    d.   written authority

6.   The theoretical basis for an employer's common law duty to employees is
    a.   fault.
    b.   assumption of risk.
    c.   contributory negligence.
    d.   ethics.

7.   An agent who works for two principals may do so if there is
    a.   an emergency.
    b.   disclosure and approval.
    c.   approval by one principal.
    d.   knowledge by a third party.

8.   The most important duty an agent owes a principal is
    a.   the duty to account.
    b.   the duty of competence.
    c.   the duty of loyalty.
    d.   the duty of obedience.

9.   The agency is terminated by operation of law if
    a.   the agent declares bankruptcy.
    b.   there is an economic depression.
    c.   the parties agree.
    d.   the principal dies.

10.   What type of termination notice must be given to third parties who have dealt with the principal through the agent.
    a.   constructive.
    b.   none.
    c.   actual.
    d.   written.

11.   A master-servant relationship arises when a person employs another
    a.   to enter into contracts with third parties.
    b.   to perform menial physical tasks.
    c.   to work for the employer.
    d.   to act as a principal.

12.   Implied authority arises from

a.   express authority.
b.   apparent authority.
c.   the employment contract.
d.   emergency authority.

13.   Ratification by the principal must be of
a.   some of the transaction.
b.   none of the transaction.
c.   all of the transaction.
d.   none of the above.

14.   An agent for a nonexistent principal
a.   is not liable on the contract to third parties.
b.   may be liable on the contract to third parties.
c.   is not liable if he/she signs properly.
d.   is liable on the contract to third persons.

15.   If an employer tells an employee to commit a crime and the employee obeys,
a.   both are criminally liable.
b.   the employer is criminally liable.
c.   the employee has a defense.
d.   the doctrine of respondent superior applies.

Short Answer

1.   List the three types of employer-employee legal classifications.

a.   _____

b.   _____

c.   _____

2.   List three types of agents.

a.   _____

b.   _____

c.   _____

3.   List two factors considered in hiring an independent contractor as opposed to a servant.

    a.   _____

    b.   _____

4.   List the four ways in which agency authority can be created.

    a.   _____

    b.   _____

    c.   _____

    d.   _____

5.   List the four common law duties agents owe principals.

    a.   _____

    b.   _____

    c.   _____

    d.   _____

6.   List three duties principals owe to agents.

    a.   _____

    b.   _____

    c.   _____

7.   Describe the doctrine of respondeat superior.

_____

_____

_____

8.   If a corporate director commits a crime in the scope of employment and in furtherance of corporate business, who can be held criminally liable?

_____

_____

9.   List four ways an agency can be terminated.

a.   _____

b.   _____

c.   _____

d.   _____

10.   What are three ways courts have treated employment situations concerning dismissal when presented with "at-will" relationships?

a.   _____

_____

b.   _____

_____

c.   _____

_____

Answers to Review Questions

True/False

1. F	3. T	5. F	7. T	9. T
2. F	4. T	6. T	8. F	10. T

Multiple Choice

1.	c.	4.	d.	7.	b.	10.	c.	13.	c.
2.	a.	5.	b.	8.	c.	11.	b.	14.	d.
3.	b.	6.	a.	9.	d.	12.	a.	15.	a.

Short Answer

1. a. master-servant
   b. principal-agent
   c. employer-independent contractor

2. a. general agent
   b. special agent
   c. del credere agent

3. a. degree of control
   b. cost--higher taxes for servants than for independent contractors

4. a. express authority
   b. implied authority
   c. apparent authority
   d. ratification

5. a. duty to account
   b. duty to use care and skill
   c. duty to follow instructions
   d. fiduciary duty

6. a. duty to reimburse
   b. duty to indemnify
   c. duty to compensate

7. Principal or master is legally answerable for the acts or omissions of his/her servants or agents when committed within scope of their employment.

8. a. corporate director
   b. corporation

9. a. voluntarily
   b. death of principal or agent
   c. bankruptcy of principal
   d. illegality of conduct
   e. completion of task
   f. contract expires

10. a. follow the general rule for employment-at-will and uphold the firing
    b. create an implied contract and allow dismissal only for good cause
    c. refuse to terminate based upon public policy grounds

Key Terms

<u>master-servant relationship</u>: performing physical tasks for another not involving the making of contracts with third parties.

<u>principal</u>: employer or one employing another to enter into business relations.

<u>agent</u>: one acting on behalf of another in forming business relations (usually contracts.)

<u>independent contractor</u>: employer does not have the right to control the means by which the work is performed.

<u>nondelegable duties</u>: responsibilities principal cannot give agent to perform.

<u>respondent superior</u>: "let the master answer" liability concept.

<u>tort</u>: civil wrong committed against another.

<u>gratuitous agent</u>: agent acting without compensation.

<u>general agent</u>: someone having authority to act for another in many different types of transactions.

<u>del credere agent</u>: one who sells goods for another on credit and guarantees that if the buyer does not pay, he or she will.

<u>special agent</u>: agent employed to accomplish a particular task.

<u>express authority</u>: authority given orally or in writing to an agent, servant or independent contractor.

<u>implied authority</u>: authority given by inference from express authority, by conduct of principal and agent, and by circumstances creating an emergency or necessity.

<u>apparent authority</u>: authority acquired by agent by words or conduct of principal leading a third party to believe the agent has authority.

<u>ratification</u>: acceptance by one of all benefits or burdens of an act done on his/her behalf by another, who at the time of the action had no authority.

<u>contributory negligence</u>: negligent conduct on the part of the plaintiff; may be a bar to recovery.

<u>fellow servant doctrine</u>: if a servant is injured by the negligence of a fellow servant, the injured servant may not recover from the employer.

<u>fraud</u>: intentional misrepresentation.

conversion: use or taking of another's property for one's own benefit.

advance: money obtained by agent prior to making a sale.

dual agency: agency in which one agent represents both parties to a transaction.

reimbursement: right of agent to be reimbursed by principal for expenses incurred during course of agency.

indemnification: right of agent to have principal stand liable for agent's liability in course of employment.

fiduciary: one who owes great faith, loyalty and accountability to another.

scope of employment: those actions taken within the agent's authority.

breach of warranty authority: agent breaching promise made to act only within the scope of authority.

nonexistent principal: agent acting for unincorporated association or other nonlegal entity.

undisclosed principal: agent and principal's identity are both undisclosed to third party.

partially disclosed principal: agent discloses existence of principal but not identity.

criminal conspiracy: cooperative conduct or agreement to engage in a criminal act.

strict criminal liability statute: statute imposes criminal liability even though the wrongdoer has no criminal intent.

superior agent rule: corporations are liable for criminal acts of high-level executives.

operation of law: effect of law is automatic as in termination of agencies.

employment-at-will: a working relationship without a written contract for a definite term.

whistleblower statutes: laws which protect against wrongful dismissals based upon lawful employee disclosures.

actual notice: personal notice.

constructive notice: public notice.

EMPLOYER-EMPLOYEE RELATIONS: SOME IMPORTANT STATUTES

Chapter Summary

Federal and state statutes have reshaped the entire area of employer-employee relations. Such statutes address two major employee concerns--on the job safety and financial security.

Workers' compensation laws pay workers or dependents for job-related injuries. Liability is imposed on an employer regardless of fault. These are state laws and vary from state to state. A worker may recover only for injuries, diseases, or death occurring on the job. Courts tend to construe this work related requirement liberally. See Cable v. Union Carbide Corp., 644. W.W.2d 397 (1983). The employee died of a heart attack on the job after a heated argument with a subordinate concerning his failure to wear required safety glasses while working. The court ruled that this was work related and remanded for determination of plaintiff's award.

One feature of workers' comp is the certain recovery given to all covered employees. Common law defenses do not apply. The remedy against the employer is exclusive and the injured employee recovers only the scheduled amount. This benefits employers. An employee may sue a third party on a common law or statutory theory, i.e., a products liability claim. Workers' comp does not apply to independent contractors. Programs are funded by employers through insurance, contingency funds and state funds. Systems are administered through state agencies. State workers' comp laws are either mandatory or elective.

The Occupational Safety and Health Act is a federal law passed in 1970. The law is administered by OSHA and its objectives are to make the workplace safe and preserve human resources. OSHA places a record keeping burden on employers. OSHA accomplishes its objectives by issuing regulations that set standards for workplace safety. NIOSH is a research institute that develops criteria, documents or studies hazards in the workplace. (See figure 14 for steps in OSHA's operation.) See Whirlpool Corp. v. Marshall, 445 U.S. 1 (1980). The court upheld OSHA's regulation, which let employees refuse to perform assigned work if they believe death or serious injury will result and believe there is no less dangerous way of doing the job.

OSHA is criticized by many businesses. There is a move to revoke or simplify OSHA regulations. OSHA's "hazard communication standard" attempts to inform all workers OSHA covers about the hazards of "all" chemicals they encounter in their work. Labor has criticized this standard as not being effective since it does not include "all" chemicals.

The Fair Labor Standards Act (FLSA) was passed in 1938 and its purpose was to eliminate working conditions that did not allow employees to maintain minimum living standards. Provisions of FLSA include minimum wages, limited work hours unless paid overtime, equal pay, record keeping and child labor standards. Covered workers or businesses include those workers engaged in interstate commerce, laundries/dry cleaners, construction firms, hospitals, schools, retail and services businesses with gross annual incomes of at least $362,500 and other businesses with gross sales in excess of $250,000. Exceptions include family employees, government employees with some limitations and other employees if they individually engage in interstate commerce. FLSA wage standards require $4.25 per hour starting April 1, 1991. Overtime for over 40 hours at no less than one-and-one-half times the employees' regular rate. Learners, apprentices and handicapped workers may, under certain circumstances, be paid less than the minimum rate. Some employees are exempt from both the FLSA's overtime and minimum wage provisions. See Donovan v. Burger King Corporation, 675 F.2d 516 (1982). Assistant managers' $250 or more per week are held to be "executive" and exempt from FLSA overtime and record keeping requirements. "Long test" managers clearing less than $250 per week must be paid overtime in weeks when they spend more than 40% of their time in nonsupervisory work.

FlSA child labor standards are designed to keep children in school and out of harmful working conditions. The FLSA requires employers to keep records on wages and hours. The U.S. Department of Labor's Wage and Hour Division administers and enforces the FLSA. Willful violations are crimes with fines up to $10,000 and possible imprisonment. Civil penalties are possible for violators of the child labor provisions. Back wages can be recovered if workers are underpaid. The statute of limitations is two years on back pay and three years for a willful violation.

The Equal Pay Act of 1973 amends the FLSA. This amendment makes it illegal to pay different wages based on sex to men and women doing substantially the same work. Jobs do not have to be identical for the Act to apply. The Act does allow wage differences if based on other factors than sex, i.e., bona fide seniority systems, merit systems and systems rewarding productivity.

The Social Security Act of 1935 established today's federal-state unemployment insurance system. The idea is to pay workers when they lose their jobs due to adverse business conditions. The money comes from federal payroll taxes imposed on employers. Covered employers include one or more employees who worked some part of 20 or more weeks per year and employers paying wages of $1,500 or more in any calendar quarter. Exemptions include employers of educational, religious and charitable institutions; certain farm labor; family labor and federal and state government labor. States may set how long a person must have worked to be eligible for unemployment benefits. The length and amount of unemployment benefits vary from state to state. All states give at least 26 weeks and federal benefits may provide supplemental income. Only certain causes entitle one to collect unemployment benefits. Striking workers are generally not entitled to benefits, but see <u>New York Tel. Co.</u> v. <u>New York State Dept. of Labor</u>, 440 U.S. 519 (1979). The Court in a non-majority opinion decided that the New York statute letting striking union workers collect unemployment insurance was not preempted by the NLRA.

An employer may reduce its unemployment tax liability if its employees are unemployed less than the average. The experience rating factor is utilized. When unemployment benefits are exhausted, a worker is left to public works employment, welfare or charity.

The original purpose of the Social Security Act was to provide a minimal income for retired workers. The Act has been amended to cover dependants, disability benefits and Medicare. Most workers in the U.S. are covered today. Social security administration administers the program and employers and the self-employed are required to keep records. People can start receiving retirement benefits at 62, larger benefits if delayed until 65. The size of benefits are based on average yearly earnings, age of retirement and number of dependents. In addition to retirement benefits, there are disability and survivors' benefits. Work credits are earned in quarters. The amount of Social Security benefits on average earnings during working years. The employer and employee both pay social security taxes to finance the system. Self employed pay at a rate of employer and employee combined. Key social security features include: benefits are not taxable by state or local governments, may not be garnished by creditors, benefits increase with cost of living and payments based on living longer. Changes in 1983 modified COLA, included federal workers hired after January 1, 1984 and imposed federal taxes on benefits if other income is above certain limits. A current issue is intergenerational wealth transfer.

Private retirement plans are separate from social security. The internal revenue code sets the rules for establishing qualified employee retirement plans. The Employment Retirement Income Security Act (ERISA) was enacted to protect employee plans.

1. imposes fiduciary duties on plan managers and advisors
    a. use care of prudent person
    b. good faith
2. imposes record and report requirements
    a. record participant's length of employment
    b. explanation of plan must be given to each employee
    c. must publish annual report
3. investment restrictions
    a. no loans
    b. no transactions between plan and employer
4. Pension Benefit Guaranty Corporation created
    a. employers pay in
    b. employees get vested benefits if plan fails

5.   vesting requirements
   a.   rights that cannot be taken away
   b.   one hundred percent vesting of employee contributions
   c.   employer contributions--after Dec. 31, 1988, either schedule
      (1) five year "cliff vesting"--five years or more, 100% vested as to employer's contribution
      (2) three-seven year graduated vesting, 100% vested in seven years
6.   pension offset provisions valid under ERISA; see Alessi v. Raybestos-Manhattan, Inc., 451 U.S. 504 (1981). The U.S. Supreme Court held that ERISA does not stop a private pension plan from reducing retirement benefits by the amount of money obtained from workers' compensation awards received after retirement. This does not contravene ERISA's nonforfeiture provisions.

ERISA's preemption is only partial; see Metropolitan Life Massachusetts (cited in text). ERISA problems have arisen in corporate takeovers.

Features of state plant closing legislation that require some type of preclosing notice to workers include: size of business, how much advance notice, sanctions for noncompliance and whether they are mandatory or voluntary. Federal plant closing statute (August 4, 1988) requires:

1. more than 100 employees--60 days advance notice if 50 or more employees at one site will lose jobs because of plant closing
2. layoff notice--more than 50 workers at one site and they make up 33% or more of workforce
3. notice required if 500 or more are laid off regardless of circumstances

The U.S. Supreme Court upheld the Maine plant closing statute, see Fort Halifax Packing Co. v. Coyne, 107 S. Ct. 2211 (1987). The court held that the Maine statute is not preempted by ERISA because the statute neither establishes, nor requires, an employer to maintain an employee welfare benefit "plan" under the federal statute. The Maine law is not pre-empted by the NLRA since it establishes a minimum labor standard that does not intrude upon the collective bargaining process.

Review Questions

True/False

_____ 1.   Executive, administrative and professional employees are exempt from both minimum wage and overtime provisions.

_____ 2.   Under current OSHA regulations, employees have a right to know if there are dangerous chemicals in the workplace.

_____ 3.   Federal employees are not covered under the Equal Pay Act.

_____ 4.   An OSHA regulation permits employees to refuse to do their work if they reasonably believe serious injury or death will result.

_____ 5.   Only work-related injuries and diseases are compensable under the workers' compensation systems.

_____ 6.   A recovery under workers' compensation is the exclusive remedy available against the employer.

_____ 7.   A person voluntarily leaving work is still entitled to unemployment benefits.

_____ 8.   Under federal law, striking workers cannot be paid unemployment benefits.

_____ 9.   ERISA requires employers to give an explanation of its pension plan to employees.

_____ 10.   ERISA requires all covered employers to set up pension plan.

Multiple Choice -- Please circle the best answer

1.   Workers' Compensation Statutes have as an objective paying workers
       a.   a sum certain for all injuries.
       b.   an indexed amount of money for work related injuries.
       c.   for job related injuries.
       d.   for contributory negligence.

2.   Workers' compensation systems are run by
       a.   the federal government.
       b.   state governments.
       c.   employers.
       d.   insurance companies.

3.   Temporary standards under OSHA last for
       a.   nine months.
       b.   one year.
       c.   an indefinite term.
       d.   six months.

4.   OSHA standards do not apply to
       a.   dangerous chemicals in the workplace.
       b.   wood.
       c.   tobacco.
       d.   b. and c.

5.   The Equal Pay Act covers
       a.   executive personnel.
       b.   women.

    c.   professional employees.
    d.   all of the above.

6. Employer contributions to a qualified employee retirement plan are
    a.   tax deductible.
    b.   not tax deductible.
    c.   taxed at a lower rate.
    d.   taxed at the local level.

7. Workers who have vested pension rights can
    a.   lose them by changing jobs.
    b.   not lose them by changing jobs.
    c.   not be terminated.
    d.   be terminated only for cause.

8. Employees who come under the five year "cliff vesting" requirements must be
    a.   100% vested in five years regarding their contribution.
    b.   80% vested in six years regarding their contribution.
    c.   100% vested in five years regarding the employer's contribution.
    d.   90% vested in seven years regarding the employer's contribution.

9. Workers' compensation
    a.   abandons common law fault principles.
    b.   embraces common law fault principles.
    c.   is federal law.
    d.   is administered by OSHA.

10. The National Institute of Occupational Safety and Health (NIOSH) has as its function
    a.   investigation of complaints.
    b.   research into workplace hazards.
    c.   promulgating regulations.
    d.   none of the above.

11. The Fair Labor Standards Act covers
    a.   laundries.
    b.   hospitals.
    c.   higher education.
    d.   all of the above.

12. Beginning on April 1, 1991 workers covered under FLSA have a legal right to receive ___ per hour.
    a. $3.75.
    b. $4.75.
    c. $4.25.

d. $5.25.

13.   In order for the Equal Pay Act to apply
a.   both jobs must be identical.
b.   both jobs must be substantially equal.
c.   the jobs have to be equal.
d.   wage differences are never allowed.

14.   The money to pay unemployment compensation comes from
a.   federal payroll taxes imposed on employees.
b.   federal payroll taxes imposed on employers.
c.   the social security tax.
d.   both employer and employee.

15.   The amount of Social Security benefits depends on
a.   work credits.
b.   marital status.
c.   number of dependents.
d.   all of the above.

Short Answer

1.   Describe the overtime requirements under FLSA.

_____

_____

2.   List five jobs exempt from both minimum wage and overtime under FLSA.

a.   _____

b.   _____

c.   _____

d.   _____

e.   _____

3.   Describe the remedies and penalties for violations of FLSA.

_____

_____

_____

4.   Describe the standards set under the Equal Pay Act.

_____

_____

5.   What types of records must be kept by employers under OSHA?

    a.   _____

    b.   _____

    c.   _____

    d.   _____

6.   List the key features of workers' compensation statutes.

    a.   _____

    b.   _____

    c.   _____

    d.   _____

    e.   _____

    f.   _____

    g.   _____

    h.   _____

7.   List three circumstances in which an employee would be ineligible for unemployment compensation.

    a.   _____

    b.   _____

c. _____

8.   Name the three factors influencing the size of retirement benefits under Social Security.

a. _____

b. _____

c. _____

9.   What types of benefits, in addition to retirement benefits, exist under Social Security?

a. _____

b. _____

10.   List the five ways ERISA tries to protect retirement plans.

a. _____

b. _____

c. _____

d. _____

e. _____

Answers to Review Questions

True/False

1. T	3. F	5. T	7. F	9. T
2. T	4. T	6. T	8. F	10. F

Multiple Choice

1. c.	4. d.	7. b.	10. b.	13. b.
2. b.	5. d.	8. c.	11. d.	14. b.
3. d.	6. a.	9. a.	12. c.	15. d.

Short Answer

1.   overtime at not less than one-and-a-half times employee's regular rate after 40 hours of work in work week.

2.   a.   executive, administrative and professional employees
      b.   employees of certain individually-owned and operated small retail or service establishments
      c.   employees of certain seasonal or amusement or recreational establishments, small newspapers, switchboard operators
      d.   farm workers employed by limited employers
      e.   casual baby-sitters and companions to the elderly

3.   willful violations are crimes with fines up to $10,000--second violations may result in imprisonment -- suit for back wages by employee or section of Labor Department--injunctions

4.   illegal to pay different wages, based on sex, to those doing substantially the same work

5.   a.   enforcement records
      b.   research records
      c.   job-related injury and accident records
      d.   records of job hazards

6.   a.   work-related requirement
      b.   certain but limited recovery
      c.   exclusivity of remedy
      d.   nonapplication to independent contractors
      e.   funding by employers
      f.   administered by state agencies
      g.   coverage of most employees
      h.   either mandatory or elective systems

7.   a.   voluntarily quits job without good cause
      b.   refuses suitable work
      c.   is dismissed for improper conduct

8.   a.   average yearly earnings
      b.   age at retirement
      c.   number of dependents

9.   a.   survivors's benefits
      b.   disability benefits

10.   a.   creates fiduciary duties for plan managers and advisors
      b.   requires plan records and reports

c.   set plan investment restrictions
d.   creates federal corporation to insure employee benefits if plan should fail
e.   requires vesting of employee and employer contributions

Key Terms

workers' compensation: system for paying workers or dependents for work-related injuries, diseases or death.

fault: negligence.

contributory negligence: negligent conduct of injured party; usually a bar to recovery.

assumption of risk: voluntary and knowing undertaking of dangerous conduct.

fellow servant rule: principal is not liable if fellow servant's carelessness causes injury.

malingering: pretending one has a covered injury to collect benefits.

percentage of disability: percentage figure assigned to unscheduled disability to determine benefits.

self-insuring: one who provides evidence of sufficient assets to act as own insurer.

adjudicate: process of judicial decision-making.

Occupational Safety and Health Act (OSHA): federal law passed to make workplace safe and healthy and to preserve human resources.

National Institute of Occupational Safety and Health (NIOSH): develops safety criteria.

SOSHAS: state-administered OSHA plans.

general duty standard: OSHA-imposed duty of general health and safety in the workplace.

OSHA's walkaround privilege: right of employers and employees to have representative in OSHA inspections.

OSHA's abatement period: time for correction of OSHA violation.

Standard for Hazard Communication: ("Employees' Right to Know")--OSHA standard (and similar to laws of approximately one dozen states) with purpose to inform employees within certain manufacturing sectors about hazards of all chemicals they encounter in their workplace.

Fair Labor Standards Act (FLSA): federal law establishing minimum wage rates, overtime pay, equal pay, record keeping and child labor standards (allows minimum hiring standards.)

covered workers: those workers entitled to the protection of the FLSA.

Equal Pay Act: federal law making it illegal to pay different wages based on sex for persons doing substantially the same work.

unemployment compensation: system to pay workers something when they lose their jobs so they can survive.

preempted: prevented from occurring.

experience rating: figure based on amount of time employer has employed workers.

Social Security: federal system for providing benefits to retired workers, disabled workers and their families.

Employment Retirement Income Security Act: federal law regulating and protecting employee retirement plans.

qualified employee retirement plan: plan which allows employer to deduct contributions to plan.

coverage requirement: requirement of percentage of workers covered to qualify for deduction.

noncontributory: only employer contributes monies put into a pension system or plan.

contributory: both employee and employer contribute monies put into a pension system or plan.

defined pension plan: employer promises specific benefits.

fiduciary duties: duties imposed on retirement plan managers to exercise care and act in good faith.

vested benefits: benefits that an employee is absolutely entitled to.

exclusive benefit rule: requirement that pension plans benefit only participants and their beneficiaries plus pay reasonable plan administration costs.

15 EMPLOYMENT DISCRIMINATION

Chapter Summary

This chapter discusses the most important federal laws forbidding discrimination in employment. Congress has taken positive steps to ensure that employees are judged on their individual merit.

The equal Pay Act of 1963 is of limited scope. It only forbids <u>sex</u> discrimination regarding pay. The Act looks at whether jobs are substantially equal. The two jobs must involve each of the following: equal effort, equal skill, equal responsibility and similar working conditions. There are four defenses under the Act: seniority, merit, quality or quantity of production (piecework) and any factor other than sex. Remedies include those for FLSA violations, back pay and an equal amount to back pay award as liquidated damages. Plaintiffs are not required to submit their claims to the EEOC or state agencies before filing a lawsuit. See <u>EEOC</u> v. <u>Madison Community Unit School District</u>, 818 F.2d 577 (1987). The Court of Appeals vocated the findings of the district judge in the comparisons between boys' soccer and girls' volleyball, boys' soccer and girls' basketball, and boys' track and girls' basketball. With this exception, the court concluded that the EEOC had established a violation.

Title VII of the 1964 Civil Rights Act prohibits employment discrimination based on race, color, religion, sex or national origin. Employers covered include those having 15 or more employees and affecting interstate commerce, labor unions, employment agencies and apprenticeship programs are covered. Title VII does not apply to less than 15 employees, independent contractors, bona fide tax exempt private clubs and religious organizations (Only when they discriminate on the basis of religion). Title VII is quite broad and covers almost all of the ways an employer might disadvantage an employee because of race, color, sex, religion or national origin. The Act also contains an anti-retaliation provision. The complaining party must first file a charge with a state agency or the EEOC within a specified period. If this fails, the complainant can sue in court. The government or private plaintiff

161

must prove that the employer has acted for discriminatory reasons. The most important methods of proof are Title VII's disparate treatment and disparate impact theories. The disparate treatment theory is used where some isolated instance of discriminatory behavior is alleged that cannot be proven by direct evidence. The plaintiff must show (prima facie case):

1. within protected class
2. applied and was qualified
3. was rejected
4. employer continued to seek applicants.

The defendant must then state legitimate non-discriminatory reasons for the employment decision. The plaintiff then has to show that these reasons are only a pretext for discriminatory motives. Disparate impact (adverse impact) is used in cases involving a large number of plaintiffs. The plaintiffs must show:

1. employment practice had an adverse impact on a protected class (testing, height, weight, strength, hiring-promotion systems)
2. employer must show business necessity
3. plaintiffs must demonstrate that other criteria would achieve employers ends with less impact on protected group.

See Chaney v. Southern Railway Co., 847 F.2d 718 (1988). The court affirmed the district court's dismissal of the disparate treatment claim, fired because of race for allegedly smoking marijuana. Reversed dismissal of disparate impact claim, district court did not undertake proper analysis.

Defenses to Title VII claims include BFOQ(narrow--applies to hiring job classifications and referral decisions), bona fide seniority system and various merit defenses (piecework system). See Auto Workers v. Johnson Controls, Inc., 59 U.S.L.W. 4209 (1991). Safety exception is limited to instances in which sex or pregnancy actually interferes with the employee's ability to perform the job. Fertile women, as far as it appears in the record, manufacture batteries as efficiently as anyone else. Johnson Controls cannot establish a BFOQ.

Courts have a wide range of remedies. If the discrimination resulted in lost wages, back pay is available two years prior to the charge. Attorney's fees can be recovered. The courts differ on consequential damages. Punitive damage recoveries are unlikely. Equitable remedies include: hired, reinstated, retroactive seniority and affirmative action orders. Title VII prohibits discrimination against all races and colors (including whites). The Supreme Court has upheld voluntary racial preferences. See United Steelworkers v. Weber, 443 U.S. 193 (1979). A private affirmative action plan upheld despite preferences based on race.

Title VII's ban on sex discrimination protects both sexes, although most cases deal with female claimants. This prohibition is only applicable to gender based discrimination; it does not forbid discrimination on the basis of sexual orientation. See Price Waterhouse v. Hopkins, 109 S. Ct. 1775 (1989). An employer who objects to aggressiveness in women but whose positions require this trait places women in an intolerable and impermissible Catch-22...Title VII lifts women out of this bind....

The Pregnancy Discrimination Act prohibits discrimination based on pregnancy, childbirth and related medical conditions. Women affected by pregnancy must be treated the same as other applicants and employees. Comparable worth: the idea that jobs, although not "equal" may be of comparable worth and so should be similarly compensated. The concept has not won acceptance and probably cannot be brought under Title VII. Sexual harassment which is recognized under Title VII is still a developing area of the law. Two general theories have emerged: quid pro quo harassment--sex for job related favors and offensive work environment due to sexual harassment. Employer is strictly liable for quid pro quo harassment by supervisors. Employers are liable for work environment harassment by both supervisors and coworkers only if higher level managers knew or should have known and failed to take action to stop it (case law, does not follow EEOC guidelines). See Meritor Savings Bank v. Vinson, 477 U.S. 57 (1986). For sexual harassment to be actionable, it must be sufficiently severe or pervasive to alter the conditions of the victim's employment and create an abusive working environment. The gravamen of any sexual harassment claim is that the alleged sexual advances were "unwelcome." The court of appeals decision reversing the district court's decision was affirmed.

Title VII's ban on national origin discrimination includes discrimination based on:

1. person's or ancestor's place of origin or

2. a person's possession of physical, cultural, or linguistic characteristics shared by people of a certain national origin. The EEOC does not flatly ban "speak-English-only" rules in the workplace.

Title VII prohibits most employment discrimination based on a person's religion.
Religious organizations can discriminate on the basis of religion only. Title VII also prohibits discrimination based on religious observances or practices (grooming, apparel and refusal to work on the Sabbath). See Ansonia Board of Education v. Philbrook, 479 U.S. 60 (1986). The employer need not further show that each of the employee's alternative accommodations would result in undue hardship. The Court of Appeals erred by requiring the board to nonetheless demonstrate the hardship of Philbrook's alternatives where the employer had already accommodated the employee's religious needs.

The Civil Rights Act of 1866 (section 1981) covers employment discrimination based on race, national origin and ancestry. Executive order 11246 requires certain federal contractors not to discriminate and undertake affirmative action to prevent such discrimination.

The Age Discrimination in Employment Act of 1967 (ADEA) protects those who are at least 40 years of age with no upper age limit. The ADEA applies to almost all terms, conditions and benefits of employment. Firefighters, law enforcement officers, prison guards and tenured higher education professors (retire at 70) are exempted from the act until December 31, 1993. Defenses include seniority, bona fide employment benefit plans, discharge for good cause and BFOQ. Remedies include unpaid back pay, willful-liquidated damages and equitable remedies (hiring, reinstatement and promotion). See Tullis v. Lear School, Inc., 874 F.2d 1489 (1989). A 68 year old school bus driver was fired from his job. Employee's reactions had slowed and he possessed an aged appearance. Because the school failed to present any evidence to suggest the finding that age is a BFOQ for the position of school bus driver, employee must prevail.

The American with Disabilities Act prohibits discrimination against qualified individuals with a disability on the basis of that disability. Apples to hiring, firing, pay, promotion, job training, and many others. Sexual orientation is not a disability. The ADA protects impaired people who can perform the essential functions of the relevant job without any extra assistance from their employers, but also protects those who could so perform with "reasonable accommodation" on their employers part. Covered entities are not required to make such accommodations when doing so would impose an undue hardship.

Review Questions

True/False

_____ 1.   Labor unions with 15 or more members are covered by Title VII.

_____ 2.   The statute of limitations for Title VII charges is 300 days.

_____ 3.   Employers may refuse to hire handicapped persons if they do not have facilities to accommodate them.

_____ 4.   BFOQ is a defense to racial discrimination.

_____ 5.   Title VII prohibits discrimination on the basis of sexual preference.

_____ 6.   Sexual harassment is not covered by Title VII.

_____ 7.   Under the Pregnancy Discrimination Act, employers' health insurance plans must also include pregnancy-related conditions.

_____ 8.   Affirmative action is required of all employers under Title VII.

_____ 9.   The Age Discrimination Act applies to workers from ages 40 - 70.

_____ 10.   To establish age discrimination, the job at issue must have been given to a younger person.

Multiple Choice -- Please circle the best answer.

1.   What federal agency enforces many of the employment discrimination statutes?
        a.   Federal Trade Commission.

b.   Department of Labor.
c.   Office for the Handicapped.
d.   Equal Employment Opportunity Commission.

2.   The Equal Pay Act forbids
   a.   all employment discrimination.
   b.   sex discrimination regardless of pay.
   c.   sex discrimination regarding pay.
   d.   sexual preference.

3.   An EPA plaintiff
   a.   must submit case for evaluation.
   b.   does not have to submit case for evaluation.
   c.   must consult with the Department of Labor.
   d.   must receive a "right to sue" letter.

4.   Title VII covers those employers and industries
   a.   that employ 20 or more employees.
   b.   that affect interstate commerce.
   c.   that engage in religious education.
   d.   that discriminate.

5.   Employment discrimination includes
   a.   hiring.
   b.   firing.
   c.   pay.
   d.   all of the above.

6.   What test would generally be acceptable under Title VII?
   a.   typing test.
   b.   aptitude test.
   c.   achievement test.
   d.   personality test.

7.   What damages would a plaintiff likely recover under Title VII?
   a.   punitive damages.
   b.   attorney's fees.
   c.   consequential damages.
   d.   back pay for three years.

8.   Title VII does not protect
   a.   men.
   b.   women.
   c.   homosexuals.

       d.   pregnancy.

9.   Sexual harassment would include
       a.   activities between consenting adults.
       b.   compliments about a woman's work.
       c.   all forms of dating.
       d.   sex related jokes.

10.   Under the Age Discrimination Act,
       a.   a private party may file a civil suit.
       b.   a private party may not file a civil suit.
       c.   the private party must file suit within 90 days.
       d.   a "right to sue" letter is required.

11.   Under the Equal Pay Act, a woman must show that she has received lower pay than a male employee
       a.   for equal work.
       b.   for substantially equal work.
       c.   for unequal work.
       d.   for jobs requiring equal effort.

12.   Title VII of the 1964 Civil Rights Act covers
       a.   race.
       b.   sex.
       c.   religion.
       d.   all of the above.

13.   Disparate impact under Title VII involves
       a.   an isolated instance of discriminatory employer behavior.
       b.   an adverse impact on a Title VII protected class.
       c.   a legitimate nondiscriminatory reason for the employment decision.
       d.   an employers pretext for an employment decision.

14.   Section 1986 of the 1866 Civil Rights Act prohibits discrimination based on
       a.   race.
       b.   sex.
       c.   religion.
       d.   national origin.

15.   What is not a disability under the ADA?
       a.   blindness.
       b.   missing a limb.
       c.   deafness.
       d.   compulsive gambling.

Short Answer

1.   List the five types of discrimination prohibited under Title VII.

    a. _____   d. _____

    b. _____   e. _____

    c. _____

2.   List the persons covered under Title VII

    a. _____

    b. _____

    c. _____

    d. _____

3.   List three defenses available for those charged with violations under Title VII.

    a. _____

    b. _____

    c. _____

4.   List the steps and time limits involved in a Title VII case.

    a. _____

    b. _____

    c. _____

    d. _____

5.   List the elements in a prima facie sex discrimination case.

    a. _____

    b. _____

c. _____

d. _____

6.   List three examples of sex discrimination.

a. _____

b. _____

c. _____

7.   What constitutes sexual harassment under EEOC guidelines?

a. _____

_____

b. _____

_____

c. _____

_____

8.   Define discrimination on the basis of national origin.

_____

_____

9.   Must an employer accommodate religious beliefs in scheduling employees?

_____

10.   Name the protected disabilities under the Americans with Disabilities Act.

a. _____

b. _____

c. _____

Answers to Review Questions

True/False

1. T	3. F	5. F	7. T	9. F
2. F	4. F	6. F	8. F	10. F

Multiple Choice

1. d.	4. b.	7. b.	10. a.	13. b.
2. c.	5. d.	8. c.	11. b.	14. a.
3. b.	6. a.	9. d.	12. d.	15. d.

Short Answer

1. a. race   d. color
   b. sex   e. national origin
   c. religion

2. a. employers having 15 or more employees
   b. private and public employment agencies
   c. labor unions with 15 or more employees
   d. state and local governments

3. a. BFOQ
   b. employers bona fide seniority or merit system
   c. differences in employee locations
   d. business necessity
   e. employer not covered by Title VII
   f. procedural defenses

4. a. violation occurs
   b. file charges within specified time limit
   c. obtain a "right to sue" letter from EEOC
   d. 90 days to sue as a private party

5. a. woman
   b. applied for and was qualified for a job for which employer was seeking applicants
   c. rejected despite qualifications
   d. after rejection, position remained open

6. a. separate lines of progression and seniority based on sex

b.   advertising for job for one sex only
c.   sexual harassment
d.   discrimination against married women
e.   discrimination in fringe benefits
f.   discrimination through pre-employment inquiries

7.   a.   submission to sexual advances, favors explicitly or implicitly a term or condition of employment
   b.   submission to or rejection of sexual advances is used as a basis for employment decisions
   c.   such conduct interferes with work performance

8.   discrimination because of a person's or ancestor's place of origin; also, discrimination because of physical, cultural or linguistic characteristics

9.   yes, but need only make reasonable attempts

10.   a.   physical or mental impairments that substantially limit one or more of a person's major life activities
    b.   any record of such an impairment
    c.   a person's being regarded as having such an impairment

Key Terms

Equal Employment Opportunity Commission (EEOC): independent federal agency that enforces various employment discrimination statutes.

Equal Pay Act: federal statute prohibiting wage differentials based on sex.

Title VII: section of the Civil Rights Act prohibiting discrimination in employment on basis of race, sex, color, religion or national origin.

unfair employment practice: act or conduct violative of Title VII.

business necessity: defense to Title VII discrimination based on business purposes and needs.

Office of Federal Contract Compliance Programs (OFCCP): enforces affirmative action in federal contractors.

right to sue letter: letter indicating administrative remedies have been exhausted and suit may be filed.

prima facie case: a case strong enough to require some rebuttal by the defendant.

Uniform Guidelines on Employee Selection Procedures (UGOESP):   EEOC guidelines on job discrimination.

comparable worth: pay should be based on value of job to employer, to eliminate traditional differentials between "men's" and "women's" jobs.

adverse impact: discrimination resulting from employer procedures that significantly affect one group.

sexual harassment: violation of Title VII involving the requirement or display of sexual advances or favors.

Pregnancy Discrimination Act: amendment to Title VII; affords protection for pregnant women and prohibits discrimination.

Affirmative Action: program of specifically recruiting or preferring members of certain groups in hiring and promotion processes.

Executive Order 11246: order requiring businesses furnishing the U.S. Government with goods or services to use affirmative action programs.

Civil Rights Act of 1866: act giving all citizens the right to enforce contracts and sue for legal protection.

Age Discrimination in Employment Act: act prohibiting discrimination for workers from ages 40 and up.

Americans with Disabilities Act: act prohibiting discrimination against qualified individuals with a disability on the basis of that disability.

CHAPTER
16

FEDERAL LABOR LAW: UNIONIZATION AND COLLECTIVE BARGAINING

Chapter Summary

Unions have historically organized themselves into skilled crafts or industrial unions. The National Labor Relations Act (Wagner Act) was passed in 1935 and led to a spurt in union growth. By 1955 the AFL and CIO were reunited into the AFL-CIO. The legal environment for organized labor changed in the 1980s due to Reagan's free market philosophy and appointments to key legal bodies. The effect of unions is an improved status for workers, a leveling of wages and improved fringe benefits.

The Norris-La Guardia (1932) removed jurisdiction to enjoin peaceful labor disputes from the federal courts but not state courts. The National Labor Relations Act (1935) provided for union elections and set forth a code of unfair labor practices binding on employers only. The Taft Hartley Act (1947) provided a code of unfair labor practices for unions, outlawed secondary boycotts and instituted an 80 day injunction before a strike could be called. The Landum-Griffin Amendment (1958) regulated the internal affairs of unions and placed further restrictions on secondary boycotts and picketing during organizational campaigns.

The National Labor Relations Board (NLRB), an administrative agency, was established by the National Labor Relations Act. Its two main purposes are to prevent unfair labor practices and settle representation questions. The NLRB has maximum jurisdiction allowable under the commerce clause. Anyone except the NLRB can initiate proceedings. Two types of proceedings can be initiated with the NLRB: complain case which alleges an unfair labor practice and a representative case--union election. The NLRB has exclusive jurisdiction over unfair labor practices. Some employers are not covered by the NLRA: governments, managers, agricultural workers, independent contractors, domestic workers and workers covered by the Railway Labor Act.

An unfair labor practice is a legal wrong that gives rise to a cause of action. Employer unfair labor practices:

1. employer interference with or coercion of employees' rights to form and join unions

2. employer dominance or interference with formation of labor organizations

3. employer discrimination in hiring or tenure to discourage union membership

4. employer discharge or discrimination against employee for union activities

5. refusal to bargain collectively

6. agreement to commit secondary boycott.

The remedies are damages and injunctions. Union unfair labor practices:

1. restraining or coercing employees in union joining

2. causing employer to discriminate on basis of union membership

3. refusal to bargain with employer

4. engaging in secondary strike or picketing activity

5. requiring excessive or discriminatory fee as condition to union membership

6. causing employer to pay for services not performed

7. picketing employer for employer's refusal to recognize unauthorized union

8. agreeing with employer to engage in secondary boycott.

The steps in an unfair labor practice case are as follows:

1. begins with party filing charges with NLRB

2. six-month statute of limitations--measured from time wrong committed

3. settlement short of issuance of complaint
    a. adjustment
    b. dismissal
    c. withdrawal of complaint

4. complaint issued for NLRB

5. hearing held
    a. before administrative law judge
    b. both parties participate
    c. preponderance of evidence

6. administrative law judge makes an Intermediate Report

7. NLRB adopts decision/issues cease and desist order

8. NLRB decision reviewable by Court of Appeals.

There are three ways to unionize:

1. voting at a representation election

2. signing authorization cards

3. NLRB's ordering the employer to bargain with a union.

The usual way to unionize is by voting in a representation election, (R election):

1. election run by NLRB

2. secret ballot and majority vote

3. petition from employees prompts NLRB to hold election
    a. thirty percent showing of interest
    b. must have signed authorization cards for R election
        (1) employer can object to their validity
        (2) NLRB may hold hearing if cards challenged

4. Employer has the right of free speech, can state its views but no threats of reprisal or force are allowed. See Dal-Tex Optical, 132 NLRB1782 (1962). Example of employer statements that were threats and hence exceeded the free speech right. (The NLRB attempts to conduct elections in laboratory conditions--clinical dispassionate atmosphere.) If an employer commits ULPs in pre-R election campaign statements, several outcomes are possible:

1. union wins, nothing happens

2. union loses, election could be rerun

3. NLRB will order the employer to bargain with the union (NLRB declares union the winner). See

NLRB v. Gissel Packing Co., 395 U.S. 575 (1969). The U.S. Supreme Court ordered that the unions be recognized by the employers as the employees' collective bargaining agents and that the employer bargain with the union even though the union had not won a representation election because of employer's preelection statements.

If union wins the election, employer can refuse to bargain, a ULP will be filed, goes to the NLRB and then employer can raise the issue in the court of appeals. Union cannot get court review of the NLRB refusal to certify the union. The election bar rule prevents and R election if one was held in the previous 12 months and the union was defeated. Also applies if the union wins. The contract bar rule prohibits an R election while a collective bargaining agreement is in force. Exceptions to the contract bar rule are: collective bargaining agreement is longer than three years; union schism or union is defunct and employer greatly expanded operations. If an employer relocates for economic reasons, no ULP. If the move is to discourage or escape unions, a ULP is committed. The remedy for this ULP is union employees will be offered first opportunity on jobs at the new location and will be awarded relocation expenses. See Milwaukee Springs Division v. NLRB (II), 268 N.L.R.B. 87 (1984). The respondent decided to transfer the assembly operations to a different plant where different workers (who were not subject to the contract) would perform the work. The respondent did not disturb the wages and benefits at its Milwaukee facility. The shift of work from one plant to another solely for economic reasons is legal.

Bankruptcy to escape collective bargaining is sometimes available to escape union contracts. the U.S. Supreme Court has held that employers may shut down a plant forever without committing a ULP, provided that the employer does not have the intent to discourage unionization at other plants.

Employers have a duty to bargain with a certified union. This includes:

1. good faith discussion of wages, hours and working conditions

2. need not agree

3. economic pressures are proper during bargaining (strikes and lockouts)

4. employer must document inability to pay

5. employer cannot increase wages without first bargaining with union

6. Boulwareism--presenting best offer on take-it-or-leave-it basis is ULP

7. must discuss wages, hours and working conditions.

See Airline Pilots Association, International v. Joseph E. O'Neil, 59 L.W. 4175 (1991). If the union settlement with the employer is not "wholly irrational or arbitrary," then the union has met its duty to its members. A union's actions are arbitrary only if, in the light of the factual and legal landscape, the union's behavior is so far outside a "wide range of reasonableness."

The collective bargaining agreement is a contract between the union and employer on behalf of the employees. It can contain a number of terms relating to employment. There can be no enforcement of a no strike clause unless the CBA contains an arbitration agreement (Boys Market case-text). Arbitration provisions are put into CBAs to settle labor disputes by using a neutral third party. Courts and Congress favor arbitration. See <u>United Paperworkers International Union</u> v. <u>Misco, Inc.</u> 108 S.Ct. 364 91984). a Court's refusal to enforce an arbitrator's "interpretation" of a collective bargaining agreement is limited to situations where the contract as interpreted would violate "some explicit public policy..." Fact finding is the task of the arbitrator, not the reviewing court. Reinstatement of Cooper does not pose a threat to the asserted public policy. Does a successor employer have to honor a CBA? See <u>Fall River Dyeing and Finishing Corp.</u> v. <u>NLRB</u>, 107 S. Ct. 2225 (1987). Where a union certified for more than one year has a rebuttable presumption of majority status, the status continues despite the change in employers. The new employer is not bound by the terms of the predecessor's bargaining agreement, it has an obligation to bargain with the union.

Four devices that affect union security:

1. right-to-work-laws--employees of unionized employers do not have to join

2. closed shops--must hire only union workers

3. union shops--those hired must become union members

4. agency shop--non-members must pay equivalent of union dues.

Strikes/lockouts are devices used to influence the terms of the CBA. Employers may hire temporary or permanent replacements for employees on economic strikes--if permanent replacement leaves striker entitled to reinstatement. In a ULP strike, striker can only be temporarily replaced--if striker offers to return, must be reinstated. Secondary boycotts require someone to stop handling another's products or doing business with another person. This is usually a ULP. See <u>National Woodwork Manufacturers Ass'n</u> v. <u>NLRB</u>, 386 U.S. 612 (1967). This was not a secondary boycott. The "will not handle' clause was not designed to preserve carpenters' on-site work, not to expand carpenters' work. This was not aimed at a secondary party. Employees can eliminate a union by a decertification election. Employees, another person or another union may file a decertification petition but must contain an indication that 30% of the employees want decertification. Employers may not file decertification petitions.

The Federal Relations Authority hears unfair labor practice complaints from federal workers. Federal workers may not bargain about wages, hours and fringe benefits. Federal employees have no right to strike. Most states allow public employees to form unions but they cannot strike.

Review Questions

True/False

_____ 1.   The Norris-LaGuardia Act is the anti-injunction act.

_____ 2.   The Labor-Management Relations Act regulates union internal affairs.

_____ 3.   The NLRB has exclusive jurisdiction over unfair labor practices in interstate commerce.

_____ 4.   NLRB orders are reviewable by administrative law judges.

_____ 5.   A union election will be held upon support of 30% of the employees.

_____ 6.   An employer may object to the authenticity of authorization cards.

_____ 7.   If an employer commits a ULP prior to an election, the NLRB may waive the election.

_____ 8.   Unions have the right to seek court review of an NLRB refusal to certify.

_____ 9.   The election bar rule applies for a 12 month period.

_____ 10.   An employer can increase wages validly without first bargaining with the union.

Multiple Choice -- Please circle the best answer

1.   Unions have responded to increased worldwide competition in the 1980s by
         a.   decertification.
         b.   givebacks.
         c.   shifting plants.
         d.   voting for George Bush.

2.   An important pro-union aspect of the Norris-LaGuardia Act is
         a.   the Danberry Hartley Doctrine.
         b.   that it outlawed the use of injunctions.
         c.   that it removed federal court jurisdiction.
         d.   that it established the NLRA.

3.   The Taft-Hartley Act outlawed
         a.   decertification.
         b.   primary boycotts.
         c.   work shifting.
         d.   secondary boycotts.

4.   The administrative agency that oversees labor-management relations is the
         a.   Federal Mediation Service.
         b.   Federal labor Commission.
         c.   National Labor Relations Board.
         d.   National Arbitration Service.

5. The length of the Statute of Limitations for an unfair labor practice is
    a.   six months.
    b.   one year.
    c.   none.
    d.   nine months.

6. The level of proof that a complainant must establish for an unfair labor charge is
    a.   beyond a reasonable doubt.
    b.   a preponderance of the evidence.
    c.   cease and desist standard.
    d.   determined by the ALT.

7. NLRB orders are reviewable in the
    a.   Federal District Court.
    b.   Supreme Court.
    c.   Federal Court of Appeals.
    d.   Department of Labor.

8. A "showing of interest" in a union is usually demonstrated by
    a.   signing a petition.
    b.   signing authorization cards.
    c.   a voice vote of the employees.
    d.   meetings with the employer.

9. The employer can make the following preelection campaign statement:
    a.   This company has been prosperous over the years.
    b.   If the union wins this election, the company will be tied up in court for years.
    c.   Remember, we have non-union plants in the south.
    d.   Do you want to gamble your present benefit package?

10. An employer must
    a.   agree to all demands of the union.
    b.   bargain in good faith.
    c.   bargain for an indefinite period of time.
    d.   present its best offer at the beginning of the bargaining process.

11. The National Labor Relations Act of 1935
    a.   required employees to join unions.
    b.   set forth unfair labor practices binding on employees.
    c.   set forth ULPs binding on unions.
    d.   set forth ULPs binding on employers.

12. The jurisdiction of the NLRB is based on
    a.   the due process clause.

       b.   the commerce clause.

       c.   the equal protection clause.

       d.   First Amendment.

13.   A ULP practice filed by an individual can be disposed of by

       a.   adjustment.

       b.   dismissal.

       c.   withdrawal.

       d.   all of the above.

14.   The election bar rule prevents another representative election for

       a.   12 months.

       b.   6 months.

       c.   2 years.

       d.   3 years.

15.   It is not an ULP if an employer relocates a plant

       a.   to discourage unionization.

       b.   to escape unions.

       c.   to take advantage of lower taxes.

       d.   to intimidate workers.

Short Answer

1.   List four federal statutes dealing with unions and employers.

       a.   _____

       b.   _____

       c.   _____

       d.   _____

2.   List two types of proceedings that can be initiated with the NLRB.

       a.   _____

       b.   _____

3.   List three employer ULPs.

       a.   _____

    b. _____

    c. _____

4.   List three union ULPs.

    a. _____

    b. _____

    c. _____

5.   List two types of cases which receive priority from the NLRB.

    a. _____

    b. _____

6.   List three ways in which employees can unionize.

    a. _____

    b. _____

    c. _____

7.   What happens if an employer commits a ULP during an election campaign?

_____

_____

_____

8.   List two bars on repeating union elections.

    a. _____

    b. _____

9.   Determine if each of the following is permitted or a ULP.

    a. shutting down a plant _____

b.   boulwareism _____

10.   Define the following:

a.   closed shop _____

b.   union shop _____

c.   secondary boycott _____

Answers to Review Questions

True/False

1. T   3. T   5. T   7. T   9. F
2. T   4. F   6. T   8. F   10. F

Multiple Choice

1.   b.   4.   c.   7.   c.   10.   b.   13.   d.
2.   b.   5.   a.   8.   b.   11.   d.   14.   a.
3.   d.   6.   b.   9.   a.   12.   b.   15.   c.

Short Answer

1.   a.   National Labor Relations Act--Wagner Act
      b.   Labor Management Relations Act--Taft-Hartley
      c.   Norris-LaGuardia Act
      d.   Landrum-Griffin Amendment to Labor Management Relations Act

2.   a.   complaint case--ULP
      b.   representation case--union election
      c.   refusing to bargain with employer
      d.   engaging in secondary strike
      e.   requiring discriminatory or excessive fee for union membership
      f.   causing employer to pay for services not performed
      g.   forcing employer to deal with noncertified union
      h.   secondary boycotts

3.   a.   employer interference with, restraint or coercion of employees in union activities
      b.   employer dominance or interference with formation or administration of labor unions

    c.   employer discrimination for union activities
    d.   discharge for union activities
    e.   refusal to bargain collectively
    f.   entering into secondary boycott

4.   a.   restraining or coercing employees in exercise of their rights
       b.   causing employers to discriminate

5.   a.   secondary boycott
       b.   hot cargo contracts
       c.   organizational and recognition picketing
       d.   employee discrimination

6.   a.   voting in a representation election
       b.   authorization cards
       c.   by NLRB ordering collective bargaining

7.   if union wins, nothing; if union loses, election could be rerun, or NLRB could order employer to bargain

8.   a.   election bar rule
       b.   contract bar rule

9.   a.   okay if employer is not discouraging unionization elsewhere
       b.   ULP

10.   a.   must be union member to be employed
       b.   must join union within certain time after beginning work
       c.   boycott against one not the employer

Key Terms

craft unions: organizations of employees according to common skills.

industrial unions: organizations of employees according to industry regardless of skills.

American Federation of Labor: large national craft union of the 1930s.

Congress of Industrial Organizations: national industrial union formed in the late 1930s.

National Labor Relations Act (Wagner Act): first federal labor legislation.

Labor-Management Relations Act (Taft-Hartley): federal act restricting union activity.

givebacks: existing agreement is reopened so employees will cut wages and fringes in exchange for profit-sharing arrangements.

Sherman Act: antitrust law originally used to prevent union activity.

Danberry Hatters Case: decision in which Sherman Act was applied to halt striking and picketing.

Clayton Act: antitrust act that attempted to halt injunctions in labor cases.

Norris-LaGuardia Act: act removing jurisdiction from federal courts to enjoin peaceful labor disputes.

Railway Labor Act: federal law regulating labor in the railroad industry.

Landrum-Griffin Amendment: federal law regulating internal affairs of labor unions.

National Labor Relations Board (NLRB): federal administrative agency responsible for enforcement of NLRA.

complaint case (C case): case brought to NLRB charging an ULP.

representation case (R case): case brought to NLRB charging inadequate or unfair representation.

unfair labor practices (ULPs): legal wrong or cause of action based on federal labor laws.

union ULPs: unfair labor practices by unions.

employer ULPs: unfair labor practices by employers.

adjustment of ULP: settlement of ULP charge.

dismissal of ULP: dismissal of ULP charge.

withdrawal of ULP: complaining parties withdraw ULP.

showing of employee interest: basis for union election; 30% of employees desiring vote.

laboratory conditions: clinical, dispassionate atmosphere for union vote.

election bar rule: twelve-month bar on elections once one has been held.

contract bar rule: bar to other contracts once union and employer have a collective bargaining agreement.

<u>schism</u>: conflict or split among union officials on policy; exception to contract bar rule.

<u>defunctness</u>: situation where union on longer operates.

<u>union certification</u>: recognition of a union as an official representative of employees.

<u>runaway shop</u>: employer moving plant to avoid effects of certified union.

<u>collective bargaining agreement</u>: contract between union and employer on employment terms and
    conditions

<u>duty to bargain</u>: duty of parties to meet and in good faith discuss wages and labor issues.

<u>mandatory bargaining topics</u>: those topics parties must discuss in bargaining.

<u>binding arbitration</u>: arbitration in which the parties are bound by the decision of the mediator.

<u>boulwareism</u>: violation of duty to bargain in good faith; a closed mind at the start of negotiations.

<u>right to work laws</u>: state laws letting persons work without having to join unions.

<u>closed shop</u>: employers required to hire only union member job applicants.

<u>union shop</u>: employee required to join union after certain time of employment.

<u>agency shop</u>: employee required to pay union dues and fees after beginning work.

<u>strike</u>: weapon of employees that stops work.

<u>whipsaw strike</u>: strike of one of a few employers in a multiemployer union.

<u>economic strike</u>: strike by employees to obtain economic advantage in bargaining.

<u>lockout</u>: economic weapon of employers to stop employees from working.

<u>ULP strike</u>: strike responding to a ULP.

<u>secondary boycott</u>: requiring or forcing someone to stop handling another's product or doing business
    with another person.

<u>decertification election</u>: election to have union removed as certified representative.

BUSINESS ORGANIZATIONS

Chapter Summary

A sole proprietorship is any person in business to make an individual profit. May operate under an assumed or fictitious name--must register. Reasons for a sole proprietorship are simplicity, control, convenience and privacy. See Rushing v. Powell, 130 Ca. Rptr. 110 (1976). A building contractor did not have an occupational license or comply with the fictitious name statute. The court found that the filing of a certificate showing that the plaintiff was doing business as an individual complied with the fictitious name statute. Failure to have the occupational license to build pools was fatal to the contract recovery.

A partnership is easy to form and does not require state approval. This is not double taxation. A major disadvantage is liability exposure. A partners individual assets can be seized to pay damages. Partners must keep minutes of meetings and business records. The UPA's definition of a partnership is an "association of two or more persons to carry on, as co-owners, of a business for profit." No express agreement is needed. A partnership can be implied by the conduct of the parties. Courts look to a number of factors to determine if a partnership exists. Two of the most important are joint right to manage the business and sharing of profits and losses. The partnership contract should be in writing. Has to be in writing if lasts longer than one year. See Dalton v. Austin, 432 A.2d 774 (1981). The record sufficiently supports the existence of co-ownership since one party actively managed the business for several months with the supervision of the defendant. Sharing is not required if, as the evidence shows, the agreement itself implies the contemplated sharing of profits. Austin and Dalton were engaged in a partnership.

The UPA sets our the rights and duties of partners with respect to one another:

1. right to profits
2. right to repayment of capital contributions
3. fiduciary duty to each other
4. right to inspect and copy books--duty to keep books
5. right to an accounting
6. duty to contribute toward partnership losses
7. right to be indemnified
8. right to manage
9. duty to render information.

The UPA allows partners to vary rights and duties by agreement (management and profits). Partners are not entitled to salaries (agreement can provide otherwise in some instances). Partners may not sue each other except to end the partnership. Partners liability for copartners' contracts and torts:

1. partner an agent for the partnership while acting for purpose of business
2. authority issue '
3. express, implied, apparent authority or ratification
4. joint and several liability for torts
5. joint liability for contracts.

Partnership property has the following characteristics:

1. may own property in partnership name
2. all property acquired with partnership funds or brought into the partnership
3. own property in tenancy in partnership
       a. partners can possess property for partnership purposes
       b. no right to use for individual purposes
4. partners right in specific partnership property not subject to attachment or execution
5. partnership creditors may execute or attach against partnership property
6. no exemptions--not subject to dower or courtesy.

See Patel v. Patel, 260 Cal. Rprt. 255 (1989). In the present case, the usual partnership business is to run a business, rather than to hold it in anticipation of its eventual sale. The partnership is not bound by a contract selling that business without the approval of all partners.

The person asserted to be a partner by estoppel is not, in fact, a partner. Partnership by estoppel has three elements: reasonable reliance, change of position, and damages.

Limited Partnerships are governed by the Uniform Limited Partnership Act. The requirements are articles that must be filed, at least one general partner, limited partners liability is limited to their contribution and be passive with respect to management. The more active the limited partner in management, the greater the risk of general liability. See Obert v. Environmental Research & Dev., 771 P.2d 340 (1989). The court held that Campus Park LP was not dissolved, denied specific performance of the subordinated profits clause, no breach of fiduciary duties.

Must first examine the trust device and terms when examining business trusts:

1. settlor--party setting up the trust
2. trustee--party managing the trust
3. beneficiary--party receiving income from the trust
4. res--subject matter of the trust.

The trustees are the managers of the business while the beneficiaries receive benefits. Examples are a business trust, Massachusetts trust and real estate investment trust (REIT).

A corporation is a legal body or entity with many owners (shareholders). Features of the corporate structure are limited liability and transferability of shares. Corporations are not given all the protections possible under the Federal Constitution. Almost all business corporations are creatures of state law. Basic corporate definitions include:

1. domestic corporation--in state where it is incorporated
2. foreign corporation--corporation in state other than its incorporation
3. governmental corporation--no profit motivation--social goal
4. municipal corporation--cities and towns
5. nonprofit corporation--charity
6. professional corporation--attorneys, accountants and physicians.

The Model Business Corporation Act (MBCA) has been adopted in about half the states. The Model Act is a liberal act from management's viewpoint. Corporations are formed by compliance with state enabling statutes. The job of generating the idea for forming a new corporation belongs to the corporate promoter. This person usually sells corporate share subscriptions. Promoter can be liable for fraud or breach of a fiduciary duty to subscribers. Promoter is liable on pre-incorporation agreements. Four legal theories have been utilized to substitute the corporation for the promoter: novation, continuing offer, adoption and ratification. The corporation begins when the certificate of incorporation is issued (MBCA). Conduct before the certificate is issued; see Robertson v. Levy, 197 A.2d 443 (1964). The certificate of incorporation provides the cut off point; before it is issued, the individuals, and not the corporation, are liable.

The MBCA declares that directors:

1. corporate mangers
2. need not be residents or shareholders
3. need at least one
4. elected at annual meeting--1 share, 1 vote
5. term--provided for in charter
6. vacancies--filled by remaining board members
    a. can be removed by shareholders with or without cause by majority vote of shares
7. quorum--majority
8. adopt by-laws--govern internal operation

9. meetings--time and place prescribed in the by-laws.

The payment of dividends are within the directors' discretion. Unrestricted earned surplus must be available to pay dividends. Dividends may be declared and paid using treasury shares. Directors owe the corporation a duty to avoid conflicts of interest. MBCA takes a liberal view--transactions are not invalidated provided there is disclosure of the director's interest. Corporate directors have a legal duty to exercise independent judgement. The standard of director care does not make directors insurers of the success of their decisions--business judgement rule. See Grobow v. Perot, 526 A.2d 914 (1987). It becomes difficult to argue that the business judgement rule should not apply where an independent disinterested board of directors decides not to abdicate control of a wholly owned subsidiary and principal supplier.

Shareholders must authorize director loans. A number of particular problems involve director liability: dividend declarations and voting at meetings. Each outstanding share of stock has one vote and when first issued full value must be paid. One vote requirement can be changed by corporate charter. Stock proxies last for a maximum of 11 months unless proxy says otherwise. Corporate officers consist of a president, one or more vice presidents, a secretary and a treasurer. Offices of president and secretary must be held by different people. Their authority is controlled by agency law and they serve at the pleasure of the board.

Review Questions

True/False

_____ 1.   A sole proprietor can hold business property in a fictitious name.

_____ 2.   Sharing of gross returns in prima facie evidence of the existence of a partnership.

_____ 3.   Under the UPA, profits are split according to the proportion of the partner's capital contribution.

_____ 4.   Partners are jointly liable for co-partners' torts committed in the ordinary course of business.

_____ 5.   Property purchased with partnership funds is presumed to belong to the partnership.

_____ 6.   A limited partnership requires at least one general partner.

_____ 7.   In a business trust, the trustees are the equivalent of the shareholders.

_____ 8.   Shareholders in corporations are liable only to the extent of the amount paid for their shares.

_____ 9.   Adoption of a pre-incorporation contract by a newly formed corporation relieves the promoter of all liability.

_____ 10.   Bylaws govern the internal operation of the corporation.

Multiple Choice

1.   Failure to comply with state fictitious name statutes will result in
   a.   the sole proprietorship being declared illegal.
   b.   a fine and/or imprisonment
   c.   a small fine
   d.   the name being withdrawn

2.   Sole proprietorships have to
   a.   register with the secretary of state.
   b.   file federal income tax returns.
   c.   keep minutes of all meetings.
   d.   pay an annual franchise fee.

3.   A partnership must do one of the following before commencing operations.
   a.   file with the proper state officials
   b.   seek the approval of the IRS
   c.   receive a charter in order to do business
   d.   none of the above

4.   If the parties intend a one time business arrangement, it is called a
   a.   partnership.
   b.   joint venture.
   c.   business trust.
   d.   none of the above.

5.   A factor that courts utilize in determining if a partnership exists is
   a.   joint ownership of property.
   b.   complying with state filing requirements.
   c.   a joint debt repayment plan.
   d.   right to share in management decisions.

6.   Partnership property may be held in the
   a.   partnership name.
   b.   partner's name.
   c.   creditor's name.
   d.   a and c

7.   The law governing corporations is
      a.   federal law.
      b.   state law.
      c.   the UPA.
      d.   municipal law.

8.   The corporate promoter can
      a.   sell stock subscriptions.
      b.   purchase property.
      c.   hire employees.
      d.   all of the above.

9.   The corporate directors
      a.   must be residents of the state of incorporation.
      b.   must be shareholders.
      c.   have authority to fix their compensation.
      d.   have the authority to suspend shareholders meetings for two years.

10.   The standard of care for a director is
      a.   independent judgement
      b.   an insurer
      c.   reasonable care
      d.   honest judgement

11.   The major disadvantage of a partnership is
      a.   ease of formation.
      b.   no state approval.
      c.   liability exposure.
      d.   record keeping.

12.   Partners may sue one another on partnership matters
      a.   over disagreements.
      b.   over tax matters.
      c.   to end the partnership.
      d.   involving torts.

13.   Partners have _____ authority.
      a.   express
      b.   implied
      c.   apparent
      d.   none of the above.

14.   A corporation organized under the laws of a state other than the state one is in is a
      a.   municipal corporation.

    b.   foreign corporation.

    c.   domestic corporation.

    d.   professional corporation.

15.   The directors owe a duty to the corporation to

    a.   make money.

    b.   pay dividends.

    c.   avoid conflict of interests.

    d.   communicate with the shareholders.

Short Answer

1.   List three advantages of the sole proprietor form of business.

    a.   _____

    b.   _____

    c.   _____

2.   List two advantages of the partnership form of business over the corporate form.

    a.   _____

    b.   _____

3.   What are the two most important factors used by courts to determine whether a partnership exists.

    a.   _____

    b.   _____

4.   In forming the ABC Partnership, A contributed $10,000, B $5,000 and C $2,000. A, B and C have no agreement. How are profits split among A, B and C?

    _____

    _____

5.   How can a limited partner lose his or her liability status?

    _____

_____

6.   List three types of corporations.

   a.   _____

   b.   _____

   c.   _____

7.   List the four theories used to substitute the corporation for the promoter in pre-incorporation contracts.

   a.   _____

   b.   _____

   c.   _____

   d.   _____

8.   Who may declare a corporate dividend?

_____

9.   List the corporate officers required under the MBCA.

   a.   _____

   b.   _____

   c.   _____

   d.   _____

10.   What six factors can be used to compare the various business forms?

   a.   _____

   b.   _____

   c.   _____

   d.   _____

e. _____

f. _____

Answers to Review Questions

True/False

1.	T	3.	F	5.	T	7.	F	9.	F
2.	F	4.	F	6.	T	8.	T	10.	T

Multiple Choice

1.	c.	4.	b.	7.	b.	10.	c.	13.	d.
2.	b.	5.	d.	8.	d.	11.	a.	14.	b.
3.	d.	6.	b.	9.	c.	12.	c.	15.	c.

Short Answer

1. a. simplicity
   b. control
   c. convenience

2. a. ease of formation
   b. less red tape in government reports

3. a. joint right to manage the business
   b. sharing of profits

4. profits are split equally among the three

5. by becoming active in the management of the partnership business

6. a. governmental
   b. municipal
   c. professional

7. a. novation theory
   b. continuing offer
   c. adoption
   d. ratification

8.   only the board of directors

9.   a.   president
      b.   vice-president
      c.   secretary
      d.   treasurer

10.   a.   ease of formation
      b.   ease of operation
      c.   attractiveness as an investment vehicle
      d.   tax considerations
      e.   privacy
      f.   control

Key Terms

sole proprietorship: any person engaged in business to make individual profit.

partnership: association of two or more persons carrying on as co-owners in a business for profit.

Uniform Partnership Act (UPA):   uniform law adopted by nearly all of the states governing partnerships.

prima facie evidence: evidence sufficiently presented to allow case to go to jury.

minors: persons below legal age for contracting.

incapacity: lack of contractual capacity; age or mental.

statute of frauds: statute which dictates the types of contracts that must be in writing to be enforceable.

specific performance: equitable remedy whereby party is ordered to perform pursuant to a contractual obligation.

damages: money awarded to compensate a party for a wrong or contractual breach.

fiduciary responsibility: duty of loyalty and trust to another.

tort: civil wrong committed against another.

express authority: authority, either written or spoken, given to an agent.

implied authority: authority that can reasonably or customarily be implied from given express authority.

apparent authority: authority that an agent appears to third parties to possess.

ratification: principal's recognition and acceptance of act of agent done without authority.

tenancy in partnership: form of ownership by partners of partnership property.

partner's interest: partner's share of profits and surplus.

tenant in partnership exemptions: property entitled to protection from judicial attachment for debt.

execution: judicial remedy of creditor to obtain payment for judgment.

dower: claims by a wife against a husband's realty because of marriage.

curtesy: claims by a husband against his wife's realty because they were married and had a child.

partnership by estoppel: legal theory imposing liability on a party even though they are not a member of the partnership.

limited partnership: form of partnership where some partners have limited liability.

general partner: partner whose personal assets can be used to satisfy partnership liability.

Uniform Limited Partnership Act: uniform law adopted in nearly all states governing limited partnerships.

trust: property arrangement set up to benefit certain persons.

trustee: party holding legal title to trust property who administers trust.

beneficiary: party benefiting from trust income.

res: property placed in trust.

business trusts: form of business organization where trustees manage property for the benefit of the beneficiaries.

Massachusetts trust: business organization where property is legally owned by trustees.

real estate investment trust (REIT): financial device in which investors buy shares in a trust and the res is invested in real estate.

corporation: legal body created to operate business for the benefit of many owners.

legal fiction: a creation of the law to satisfy social and economic needs.

qualified: (relating to corporations) able to do business.

domestic corporation: corporation organized under the state corporation law of the state one is in.

foreign corporation: corporation organized under the laws of a state other than the state one is in.

Model Business Corporations Act (MBCA): model corporate law act giving states guidelines for their acts (over one-half of states have adopted some form of the MBCA).

registered agent (corporate): agent of record for corporation for receipt of service of process.

promoters: parties organizing the formation and financing of a corporation.

share subscriptions: offer to buy shares in a corporation.

corporation by estoppel: corporate existence by attempted formation and reliance.

directors: corporate managers.

cumulative voting: method of electing directors to the board giving minority shareholders a greater voice.

treasury shares: shares once issued and repurchased by the corporation.

earned surplus: account reflecting cumulative losses and profits of a corporation.

paid-in capital: account reflecting the number of shares sold times the par value.

stock dividend: payment of dividend in shares of corporation's stock.

stock split: no movement in capital accounts but a further division of corporation equity.

business judgement rule: standard of care for directors.

stock proxy: authorization for non-owner to vote shares of stock.

SECURITIES REGULATION

Chapter Summary

When we speak of the federal security laws, referring to ten federal laws.

1. Securities Act of 1933
   a. selling securities to public in primary market
   b. requires registration before sale
2. Securities Exchange Act of 1934
   a. sale of securities in secondary market
   b. set up Securities and Exchange Commission
3. Public Utility Holding Company Act of 1935
   a. stop abuses in financing and operations of gas and electric public utilities
   b. administered by SEC
4. Trust Indenture Act of 1937
   a. regulates sales of debt securities (bonds)
   b. requires certain provisions and supervision
5. Investment Company Act of 1940
   a. regulation of publicly-owned companies selling securities
   b. regulation of management also
6. Investment Advisors Act of 1940--regulation of investment advisors
7. Williams Act of 1968--regulates tender offers, response to hostile takeovers
   a. disclosure requirements
   b. procedural rules
   c. state laws have been declared valid; see, CTS Corporation v. Dynamics Corporation (text)
8. Securities Investory Protection Act of 1970
   a. set up Securities Investor Protection Corporation
   b. administers liquidation of brokerage firms having financial problems

9.   Foreign Corrupt Practices Act of 1977
        a. prohibits bribes to foreign officials
        b. requires certain businesses to set up systems of internal control
10.   Insider Trading Sanctions Act of 1984--to increase punishment for insider trading

What is a security? The Securities Act of 1933 provides a broad definition. Any note, stock, treasury stock, bond debenture, etc. The Howey definition: investment in a common enterprise with profits expected solely from the efforts of others. In recent years, the Supreme Court has narrowed the definition. See Landreth Timber Co. v. Landreth, 471 U.S. 681 (1985). The stock at issue here is a "security" within the definition of the acts, and the "sale of business" doctrine does not apply.

The main objective of the SEC Act of 1933 is to provide the public with full and fair disclosure about new securities offered for sale. Securities must be registered with the SEC by filing a registration statement. A registration statement consists of two parts: a prospectus and Part II. A prospectus:

1. must be given to buyer before or after purchase occurs
2. includes information about issuer--its officers, assets directors, liabilities.

A Part II statement:

1. not given to investor
2. available for inspection at SEC office
3. contains expert opinions (accountants, lawyers, geologists).

The registration is effective 20 days after filing. The SEC may delay or accelerate. Approval is only for full and fair disclosure--no decision on the validity of the investment. Steps in the registration process:

1.   pre-filing period
        a. no offers or selling
        b. issuers may negotiate with underwriters
2.   waiting period--20 days
        a. period between filing and effective date
        b. SEC may ask for amendments
        c. may run "tombstone" ads
        d. may distribute "red herring" prospectus
        e. offers may be made--contracts to sell illegal
3.   post-effective period
        a. no limitations on sales
        b. final prospectus must be given to all, even those with red herring

The purpose of a shelf registration is to reduce the time-lag problem. Permits issuers to prepare one registration statement covering any securities offered by the issuer for two years. Puts securities "on the shelf" until the market is receptive.

Not all new securities or securities transactions have to go through the full registration process. Certain securities and transactions in securities are exempt. Exemptions are valuable because they save time, money and red tape. There are two kinds of exemptions under the SEC Act of 1933. Exempt securities never have to be registered before being offered for sale. An exempt transaction means that when a particular sale of a security occurs, the seller does not have to register the security. This lasts for only one sale or round of sales. Exemptions are costly for business and generally lower investor protection.

Exempt transactions under the 1933 Act:

1.   secondary trading
2.   private placements--no public offering
3.   interstate offerings
    a. can use mails and telephone
    b. all offerees and offeror in one state
4.   small offerings
    a. Regulation A
        (1) short form registration
        (2) $1,500,000 issue maximum in any 12 month period
    b. Regulation D
        (1) Rule 501: defines accredited (sophisticated) investor
            (a) any bank, insurance company, investment company, or employee benefit plan
            (b) any business development company
            (c) any charitable or educational institution with assets of more than $5 million
            (d) any director, executive officer, or general partner of the issuer
            (e) any person buying at least $150,000 of securities if the purchase is 20% or less of the person's net worth
            (f) any person with a net worth of more than $1 million
            (g) any person with an annual income of more than $200,000
        (2) Rule 502--three Regulation D matters
            (a) integration: if more than one offering in less than six months--may be treated as one offering and lose small offering exemption
            (b) five factors to determine
                -part of one financing plan
                -same class of security
                -made about the same time
                -for the same purpose
                -for same consideration
            (c) special information requirements if integrated and sold to unaccredited buyer under 505 or 506 (short-form prospectus)
            (d) limits on resale
        (3) Rule 503: seller must give SEC notice of Regulation D sales
        (4) Rule 504: exemption if issuer sells less than $500,000 of securities in 12 month period

>   (5) Rule 505: exemption where issuer may sell up to $5 million of securities in 12 month period to accredited investors and up to 35 unaccredited investors
>   accredited and up to 35 unaccredited investors--if any are unaccredited, a short-term prospectus required for all
>   (6) Section 4(b): exempt securities offerings up to $5 million when made only to accredited investors.

Exempt securities under the 1933 SEC Act of 1933--not exempt from SA's antifraud and civil liability provisions:

1. securities issued by federal, state or municipal governments
2. commercial paper--maturity under nine months
3. banks, religions, and charitable organizations' securities
4. securities of common carriers subject to Interstate Commerce Commission regulation
5. bankruptcy certificates
6. annuity contracts
7. insurance policies

People can be civilly liable under the SEC Act of 1933. Section 11 deals only with securities registered under the SA. Section 12 of the SA puts civil liability on those committing fraud in the sale or offer of any security even if not registered under the SA. Requirements for recovery under Section 11:

1. person purchased recovery
2. security is covered by registration statement
3. material misstatement or omission in registration statement
4. loss of money on security
5. reliance need not be established.

Who is liable?

1. anyone who signed the registration statements
2. all directors
3. all experts preparing part of the statement (lawyers-accountants)
4. all underwriters.

Extent of liability?

1. joint and several liability
2. experts liable only for their portion of the registration statement.

Defenses to Section 11:

1. due diligence--reasonable grounds to believe no error after reasonable investigation (not available

to issuer)
2. immateriality--not important information
3. purchaser knew of error or omission and bought anyway
4. other cause of purchaser's loss--economic depression
5. no reliance (for cases brought over one year after the registration statement took effect)
6. statute of limitations--one year, three year

SEC Act of 1933 has criminal sanctions. Committing fraud in the sale of securities or willfully violating the SA is a crime. Punishment is up to five years in prison, a maximum of $10,000 fine, or both. See <u>Escott</u> v. <u>BarChis Construction Corp.</u>, 283 F. Supp. 643 (1968). Leading case in interpreting Section 11 of the SEC Act of 1933. Some investors bought bonds that BarChris issued. A registration was filed for the bonds and the bonds were sold. BarChris defaulted on the bonds. Bond investors lost money and pointed out errors in the bond registration statement. The court ruled that there were material misrepresentations and omissions in the registration statement. Bond buyers could recover from accountants, directors, signers, and certain others if they did not establish a defense.

The Securities Exchange Act of 1934 covers many different securities areas. The SEA concentrates on the secondary (used) securities and their markets. The SEA establishes the Securities and Exchange Commission (SEC) and regulates the securities exchanges, dealers, brokers, and public held companies. The SEC is the leading enforcer of the federal securities laws. SEC promulgates rules and regulations, enforces them and adjudicates cases--a federal administrative agency. Registration under the 1934 Act:

1. broker-dealers must register
2. certain securities must be registered
    a. any security (debt or otherwise) traded on national stock exchange
    b. any equity security of company with 500 or more shareholders and over $5 million in assets
    c. exemptions such as securities of government agencies.

Reporting under the 1934 Act:

1. 10-K report--annual report
2. 10-Q report--unaudited quarterly report
3. 8-K report--current report filed when major corporate events occur such as change in directors.

A proxy is a person who acts for another. Common practice for shareholders to give the right to vote their shares to incumbent management or a challenging group. SEA imposes certain requirements:

1. proxy statement must be used
    a. provides information about solicitor of proxies
    b. if company is soliciting, information about directors, salaries, etc.
2. must be submitted to SEC if shares are required to be registered
3. proxy is actual form for shareholder's signature and instructions on voting
4. management must provide room in proxy statement for shareholder proposals

Buyers sometimes want to give themselves leverage by putting a small amount down on securities and borrow the rest (buying on margin). Credit restrictions:

1. regulate amount of credit a broker can extend to a securities buyer
2. margin requirements
3. restricts broker using customer's securities as collateral.

Short swing profile rule--16(b) 1934 Act:

1. insider--officer, director or large shareholder of more than 10% of an equity class
2. 16-6--if prohibited acts occurred within six month period, presumed to have used inside information
3. insider reports--when they engage in stock transactions
4. exceptions--fewer than 100 shares and low dollar amount transactions
5. may not use "straw people"

Section 10(b) and Rule 10b-5 is aimed at preventing fraud in the buying and selling of securities. Rule 10b-5 can stop profit taking in the firm's securities by corporate insiders who have inside information. The Act prohibits churning. See Zaretsky v. E. F. Hutton and Co., 509 F. Supp. 68 (1981). Rule 10b-5 of the SEC Act of 1934 views churning as a fraudulent act. Churning occurs when (1) the broker trades excessively in light of the type of account, and (2) the broker effectively controls the account.

Rule 10b-5 applies to any device, scheme or artifice to defraud. Applies to exempt or unregistered securities. See SEC v. Texas Gulf Sulphur Co., 401 F.2d 833 (1968). Various insiders violated rule 10b-5. Between announcements that a mineral company made a lucrative discovery, corporate officers and their relations bought or placed orders to buy company stock. The stock zoomed up in price after the second announcement which was quite specific.

Is tipee trading in the company's security illegal? It depends if the insider breaches a fiduciary duty in disclosing information to the tipee. If so, it is illegal for the tipee to trade in the issuer's securities unless the tipee discloses. See Dirks v. SEC, 463 U.S. 646 91983). All insider disclosures are not illegal. It depends largely on the personal benefit the insider gets as a result of the disclosure. Here, the inside tipper got no personal benefit from tipping Dirks, so Dirks did not inherit the insider's duty to disclose or abstain.

In 1984, Congress enacted the Insider Trading Sanctions Act to regulate insider trading. Act has the following provisions:

1. SEC authorized to seek civil penalties
2. damages of up to three times the profit made
3. criminal penalties increased from $10,000 to $100,000
4. insider trading in stock options illegal
5. aiders and abettors are also liable
6. the act does not define insider trading or material nonpublic information
7. five year statute of limitations.

A takeover bid, or tender offer, occurs when someone publicly offers to buy stock from a corporation's shareholders at a set price. Regulated by two federal statutes:

1. way to take over control of corporation ("target corporation") by purchase of a majority of its shares
2. tender offeror must set uniform price and it may be contingent on a certain percentage of shares accepting the offer
3. shareholders may withdraw tendered stock for fist seven days of offer
4. may also withdraw if not purchased after 60 days
5. regulated by 1934 Act and Williams Act of 1968--if tender offer would result in offeror's owning more than five percent of a class of securities registered under the SEA, offeror must file with the SEC and provide information to all offerees
6. why regulated?
    a. to let management know
    b. to help shareholders make an intelligent decision by requiring that they receive information
7. misstatements, omitting a material fact or engaging in any deception in connection with a tender offer unlawful
8. criminal sanctions
    a. must be willful violation
    b. five years and/or $100,000.

See Schreiber v. Burlington Northern, Inc., 472 U.S. 1 (1985). Shareholder claims that a series of tender offers resulted in her not benefiting as much had the first tender offer been the only one. Manipulative acts under 14(e) require misrepresentation or nondisclosure. Section 14(e) does not oversee the substantive fairness of tender offers; the quality of any offer is a matter for the market place.

The Foreign Corrupt Practices Act (FCPA) has three principal sections:

1. Section 102--Internal Reporting Requirements
2. Section 103--prohibits bribes by 1934 registered securities
3. Section 104--prohibits foreign corrupt practices by domestic concerns
4. Violation is a felony
    a. $1 million fine maximum for corporation
    b. officers/directors--$10,000 and/or five years

Each individual state has the power to regulate securities within its borders. These are called blue sky laws. About half the states have passed the Uniform Securities Act as their blue-sky law.

Review Questions

True/False

_____ 1.   The Securities Exchange Act of 1934 deals primarily with selling securities in the primary market.

_____ 2.   Copies of the registration statement must be given to security buyers before the purchase occurs.

_____ 3.   By allowing the registration statement to take effect, the SEC is indicating the securities are good investment.

_____ 4.   Only tombstone ads and red herrings are permitted during the pre-filing period.

_____ 5.   Regulation A is an exemption allowing a short form registration.

_____ 6.   Securities of local governments are exempt from SEC registration requirements.

_____ 7.   Proof of a Section 11 violation requires establishing that there is a material omission or misstatement in the registration statement.

_____ 8.   All securities, including bonds, must be registered under the 1934 Act if those securities are traded on a national exchange.

_____ 9.   Margin requirements refer to restrictions on the use of credit to purchase securities.

_____ 10.   For purposes of Rule 16b, insiders are officers, directors, and 10% shareholders.

Multiple Choice -- Please circle the best answer

1.   The Securities Act of 1933 regulates securities in the
   a.   primary market.
   b.   secondary market.
   c.   in all markets.
   d.   in the hostile takeover market.

2.   This act gives the SEC authority to regulate tender offers
   a.   Investment Advisers Act.
   b.   Trust Indenture Act.
   c.   Williams Act.
   d.   Davis Act.

3.   The term security could include
   a.   rows of orange trees.
   b.   farmlands.
   c.   stock.
   d.   all of the above.

4. The main purpose of the 1933 SEC Act is
   a. punitive.
   b. informational.
   c. regressive.
   d. to regulate.

5. During the waiting period under the 1933 Act, parties may
   a. enter into contracts.
   b. file a registration statement.
   c. make sales to public.
   d. make offers to the public.

6. The SEC has developed the following to deal with the problems of timing and red tape in the sale of securities
   a. red herring prospectus.
   b. shelf registration.
   c. tombstone ad.
   d. prefiling period.

7. An initial sale of bonds to an insurance company is an example of a(an)
   a. exempt security.
   b. intrastate offering.
   c. Regulation D-105.
   d. private placement.

8. Regulation A (small security issues) of the 1933 Act provides
   a. an exemption from registration.
   b. for a 20 day waiting period.
   c. for an exemption up to $2 million.
   d. for short form registration.

9. Under Section 11 of the 1933 Act, experts have
   a. primary liability.
   b. limited liability.
   c. no liability.
   d. strict liability.

10. A director who owns more than ____ of an equity class is considered an insider under Section 16(b).
    a. 5%   c. 20%
    b. 10%   d. 50%

11. The waiting period in the registration process under the 1933 SEC Act is
    a. always 20 days.

b.   the period between the filing and the registration statement's effective date.
c.   the period between the filing and the date of SEC approval.
d.   45 days.

12.   Who may not raise the due diligence defense under Section 11 of the 1933 SEC Act?
a.   accountants.
b.   underwriters.
c.   issuers.
d.   attorneys.

13.   The SEC Act of 1934 applies to
a.   new securities.
b.   secondary securities.
c.   primary securities.
d.   first issues.

14.   A 10-K report under the 1934 SEC Act
a.   is an unaudited quarterly report.
b.   is an annual report of the issuer's operations.
c.   is a current report that must be filed during the first 10 days of the month.
d.   need not be audited by independent auditors.

15.   This section or rule is aimed at preventing fraud in buying and selling securities.
a.   Rule 10b-5.
b.   Rule 16-(b).
c.   Section 11.
d.   Section 17.

Short Answer

1.   Give the Supreme Court definition of a security.

_____

_____

2.   List three examples of exempt securities under the 1933 Act.

a.   _____

b.   _____

c.   _____

3.   List the elements required to establish a violation of Section 11.

a. _____

b. _____

c. _____

d. _____

4.   Describe the types of securities required to be registered under the 1934 Act.

a. _____

b. _____

5.   Who is subject to the short-swing (16b) profit rule?

a. _____

b. _____

c. _____

6.   Define the scope of coverage of Rule 10b-5.

_____

_____

_____

_____

_____

7.   Why are tender offers regulated?

a. _____

b. _____

8.   What is the tender offeror normally seeking through use of a tender offer?

_____

_____

9.   What is churning?

_____

_____

_____

10.   What may an issuer legally do during the waiting period to generate interest in a forthcoming securities issue?

a.   _____

b.   _____

Answers to Review Questions

True/False

| 1. | F | 3. | F | 5. | T | 7. | T | 9. | T |
| 2. | F | 4. | F | 6. | T | 8. | T | 10. | T |

Multiple Choice

1.	a.	4.	b.	7.	d.	10.	b.	13.	b.
2.	c.	5.	d.	8.	d.	11.	d.	14.	b.
3.	d.	6.	b.	9.	b.	12.	c.	15.	a.

Short Answer

1.   investment in a common enterprise with profits to come from the efforts of others

2.
a.   securities issued by federal, state or municipal governments
b.   commercial paper
c.   securities of banks, religious organizations, charitable organizations and savings and loans
d.   securities of common carriers
e.   bankruptcy certificates
f.   annuity contracts & insurance policies

3.   a.   security acquired
      b.   security covered by a registration statement
      c.   material misstatement or omission in registration statement
      d.   loss of money on security

4.   a.   those securities (bond or equity) traded on a national exchange
      b.   securities (equity) of companies with 500 or more shareholders and over $5 million in assets if traded in interstate commerce

5.   a.   officers
      b.   directors
      c.   ten percent or more shareholders of any class of stock

6.   Rule 10b-5 applies to virtually any fraud in connection with the sale or purchase of any security where the mails or instrumentality of interstate commerce is involved. It makes illegal any device, scheme, or artifice to defraud; any untrue statement, or any act, practice, or course of business that operates as a fraud in connection with the sale or purchase of a security.

7.   a.   to let existing management know of takeover attempts
      b.   to let target shareholders get the facts from both sides

8.   control of the target corporation

9.   the buying and selling of customers' securities to make commissions for the investment advisor rather than profit for the investors.

10.   a.   issue a red herring prospectus
      b.   place a tombstone ad

Key Terms

Security Act of 1933: federal statute setting out rules for selling new securities to the investing public.

Security Act of 1934: federal statute regulating the sale of "used" securities (the secondary market).

Public Utility Holding Company Act of 1935: federal statute enacted to end abuses in gas and electric public utility financing and operations.

Trust Indenture Act of 1937: federal statute which regulates the sale of debt securities (such as bonds).

Investment Company Act of 1940: federal statute giving the SEC authority to regulate publicly owned companies that invest and trade in securities.

<u>Williams Act of 1968</u>: tender offer regulation.

<u>Security Investor Protection Act of 1977</u>: federal statute enacted to create the S.I.P.C. to administer the liquidation of brokerage firms having financial problems.

<u>Foreign Corrupt Practices Act of 1977</u>: federal statute which prohibits bribes and requires systems of internal controls.

<u>Insider Trading Sanctions Act of 1984</u>: federal statute enacted to increase punishments for insider trading.

<u>proxy</u>: authorization for another to cast a shareholder's vote or votes.

<u>Rule 10b-5</u>: antifraud provision of the '34 Act.

<u>short-swing profit rule</u>: provision of the '34 Act that prohibits directors, officers and ten percent shareholders from making six month profits on sales and purchases of shares.

<u>Securities and Exchange Commission</u>: administrative agency responsible for enforcing the 1933 and 1934 acts.

<u>registration statement</u>: informational document required to be filed and approved by SEC for sale of securities requiring registration.

<u>waiting period</u>: period between filing of registration statement and date it becomes effective.

<u>underwriters</u>: purchasers of entire issues of securities.

<u>tombstone ad</u>: plain ad (black borders) that can be run during waiting period.

<u>red herring prospectus</u>: prospectus that can be given to parties during waiting period.

<u>exempt transactions</u>: sales of securities exempt from registration.

<u>accredited persons</u>: experienced investors to whom securities can be sold without registration.

<u>exempt securities</u>: securities that never have to be registered.

<u>specific intent crimes</u>: crimes requiring proof of a specific state of mind.

<u>permanent injunctions</u>: court orders prohibiting certain conduct in the future.

<u>security</u>: investment in common enterprise with profits to come solely from the efforts of others.

prospectus: document given to each security buyer containing information about the issuer.

Regulation A: small offering exemption.

Regulation D: exempts limited offerings from the 1933 Act.

integration: exempt, small offerings may be integrated (under Regulation D) and lose their exempt status.

due diligence: defense to false or misleading registration statement.

proxy statement: statement containing facts about the party soliciting a proxy.

tipee: someone getting material nonpublic information about an issue from an insider.

tender offer: a public offer to buy stock from shareholders at a set price.

target corporation: the corporation whose stock is sought.

golden parachute: contract that gives management high severance pay.

blue sky laws: state securities regulations.

19 ANTITRUST LAW: THE SHERMAN ACT

Chapter Summary

The United States followed an economic policy of laissez-faire during much of the nineteenth century. The common law was not effective in controlling anticompetitive behavior. The industrial revolution and corporate abuses led to the Interstate Commerce Act of 1887 and the Sherman Act of 1890.

Economics deals with the study of scarce resources. Price is a way of allocating scarce resources and is set by markets. In purely competitive market the greatest amount of goods will be produced at the lowest prices--efficiency. Two types of efficiency:

1. allocative means that consumers are getting the goods and services they want
2. productive means that scarce resources used in a way that will maximize their ability to satisfy people's wants.

The characteristics of pure competition:

1. goods and services are identical--price only differs
2. consumer shave perfect market knowledge
   a. what goods and services are available
   b. where things can be purchased for less or sold for more
3. many small buyers and sellers
4. no single buyer or seller can affect the price of a good or service
5. no barriers to market entry.

Three distortions of pure competition--see how antitrust laws try to deal with these distortions:

1.   monopolies
        a. one seller of unique good or service
        b. imperfect market knowledge
        c. barriers to entry
        d. problems
            (1) lower production
            (2) higher cost
            (3) transfer of wealth to producers
        e. early controls were ineffective
        f. Sherman Act was first control
        g. Clayton Act's incipiency doctrine--illegal if merger tends to create a monopoly
        h. Section 5 of FTC Act helps prevent monopolies
2.   monopolistic competition--not illegal
        a. involves many small sellers
        b. each has some unique feature or characteristic giving it limited monopoly
        c. economic consequences
            (1) not as many goods and services
            (2) prices are higher
            (3) sellers' costs are higher
            (4) sellers' profits are the same
3.   oligopolies
        a. large sellers sell all or most of goods or services
        b. interdependent sellers-watch each others' prices and output
        c. economic effects
            (1) no price competition
            (2) output greater than monopolies but less than pure
            (3) price is higher and producers earn more profits
        d. tendency to reach express or implied agreements--interdependent on each other
            (1) conscious parallelism
            (2) can violate antitrust laws (Theater Enterprises, Inc. v. Paramount Film Distrib. Corp., Inc.-text).

        Two schools of thought have dominated antitrust analysis and enforcement. The traditional (Harvard) approach favors an economy with many independent businesses, no one of which dominates the market. The assumption is that concentrated power can lead to social, political and economic abuses. The Chicago antitrust approach focuses almost exclusively on economics. It views efficient use of scarce resources as the crucial goal of industrial organization. Big firms are not necessarily bad. This creates jobs and strengthens businesses that must compete internationally. Under the Harvard school, enforcement is strict and comprehensive. Enforcement is limited to preventing horizontal price fixing under the Chicago School. Areas exempt from antitrust laws:

1. Most labor union activities

2. Intrastate industries having no effect on interstate commerce
3. Farmer and fisherman organizations (Capper-Volstead Act)
4. Export associations
5. Baseball
6. Regulated industries
7. Small businesses
8. Right to petition--Noerr doctrine
9. Business and professional activities covered by state action
    a. theory is that sovereign should not regulate another sovereign
    b. there must be enough state involvement to warrant exemption; see Patrick v. Burget, 108 S.Ct. 1658 (1988). The state-action doctrine does not protect Oregon physicians from federal antitrust liability for their activities on hospital peer-review committees. The "active supervision" prong of the test requires that state officials have and exercise power to review such parties' particular anticompetitive acts and disapprove those that fail to accord with state policy. This requirement is not satisfied here.

The Sherman Act of 1890 has two short but important provisions. One person can violate the monopolization section (2); two persons are required to violate the restraint of trade section (1). The Justice Department can bring suit as well as any private person whose business was injured can sue (treble damages). Suit is brought in federal district court in the district where the alleged conduct occurred. There must be interstate commerce--few are not. The Sherman Act is both criminal and civil. Penalties include:

1. criminal
    a. corporations, partnerships, individuals
    b. felony
    c. individuals--three years in prison and/or $100,000
    d. corporation fine up to $1 million
2. injunctive relief
3. divestiture of firms or dissolution
4. seizure of goods
5. civil suits
    a. any private person can bring
    b. recover three times their actual damages (treble damages) and attorney fees
6. can have both civil and criminal actions; prior criminal conviction is prima facie evidence for civil suit
7. pleas and plea bargaining
    a. guilty
    b. not guilty
    c. nolo contendere.

Section 1 of the Sherman Act outlaws every contract, conspiracy, or combination in restraint of trade. Almost all contracts are in restraint of trade. The rule of reason tolerates restraints of trade as long as they are not unreasonable. What is reasonable is determined on a case by case basis. See

Business Electronics Corporation v. Sharp Electronics Corporation, 108 S.Ct. 1515 (1988). A vertical non-price restraint is not per se illegal under Sec. 1 of the Sherman Act unless it includes some agreement on price or price levels.

The courts have held that some trade restraints are so obviously harmful that they are per se offenses. Proof of a per se offense establishes illegality. Several types of competitive activities have been declared per se offenses:

1.   horizontal division of markets

    a. agreements among competitors at same level of business to divide the geographic market
    b. detrimental effect on interbrand competition

2.   horizontal price fixing
    a. agreement among competitors at same level to fix prices
    b. can be express or implied; see U.S. v. Container Corp. of America, 393 U.S. 333 (1969). The parties had a voluntary agreement to exchange the most recent price charged or quoted for their products when such information was needed and when it was not available from another source. The court found their arrangement to be in violation of Art. 1 of the Sherman Act. In this particular market, the exchange of price data tends toward price uniformity.

3.   vertical price fixing
    a. agreement between parties at different levels
    b. muss sell at minimum retail price--resale price maintenance
    c. reduces intrabrand competition
    d. Chicago school advocates rule of reason, Supreme Court disagrees; see Monsanto Company v. Spray-Rite Service Corp., --text. See Atlantic Ritchfield Co. v. USA Petroleum Co., 110 S.Ct. 1884 (1990). USA loses. Even though USA proved a per se violation (setting a maximum price), the Supreme Curt said USA proved no injury to itself which, it said, was required when a private party tries to recover under Sec. 1 of the Sherman Act.

4.   group boycotts
    a. several manufacturers refusing to sell to a distributor
    b. may prevent sales to discounters
    c. full-service distributors; see U.S. v. General Motors Corp., 384 U.S. 127 (1966). An arrangement between a single manufacturer and some of its full service dealers to boycott a discounter is illegal per se--violation of Sec. 1 Sherman Act.

5.   tying arrangements
    a. seller requires buyer to purchase one item (tied product) as a condition to purchasing another (typing product or service)
    b. extends market in typing product and restrains trade
    c. sometimes per se and sometimes not
    d. example--Northern Pacific RR requiring lessees of farm land to use only Northern Pacific for transportation of cattle, crops, etc.
    e. recent example--not violative of Section 1 of Sherman Act; see Jefferson Parish Hospital District v. Hyde, 466 U.S. 2 (1984). A hospital entered into an exclusive contract with Rowx and Associates, a corporation of anesthesiologists, to provide service to the hospital. An

excluded anesthesiologist alleged that the Rowx-hospital contract was an illegal typing arrangement. There is no evidence that the price, quality or supply or demand for either the "tying product" or the "tied product" has been affected at all by the contract.

Per se rules clearly tell a business that certain conduct is or is not legal. One really never knows if conduct is illegal under the rule of reason until a court decides. Sometimes the court will flip flop--compound the problem for business. See Continental T.V., Inc. v. GTE Sylvania Inc., 433 U.S. 36 (1977). Vertical nonprice restraints (exclusive franchised dealers--limited number of franchises for any given area--must sell at that location--no exclusive territory) that manufacturers put on retailers to reduce intrabrand competition judged under the rule of reason.

Section 2 of the Sherman Act does not outlaw all monopolies, outlaws attempts to monopolize. Section 2 requires both monopoly power and the intent to monopolize. A business that has a monopoly legally acquired can compete aggressively; see U.S. v. Grinnel Corp. (text). What is monopoly power? This question requires an analysis of the relevant product market. If the business defendant can convince the court that many functional equivalents for the product exist, the court is likely to enlarge the market, and the chances of monopolizing are much lower. The business defendant wants a broad market definition, while the government wants a narrow one. See U.S. v. E. I. du Pont de Nemours & Co., 351 U.S. 377 (1955). DuPont argued that the relevant market was not cellophane but all flexible packaging materials. The court found that cellophane and other packaging materials were reasonably interchangeable. Price, use and quality were considered.

The state attorney general may sue a business violator under the Sherman Act in the name of the citizens of the state--parens patriae.

Review Questions

True/False

_____ 1. Section 1 of the Sherman Act outlaws monopolizing.

_____ 2. For pure competition, consumers and producers must have perfect market knowledge.

_____ 3. In a monopoly there is only one seller or producer of a unique good or service.

_____ 4. At least two persons or firms are necessary to establish a violation of Section 2 of the Sherman Act.

_____ 5. Individual violations of the Sherman Act can result in penalties of up to $1 million.

_____ 6. If a criminal suit under the Sherman Act is brought by the government, there can be no civil action.

____ 7.   Private parties bringing suit under the Sherman Act can recover three times the actual amount of damages sustained.

____ 8.   All tying arrangements are per se offenses.

____ 9.   Proof of monopolization requires proof of intent to monopolize.

____ 10.   The Chicago School reflects a presumption that big businesses are always harmful.

Multiple Choice -- Please circle the correct answer

1.   Consumers getting the goods and services they want--
      a.   market efficiency.
      b.   allocative efficiency.
      c.   productive efficiency.
      d.   economic efficiency.

2.   The first antitrust legislation in the United States was the
      a.   Interstate Commerce Act of 1887.
      b.   Clayton Act.
      c.   Laissez-Faire Act.
      d.   Sherman Act.

3.   Monopolies can occur when there is
      a.   one seller of a common good.
      b.   many sellers of a unique good.
      c.   one seller of a unique good.
      d.   many sellers of common goods.

4.   Oligopolies produce the following characteristic(s)
      a.   little price competition exists.
      b.   price competition is prevalent in a given market.
      c.   industry output is more than in pure competition.
      d.   producers earn lower profits than in competitive markets.

5.   An area exempt from the antitrust laws--
      a.   professional football.
      b.   import associations.
      c.   fishermen's organizations.
      d.   interstate commerce.

6.   A defendant pleading nolo contendre to an antitrust violation can be
      a.   found innocent.

    b.   fined and sentenced to prison.
    c.   be fined only.
    d.   none of the above.

7.   Vertical restraints of trade are governed by the
    a.   rule of reason.
    b.   per se rule.
    c.   Noerr Doctrine.
    d.   Sharp Mind Rule.

8.   _____ is a per se offense.
    a.   A tying arrangement.
    b.   A vertical restraint.
    c.   A monopoly.
    d.   A group boycott.

9.   Horizontal price fixing is an
    a.   agreement at different levels to fix prices.
    b.   agreement at the same level to fix prices.
    c.   offense governed by the rule of reason.
    d.   agreement between management and labor to fix prices.

10.   Resale price maintenance is
    a.   illegal per se.
    b.   judged by the rule of reason.
    c.   legal under the Miller-Tydings Act.
    d.   legal under the Monsanto Doctrine.

11.   Once a per se offense is proven, the courts
    a.   will examine their reasonableness.
    b.   will examine the impact on competition.
    c.   will presume their illegality.
    d.   may not find the practice illegal.

12.   The incipiency doctrine under Section 7 of the Clayton Act
    a.   outlaws corporate mergers.
    b.   outlaws corporate mergers if they tend to create a monopoly.
    c.   requires the government to prove that the merger will create a monopoly.
    d.   requires a violation of the Sherman Act.

13.   The Parker doctrine requires
    a.   some state involvement in a business.
    b.   extensive state involvement in a business.
    c.   no state involvement in a business.

      d.   a violation of Section 2 of the Sherman Act.

14.   A violation of Section 1 of the Sherman Act requires at least
    a.   one person.
    b.   monopolistic tendencies.
    c.   a relevant market.
    d.   two persons.

15.   The following can sue under the Sherman Act
    a.   U.S. Justice Department.
    b.   private person whose business was injured.
    c.   State Attorney General.
    d.   all of the above.

Short Answer

1.   List the types of conduct prohibited under the following Sherman Act sections.

    a.   Section 1 _____

    _____

    b.   Section 2 _____

    _____

2.   List the characteristics of perfect competition.

    a. _____

    b. _____

    c. _____

    d. _____

    e. _____

3.   List three types of competitive markets

    a. _____

    b. _____

c. _____

4. List three areas exempt from antitrust laws.

a. _____

b. _____

c. _____

5. List the appropriate Sherman Act criminal penalties for each of the following:

a. a corporation _____

b. an individual _____

6. List the three types of pleas possible under the Sherman Act by a criminal defendant.

a. _____

b. _____

c. _____

7. List three per se violations of the Sherman Act.

a. _____

b. _____

c. _____

8. List the two elements of monopolization under the Sherman Act.

a. _____

b. _____

9. What can be done under the doctrine of "parens patriae?"

_____

_____

10.   Explain the basic difference in enforcement between the Chicago School and the Traditional (Harvard) School antitrust analysis.

_____

_____

_____

_____

_____

Answers to Review Questions

True/False

1.	F	3.	T	5.	F	7.	T	9.	T
2.	T	4.	F	6.	F	8.	F	10.	F

Multiple Choice

1.	b.	4.	a.	7.	a.	10.	a.	13.	a.
2.	d.	5.	c.	8.	d.	11.	c.	14.	d.
3.	c.	6.	b.	9.	b.	12.	b.	15.	d.

Short Answer

1.   a.   contract, combinations and conspiracies in restraint of trade.
      b.   monopolization and attempts to monopolize

2.   a.   goods or services of different competitors are presumed identical
      b.   both producers and consumers have perfect market knowledge
      c.   many small buyers and sellers
      d.   no single buyer or seller can affect the market
      e.   no barriers to market entry

3.   a.   pure competition
      b.   monopolistic competition
      c.   oligopolistic competition

4.   a.   most labor union activities

b.   intrastate industries
c.   farmer and fishermen organizations
d.   export associations
e.   baseball
f.   regulated industries
g.   small businesses
h.   business and professional activities

5.   a. $1 million
      b. $100,000 and/or three years

6.   a.   guilty
      b.   not guilty
      c.   nolo contendere

7.   a.   horizontal division of markets
      b.   horizontal price fixing
      c.   vertical price fixing
      d.   group boycotts
      e.   certain tying arrangements

8.   a.   monopoly power
      b.   intent to monopolize

9.   The state attorney general can bring action to enforce the Sherman Act on behalf of consumers.

10.   Chicago--generally more lenient, tolerates more anticompetitive practices; focuses only on horizontal price-fixing; fewer per se offenses; decriminalize many offenses; like to get rid of incipiency doctrine.
      Harvard--more strict enforcement, approval of treble damages; criminalization of acts; incipiency doctrine and Clayton Act in general; urges attacking vertical territorial and price restraints; enlarging per se offenses and stopping restraints at an early stage

Key Terms

antitrust: derived from early business practice of competitors' putting their stock in trust to minimize competition.

rule of reason: standard used for determining whether agreements restraining trade are proper.

per se offenses: trade restraints whose harm is presumed so that proof of the act establishes illegality.

laissez-faire: business is given much freedom to conduct its affairs with little government interference.

Interstate Commerce Act of 1887: act that established the Interstate Commerce Commission to regulate railroads.

allocative efficiency: allocation of scarce resources to maximize the ability to satisfy consumer wants.

Sherman Act: prohibits contracts, combinations and conspiracies in restraint of trade; prohibits monopolization.

Clayton Act: prohibits price discrimination, tying arrangements, mergers, interlocking directorates.

Robinson-Patman Act: prohibits price discrimination.

incipiency doctrine: controlling monopolies through prevention of mergers.

Federal Trade Commission Act: prohibits unfair methods of competition.

monopolistic competition: monopoly wherein output is greater and prices are higher than in pure competition.

monopoly: one seller or producer of a unique good or service, imperfect market knowledge and barriers to competitive entry.

Traditional School of Antitrust Analysis (Harvard): populist approach that favors an economy of many independent business, none of which dominates the market.

Chicago School of Antitrust Analysis: approach of antitrust that focuses on pure economics, utility, creativity and innovation and believes "big" firms are not necessarily bad.

oligopolies: markets where a few large sellers sell all or most of the goods and services.

nolo contendre: plea of no contest to criminal charges.

conscious parallelism: similar behavior evidenced by circumstances as opposed to intentional agreements.

dictum: statement not apart of a case's decision and not binding for future cases.

Noerr Doctrine: doctrine that permits lobbying for laws or expressing ideas in the political system despite its anticompetitive effects.

treble damages: recovery provision of antitrust laws permitting damage recovery of three times actual damages.

felony: classification of crime, usually a more serious offense.

dissolution: bringing legal existence to an end.

divestiture: selling off of portion(s) of a conglomerate organization.

prima facie: meeting the burden of proof or establishing all elements required in a suit.

plea bargain: negotiation for offense and penalties in a criminal action.

horizontal division of markets: division of markets among competitors at the same level of business to divide the geographic market.

resale price maintenance (vertical price fixing): the vertical fixing of pricing among buyers and sellers at different levels of the manufacturing and distribution process based upon a manufacturer's refusal to sell unless the retailer agrees to a minimum retail price.

interbrand competition: competition among similar products manufactured by different firms.

Miller-Tydings Act: federal act excluding resale price maintenance from antitrust laws, repealed in 1976.

group boycotts: sellers refusing to sell to a certain distributor.

tying arrangement: seller requires buyer to purchase one item (tied item) as a condition to purchasing another item (tying item).

parens patriae: "father of his country" doctrine permitting state officials to sue antitrust violators on the basis of federal laws.

20 ANTITRUST LAW: THE CLAYTON ACT

Chapter Summary

The Clayton Act is a federal law passed in 1914. Section 2 as amended by Robinson-Patman prohibits a seller from discriminating in price between different buyers of goods (not services) of like grade and quality. The goods must be sold for use, consumption or resale in the U.S. and the effect of price discrimination may lessen competition or tend to create a monopoly. The general objective of Section 2 is to stop large firms from driving small competitors out of business by bold use of economic power. This was passed during the depression to help "mom and pop" stores being driven out of business by large quantity discounters. The act was amended to include buyer induced price discrimination. Either a private party or the FTC can bring a Robinson-Patman case. Private party can usually recover treble damages. Elements required to violate the Robinson-Patman Act include:

1. sale
2. of goods
3. of like grade and quality
4. at different prices
5. that injures competition
6. in interstate commerce (at least one of the sales must be in another state).

A Robinson-Patman Act charge includes the following defenses:

1. cost justification
2. meeting a competitor's equally low price
3. selling perishables
4. "goods" are in reality services (janitorial)

5. no interstate contact
6. goods are of different grade or quality
7. no injury to competition; see Utah Pie Company v. Continental Baking Co., 386 U.S. 685 (1967). The U.S. Supreme Court held that there was enough evidence to show a probable injury to competition to establish a Robinson-Patman violation. The statutory test is one that necessarily looks forward on the basis of proven conduct in the past.

An actual competitive injury does not have to be shown under Robinson-Patman, one must merely prove a possible injury as a result of price discrimination. A Robinson-Patman violation can occur at several levels of competition:

1. primary-line injury--one seller's price discrimination injures another seller
2. secondary-line injury--seller discriminates in price between two buyers
3. third-line injury--injury to buyers of buyers who have been discriminated against
4. fourth-line injury--injury to buyers of buyers of buyers who have been discriminated against.

The Act has been criticized because it stifles competition--price justification defense difficult. Why can't a business beat a competitor's price?

Section 3 of the Clayton Act regulates three practices that can unreasonably restrain trade by stopping buyers from dealing with the seller competitors--tying arrangements, exclusive dealing and requirements contracts. Section 3 does not establish a per se rule. Section 3 does not cover services, only goods. The practices must substantially lessen competition or tend to create a monopoly. Section 3 does not apply to consignments.

1.   Tying arrangements
      a. e.g., requiring buyers to buy data processing cards (tied product) in order to get data processor (tying product)
      b. may also violate Section 1 of Sherman Act (criminal sanctions available there but not under Clayton)
2.   Exclusive dealing
      a. agreement in which sale of product is conditioned on the buyer's agreement to deal only in that product or not to deal in competitor's goods
      b. e.g., drug manufacturer's requiring a drugstore to carry only its brands
      c. closes off market--requirements of establishing that arrangement substantially lessens competition; see Standard Oil of California v. U.S., 337 U.S. 293 (1949). The court decided that Section 3 is satisfied by proof that competition has been foreclosed in a substantial share of the line of commerce affected. Standard's use of the contracts creates just such a potential clog on competition as it was the purpose of Section 3 to remove.
3.   Requirements contracts
      a. require business or person to buy all of its needs or requirements of some commodity from a particular seller
      b. must establish lessening of competition; see Tampa Electric Co. v. Nashville Coal Co., 365 U.S. 320 (1961). In judging the term of a requirements contract in relation to the substantiality

of the foreclosure of competition, particularized considerations of the parties' operations are not irrelevant. In weighing the various factors, we have decided that in the competitive bituminous coal marketing area involved here, the contract sued upon does not tend to foreclose a substantial volume of competition.

Section 4 of the Clayton Act sets out civil remedies available under <u>all</u> federal antitrust laws.1.

    Who can sue
    a. any person injured in business or property
    b. federal district court is appropriate forum
    c. need not meet $10,000 minimum

2.   Amount of recovery
    a. three times the amount of injury to business or property (treble damages)
    b. court costs
    c. attorney's fees
    d. simple interest from day of service of complain until judgement day--at discretion of judge

3.   Pass-on theory
    a. if discrimination or price-fixing occurs high up. the violator tries to defend on grounds that harm was passed on to others
    b. cannot be used affirmatively by consumers to recover from manufacturers engaging in price fixing
    c. may not be used defensively; see <u>Kansas</u> v. <u>Utilicorp United, Inc.</u>, 110 St.Ct. 2807 (1990). The Supreme Court upheld <u>Illinois Brick</u>. This meant the consumers were indirect purchasers and could not sue natural gas producers and a pipeline company for alleged overcharges resulting from antitrust violations.

Section 7 of the Clayton Act outlaws certain mergers. Types of combinations qualifying for Section 7:

1. merger--one corporation buys enough of the stock of another corporation to give it control
2. consolidation--two or more corporations combine to form a new corporation
3. buy another's stock
    a. one is parent
    b. acquired company is subsidiary and controlled by parent board
4. purchase of assets where one company dissolves.

An accurate statement on the purpose of Section 7 of the Clayton Act after the Celler-Kefauver Amendment came in <u>Brown Shoe Co.</u> v. <u>U.S.</u>--text:

1. plugged loophole
2. covered all types of combination
3. reduce economic concentration
4. prevent application of other acts
5. preclude anticompetitive measures

6. general terms for effect on competition
7. functional view of merger in its industry
8. prevent mergers at outset.

The Clayton Act, Sec. 7, does not make all mergers illegal. There are several keys to understanding Sec. 7:

1. tries to stop mergers before they start
2. can be illegal even if not nationwide
3. has been applied to horizontal, vertical, and conglomerate
4. mergers not illegal per se.

Defenses to Sec. 7 charges:

1. no substantial effect on interstate commerce--often not a good argument
2. failing company defense
3. merger does not substantially lessen competition or tend to create a monopoly in any line of commerce in any section of the country. See U.S. v. Von's Grocery Co., 384 U.S. 270 (1966). Section 7 "requires not merely an appraisal of the immediate impact of the merger upon competition, but a prediction of its impact upon competitive conditions in the future..." Using this incipiency doctrine, the merger was not allowed.

A conglomerate merger occurs when two or more corporations in different product markets combine into one corporation. Some of these mergers have possible marketing, financial and other advantages.   The formation of conglomerates can reduce potential competition. See FTC v. Proctor & Gamble Co., 386 U.S. 568 (1967). Possible economics cannot be used as a defense to illegality. Congress was aware that some mergers which lessen competition may also result in economics but it struck the balance in favor of protecting competition. The court upheld the Commission's order that the acquisition of Clorox by Proctor eliminated Proctor as a potential competitor.

One of the main aspects of the Hart-Scott-Rodino Antitrust Improvements Act (1976) was:

1.   premerger notification--avoids divestiture orders
2.   requires reporting of mergers to Justice Department and FTC by certain companies
       a. size tests
       b. interstate commerce
       c. ownership of $15 million or 15% of assets or voting securities of acquired company
3.   applies to corporations, partnerships, natural person, unincorporated associations and foreign governments
4.   thirty-one day waiting period after report is filed
5.   penalties of $10,000 per day.

Section 8 of the Clayton Act prohibits individuals from being directors of competing corporations. Three things must occur for a violation:

1. one corporation has a net worth of $1 million
2. corporations must be competitors
3. eliminating competition would violate federal antitrust law. See <u>Bankamerica Corp.</u> v. <u>U.S.</u>, 462 U.S. 122 (1983). The court held that Section 8 of the Clayton Act does not forbid directors from serving on boards of competing banks and insurance companies.

Review Questions

True/False

____ 1.   The Clayton Act carries criminal sanctions for violations.

____ 2.   Price discrimination applies only to the sale of goods

____ 3.   Meeting a competitor's price is a defense to price discrimination.

____ 4.   Primary-line injury occurs when one discriminating seller injures a competing seller.

____ 5.   The tied product is the product the buyer wishes to purchase initially.

____ 6.   Exclusive dealing arrangements must be shown to substantially lessen competition.

____ 7.   A merger occurs when two or more corporations combine to form a new corporation not previously existing.

____ 8.   Asset acquisitions are not covered under the merger provisions of the Clayton Act.

____ 9.   To violate Section 7, mergers must be national in scope.

____ 10.   A horizontal merger is between two firms dealing at the same level.

Multiple Choice -- Please circle the best answer

1.   The Clayton Act, unlike the Sherman Act
    a.   carries criminal sanctions.
    b.   does not carry criminal sanctions.
    c.   does not allow private party enforcement.
    d.   does not prohibit mergers.

2.   The Robinson-Patman Act prohibits
    a.   seller induced price discrimination.
    b.   buyer induced price discrimination.

c.   a. and b.
d.   price fixing.

3.   The Robinson-Patman Act covers
a.   sales of services.
b.   sales of life insurance policies.
c.   leases of goods.
d.   sales of goods.

4.   A secondary line injury occurs when
a.   one seller's price discrimination injures a competing seller.
b.   a seller discriminates in price between competing buyers.
c.   a buyer discriminates in price.
d.   a wholesaler and a wholesaler-retailer discriminate in price.

5.   Section 3 of the Clayton Act does not apply to a tying agent if
a.   the buyer can readily find substitutes for the tying product.
b.   the buyer cannot find substitutes for the tying product.
c.   the seller has significant economic power.
d.   it encourages competition.

6.   One benefit of an exclusive dealing arrangement is
a.   it lowers prices.
b.   it opens up markets.
c.   superior knowledge on the part of the retailer.
d.   it encourages competition.

7.   A requirements contract is
a.   illegal per se.
b.   inflationary.
c.   not helpful in business planning.
d.   judged under the rule of reason.

8.   The pass-on theory allows
a.   the consumer to sue the manufacturer-price fixer.
b.   the manufacturer-price fixer to use it as a defense.
c.   the consumer to sue everyone in the marketing chain.
d.   none of the above.

9.   Section 7 of the Clayton Act covers
a.   stock mergers.
b.   asset mergers.
c.   a. and b.
d.   interlocking directorates.

10. A vertical merger occurs when two corporations
    a. combine all their assets.
    b. on the same level merge.
    c. on different levels merge.
    d. in unrelated businesses merge.

11. The Robinson-Patman Act prohibits a seller from discriminating in price
    a. between different buyers of services.
    b. between different buyers of goods of like grade and quality.
    c. between different buyers of services of like grade and quality.
    d. if sold outside the boarders of the U.S.

12. An exclusive dealing arrangement is
    a. an arrangement that allows a buyer to deal in competing goods.
    b. illegal per se.
    c. judged under the rule of reason.
    d. an agreement in which a business can sell two brands of a competitor's goods.

13. A suit under the Clayton Act can be brought in the
    a. U.S. District Court.
    b. appropriate state court.
    c. U.S. Court of Appeals.
    d. Federal Trade Commission.

14. Section 7 of the Clayton Act
    a. outlaws all mergers.
    b. outlaws only national mergers.
    c. does not cover conglomerate mergers.
    d. outlaws some mergers.

15. The following defenses are available under Section 7:
    a. failing firm defense.
    b. only horizontal mergers are covered.
    c. merger not significant enough.
    d. a. and c.

Short Answer

1. List the topics covered in each of the following sections of the Clayton Act.

    Section 2 _____

    Section 3 _____

Section 4 _____

Section 7 _____

Section 8 _____

2.   List the elements needed to establish price discrimination.

a. _____

b. _____

c. _____

d. _____

e. _____

f. _____

3.   List three defenses to a charge of price discrimination.

a. _____

b. _____

c. _____

4.   In the following example, determine which is the tying and which is the tied product: An ice cream machine manufacturer requires customers to buy its rock salt in order to purchase its ice cream machines.

a. tying product _____

b. tied product _____

5.   List three business reasons for using requirements contracts (for the seller.)

a. _____

b. _____

c. _____

6.   List the types of civil damages recoverable under Section 4.

    a. _____

    b. _____

    c. _____

    d. _____

7.   If a manufacturer is price-fixing with another manufacturer, who can also be damaged under the pass-on theory?

    a. _____

    b. _____

8.   Define the following terms.

    a.   merger _____

_____

    b.   consolidation _____

_____

    c.   asset merger _____

_____

    d.   horizontal merger _____

_____

    e.   vertical merger _____

_____

    f.   conglomerate merger _____

_____

9.   List three defenses for Section 7 violations.

    a. _____

    b. _____

    c. _____

Answers to Review Questions

True/False

| 1. F | 3. T | 5. F | 7. F | 9. F |
| 2. T | 4. T | 6. T | 8. F | 10. T |

Multiple Choice

1. b.	4. b.	7. d.	10. c.	13. a.
2. c.	5. a.	8. d.	11. b.	14. d.
3. d.	6. c.	9. c.	12. c.	15. d.

Short Answer

1. Section 2--price discrimination
    Section 3--tying, requirements, exclusive dealing
    Section 4--remedies
    Section 7--mergers
    Section 8--interlocking directorates

2. a. sale
    b. of goods
    c. of like grade and quality
    d. at a different price
    e. injures competition
    f. in interstate commerce (at lease one sale in another state)

3. Any of:
    a. cost justification
    b. meeting a competitor's equally low price
    c. selling perishable goods
    d. not goods but services or intangibles
    e. no interstate contact
    f. goods are of different grade or quality
    g. no injury to competition

4.   a.   ice cream maker
      b.   rock salt

5.   a.   cut sales expenses
      b.   spread production evenly by staggering delivery dates
      c.   hedge against price variances

6.   a.   treble damages
      b.   court costs
      c.   attorneys fees
      d.   simple interest

7.   a.   distributors
      b.   customers

8.   a.   merger: one corporation buys enough of another corporation's stock or assets to give
            the buying corporation control over the company purchased
      b.   consolidation: two or more corporations combine to form a corporation not previously
            existing
      c.   asset merger: merger in which only assets and not stock are acquired
      d.   horizontal merger: merger between firms dealing with the same product on the same
            level
      e.   vertical merger: mergers between firms dealing with same product on different levels.
      f.   conglomerate merger: merger between corporations in unrelated businesses

9.   a.   purely intrastate merger
      b.   failing company
      c.   merger does not substantially lessen competition

Key Terms

Robinson-Patman Act: federal statute regulating price discrimination.

price discrimination: charging of prices that result in a lessening of competition.

primary-line injury: injury caused to one seller through price discrimination by another seller.

secondary-line injury: injury caused when seller discriminates in price between competing buyers.

third-line injury: injury from price discrimination affecting retail operations.

consignments: selling arrangement whereby third party acts as agent for seller but does not hold title.

tying: requiring a buyer of goods to buy another good (tied product) as a condition to buying what the buyer want (tying product).

exclusive dealing: arrangement in which sale of a product is conditioned on the buyer's agreement to deal only in that product, not in a competitor's.

requirement contracts: contracts requiring one person to buy all of its requirements of some commodity from a particular seller.

pass-on defense: defense that damages from price-fixing were passed along the chain of distribution to others.

defensive pass-on: use of defense by one accused of price-fixing.

offensive pass-on: use of pass-on theory to affirmatively establish action for price-fixing.

merger: one corporation buying enough stock of another corporation to give the buying corporation control over the purchased company.

stock merger: merger in which one corporation acquires the majority of another corporation's stock.

asset merger: merger in which one corporation acquires the assets of another corporation.

consolidation: two or more corporations combining to form a new corporation that did not exist previously.

conglomerate merger: merger between firms in different industries.

Celler-Kefauver Amendment: amendment to Clayton Act on asset mergers.

horizontal merger: merger between competing firms.

vertical merger: merger between firms at different levels of the product distribution scheme.

Hart-Scott-Rodino Antitrust Improvement Act of 1976: act amending Clayton Act's Section 7 merger provision to alert feds of mergers through premerger notification by certain size companies.

failing company defense: defense to anticompetitive effect of merger which states the business acquired is failing.

divest: process of selling off portions of a business.

interlocking corporate directorates: directors sitting on boards of competing firms.

21 THE FEDERAL TRADE COMMISSION

Chapter Summary

The Federal Trade Commission was created by the FTC Act of 1914. The FTC protects consumers and maintains economic competition. The FTC is an independent administrative agency with five commissioners appointed by the President for staggered seven year terms. Section 5, which prohibits unfair methods of competition, is worded in a broad and general fashion. Businesses sometimes have difficulty determining whether their activities will be attached.

The Commission uses the following devices to enforce its orders:

1. Cooperative procedures
   a. advisory opinions--requested by party to determine up front
      if conduct is illegal--not binding
   b. industry guides--FTC interpretation of statutes in lay language
   c. trade regulation rule--FTC interpretation of statutes
2. Formal FTC action
   a. begin with informal complaint
      (1) can be by FTC
      (2) any consumer or government agency
      (3) upon receipt, FTC decides whether to investigate
   b. after investigation--staff recommendations
      (1) can close case as alternative
      (2) negotiate/consent order
      (3) issue formal complaint to offending party
   c. hearing held

(1) before administrative law judge
(2) public--resembles court trial
(3) judge issues decision
  d.   FTC decision
(1) based on judge's determination after hearing
(2) thirty days to decide from judge's decision
(3) respondent can appeal
(4) FTC can stay or temporarily stop effective date.
(5) FTC agrees to hear case
    (i)   can sustain judge's decision
    (ii) can modify judge's decision
    (iii) can revise judge's decision

3.   Further action
  a.   order is issued after review or after consent order
  b.   can be appealed for 60 days to appropriate U.S. Court of Appeals
  c.   can appeal Court of Appeals decision to the U.S. Supreme Court

4.   Types of FTC orders
  a.   case and desist (normal kind)--to cease illegal behavior
  b.   affirmative disclosure
  c.   divesting of assets or stocks
  d.   restitution to injured parties
  e.   corrective advertising
  f.   consent order - FTC does not pursue further in exchange for
    promise from respondent to refrain from certain behavior
  g.   violation of order
(1) $10,000 per violation
(2) continuance of prohibited behavior--each day is a separate violation

5.   Other enforcement devices
  a.   injunctive relief
  b.   penalties for deceptive acts or practices--certain cases
(1) violation of trade regulation rule
(2) violation of a cease and desist order
(3) up to $10,000 penalty for each violation
  c.   other unfair or deceptive acts or practices
(1) trade regulation rule violated
(2) commission order through dishonesty or fraud--redress via rescission
(3) rescission: rescission and reformation, refund of money, return of property, payment of
    damages, public notice of practice.

The FTC is concerned with the broad orthodox antitrust violations prohibited by the Sherman and Clayton Act. Section 5 also gives the FTC the ability to attack anticompetitive conduct outside the letter or the spirit of the other antitrust statutes. See FTC v. Superior Court Trial Lawyers Association, 110 S.Ct. 768 (199). "Regular" attorneys, acting through the SCTLA, met and resolved not to accept any new cases unless they received a substantial fee increase. FTC filed a complaint that this boycott was an unfair method of competition under Section 5. The court ruled that the boycott constituted a classic restraint of trade within the meaning of Section 1 of the Sherman Act. This also violates Section 5 of the FTC Act.

During the 1960s and 1970s the Commission often considered the following factors when making unfairness determinations (Section 5):
1. whether the acts offend public policy
2. whether it is immoral or unethical
3. whether it causes substantial injury to consumers.

FTC, in the 1970s, was worried that modern mass advertising can be very manipulative even when it is not deceptive. In the 1980s, the FTC's ability to attack unfair acts has receded. The tests of unfairness have been modified to focus on "consumer injury." See In the Matter of International Harvester Company, 104 F.T.C. 949 (1984). The test for consumer injury includes: (1) it be substantial, (2) not outweighed by an offsetting consumer or competitive benefits and (3) one that consumers could not have reasonably avoided.

In 1983, the FTC modified the approach in cases involving deceptive ads or practices under Section 5. Advertising or other deceptive behavior now must involve a material representation, omission or practice that is likely to mislead a consumer acting reasonably under the circumstances. Critics of this approach have argued that the reasonableness standard may protect some unscrupulous advertising schemes aimed at the unsophisticated, naive and gullible. Several types of orders are possible in deceptive or unfair advertising cases: cease and desist, affirmative disclosure, corrective advertising and civil penalties or consumer redress. See Removatron International Corp. v. FTC, 884 F.2d 1489 (1989). The Commission did not abuse its discretion by requiring Removatron to obtain scientific support before making any permanency claims. The inclusion of a disclaimer statement (hair removal only temporary) in advertising was upheld.

First Amendment challenges have not seriously affected the FTC's regulation of advertising.

In 1978, the FTC issued disclosure requirements and prohibitions governing the advertising, offering, promotion and sale of franchises. A franchise is defined and a franchisor's fee of $500 or more is required for the regulation to apply. Franchisor can commit an unfair act or practice under Section 5 in any of the following ways:

1. failure to furnish certain information
2. making any representation that states a specific level of potential sales, income or profit unless there is a reasonable basis for such representations and these are furnished to the franchisee in a single written document
3. making certain statements on the cover sheet of the written documents disclaiming correctness of sale, income or profit figures.

Review Questions

True/False

_____ 1.   The 1980s have seen the FTC take a more skeptical attitude toward regulation.

_____ 2.   Industry guides written by the FTC are in layperson's language.

_____ 3.   Anyone can file an informal complaint with the FTC.

_____ 4.   A consent order is an admission of guilt.

_____ 5.   After the administrative law judge's decision on an FTC case, the case is appealed to the U.S. Court of Appeals.

_____ 6.   In cases in which the respondent business is found in violation, the FTC issues cease and desist orders after the administrative law judge's decision.

_____ 7.   The FTC has the power to impose civil sanctions for violation of a cease and desist order.

_____ 8.   The FTC has no power to order future corrective advertising for past, false advertising.

_____ 9.   The "Reasonable Consumer" test generally protects the use of subjective claims such as taste and smell.

_____ 10.   The FTC may compel affirmative disclosure of information previously omitted from ads.

Multiple Choice -- Please circle the best answer

1.   The FTC is a (an)_____ federal administrative agency.
   a.   dependent.
   b.   independent.
   c.   executive.
   d.   legislative.

2.   The FTC can enforce
   a.   the FTC Act.
   b.   the Sherman Act.
   c.   federal consumer protection measures.
   d.   all of the above.

3.   Trade regulation rules
        a.   must contain lay language.
        b.   are not binding.
        c.   do not have the force and effect of law.
        d.   have the force of law.

4.   An FTC settlement case involves a
        a.   cease and desist order.
        b.   formal proceeding.
        c.   consent order.
        d.   trade regulation rule.

5.   Section 5 of the FTC Act requires deceptive acts or practices to
        a.   actually mislead.
        b.   be likely to mislead.
        c.   mislead all consumers.
        d.   mislead selected consumers.

6.   Many advertisements do not violate Section 5 of the FTC Act because of the
        a.   materiality test.
        b.   gross deception test.
        c.   reasonable consumer test.
        d.   danish pastry test.

7.   One remedy available to the FTC is
        a.   a criminal fine.
        b.   consumer redress.
        c.   a conservative court.
        d.   corrective advertising.

8.   The First Amendment does not protect
        a.   political speech.
        b.   false and deceptive advertising.
        c.   corrective advertising.
        d.   commercial speech.

9.   The usual starting point for consumers to file a complain with the FTC is
        a.   the federal district court.
        b.   the Washington, D.C. office.
        c.   one of the regional offices.
        d.   the state attorney general's office.

10.   _____ are FTC interpretations of the laws it enforces, stated in lay language.
        a.   industry guides.

    b.   advisory opinions.
    c.   trade regulation rules.
    d.   FTC opinions.

11.   The main way the FTC enforces its statutes and rules is by
    a.   trade regulations.
    b.   criminal cease and desist orders.
    c.   formal administrative actions.
    d.   advisory opinions.

12.   If the administrative law judge's initial decision is appealed, that appeal goes to the
    a.   head of the Commission.
    b.   U.S. Court of Appeals.
    c.   full commission.
    d.   U.S. District Court.

13.   The following enforcement devices are available to the FTC
    a.   civil penalties.
    b.   injunctive relief.
    c.   redress to consumers.
    d.   all of the above.

14.   The FTC is applying the general tests of unfairness now focuses on
    a.   cause and effect.
    b.   costs-benefits.
    c.   consumer injury.
    d.   public impact.

15.   To violate Section 5, deceptive behavior must be likely to mislead consumers who have acted
    a.   with pure heart and empty head.
    b.   reasonably under the circumstances.
    c.   unreasonably under the circumstances.
    d.   foolishly but in good faith.

Short Answer

1.   List five orders the FTC may use in enforcement.

    a.   _____

    b.   _____

    c.   _____

d. _____

e. _____

2. What are two good reasons an independent agency like the FTC is said to be only "partially immune" from political control.

a. _____

_____

b. _____

_____

3. List three voluntary and cooperative procedures of the FTC.

a. _____

b. _____

c. _____

4. Number the following in the proper procedural order.

____ a. formal complaint
____ b. cease and desist order
____ c. investigation
____ d. administrative hearing
____ e. informal complaint
____ f. FTC review

5. List three options available to the FTC in reviewing administrative law judges' decisions.

a. _____

b. _____

c. _____

6. How long after the issuance of a cease and desist order does the respondent business have to appeal?

_____

Where is the appeal taken?

_____

7.   List four reasons corrective advertising is controversial.

a.   _____

b.   _____

c.   _____

d.   _____

8.   To violate Section 5 of the FTC Act on the issue of deceptiveness, advertising must contain:

_____

_____

9.   Where should consumers address complaints related to FTC violations?

_____

10.   Name three requirements of the "consumer injury test."

a.   _____

b.   _____

c.   _____

Answers to Review Questions

True/False

1. T	3. T	5. F	7. T	9. T
2. T	4. F	6. T	8. F	10. T

Multiple Choice

1. b.	4. c.	7. d.	10. a.	13. d.

| 2. | d. | 5. | b. | 8. | b. | 11. | d. | 14. | c. |
| 3. | d. | 6. | c. | 9. | c. | 12. | c. | 15. | b. |

Short Answer

1. a. cease and desist
    b. corrective advertising
    c. consent order
    d. affirmative disclosure
    e. divesting of assets
    f. restitution to parties

2. a. funding from Congress--possible elimination or reduction of budget.
    b. staffing requirements--appointed by president, confirmed by senate, president selects chair

3. a. advisory opinions
    b. trade regulation rules
    c. industry guides

4. 3. a.
    6. b.
    2. c.
    4. d.
    1. e.
    5. f.

5. a. sustain
    b. modify
    c. reverse

6. sixty days
    U.S. Court of Appeals

7. a. can affect firm's marketing program
    b. FTC Act does not expressly authorize it
    c. First Amendment free speech considerations
    d. extent of corrective advertising

8. material misrepresentation, omission or practice likely to mislead a consumer acting reasonably under the circumstances

9. to the nearest FTC regional office

10.   a.   substantial
       b.   not outweighed by consumer or competitive benefits
       c.   one that consumers could not reasonably have avoided

Key Terms

Federal Trade Commission Act: act creating the FTC and preventing "unfair methods of competition."

independent agency: agency not within the executive branch.

Wheeler-Lea Act: act amending FTC Act and covering "unfair or deceptive acts or practices."

advisory opinions: notifications by FTC informing individuals/businesses in advance of the legality of conduct.

trade regulation rules: FTC interpretation of statutes.

industry guides: FTC interpretation of statutes stated in layperson's language.

informal complaint: beginning of an FTC case by public, private or government source.

formal complaint: FTC's charge of violation of statute or regulation.

order: FTC's avenue of conduct and relief for violation.

cease and desist order: order of commissioners of FTC (based on administrative law judge's findings) requiring certain specified activities be halted.

consent order: remedies negotiated between FTC and the violating business.

respondent: the alleged violator.

administrative hearing: adjudicative proceeding before an administrative law judge.

redress: available to injured parties which may include rescission, reformation, refunds, return of property, payment of damages, or public notice of unfair or deceptive practices.

"reasonable consumer" test: to violate Section 5 of the FTC Act, a deceptive advertisement must be likely to mislead consumers who have acted reasonably under the circumstances.

deceptive advertising: advertising that includes a material misrepresentation, omission, or practice likely to mislead a consumer acting reasonably.

corrective advertising: remedy whereby party violating deceptive ad rule is required to run ads to correct consumer's mistaken present beliefs based on the prior false ads.

affirmative disclosure: compelling disclosure of information previously omitted from an advertisement.

franchise: any continuing commercial relationship in which goods and services are (a) identified by the franchisor's trademark, trade name or other commercial symbol, (b) required to meet the franchisor's quality standards, or (c) offers to sell goods or services supplied by the franchisor.

CHAPTER 22 CONSUMER PROTECTION

Chapter Summary

A consumer is any person who buys goods and services for personal consumption. Consumer protection rules are made by courts, legislators, and administrative agencies. Eight common law concepts (judge-made law) that protect consumers are:

1.   consideration
      a.   voluntarily giving up right in exchange for another's right
      b.   adequacy of right is up to parties unless unfair
2.   undue influence
      a.   trust relationship
            (1)   doctor
            (2)   lawyer
            (3)   relative
      b.   breach trust to obtain contract--contract is set aside
3.   duress
      a.   wrongful act used to obtain contractual promise
      b.   need voluntary contracts
      c.   voidable contract at option of party subjected to duress
4.   fraud
      a.   false information to obtain promise
            (1)   misrepresentation
            (2)   material fact
            (3)   knowledge
            (4)   intent

          (5)   damages
          (6)   reasonable reliance
    b.   does not cover opinions or puffing
    c.   can occur through concealment of a material fact

5.   innocent misrepresentation
    a.   false information given to obtain promise
    b.   one misrepresenting lacks knowledge and intent elements of fraud
    c.   contract is rescinded

6.   contracts contrary to public policy
    a.   public policy--desirable social goals and conduct
    b.   example--exculpatory or hold-harmless clauses

7.   illegal contracts
    a.   void contracts
    b.   illegal subject matter or illegal act
    c.   if both parties wrong (in pari delicto), no remedy

8.   unconscionability
    a.   lopsided contracts--extremely favorable to one party and extremely unfavorable to another party
    b.   focus on parties
          (1)   knowledge
          (2)   intelligence
          (3)   business sophistication
          (4)   bargaining power
    c.   applied in extreme cases: see Williams v. Walker Thomas Furniture Company, 350 F.2d 445 (1965). In determining fairness, the primary concern must be with terms of the contract considered in the light of the circumstances existing when the contract is made. Corbin suggests the test as being whether the terms are "so extreme as to appear unconscionable according to the mores and business practices of the time and place." The court accepted this test in those cases where no meaningful choice was exercised upon entering the contract.

The main weakness with these common law remedies is that the consumer must sue the business. Consumers often lack the time, money or desire to take the trouble to sue. This has resulted in federal and state legislatures passing statutes increasing consumer protections. One of the FTC's main jobs is consumer protection. The FTC has authority to promulgate consumer protection regulations. Four important regulations are:

1.   bait and switch
    a.   business advertises goods or services at very low price to attract buyers
    b.   seller then switches buyer to a more expensive product
    c.   prohibited practices
          (1)   refusing to show lower-priced product
          (2)   indicating bait item won't be available for awhile
          (3)   having an inadequate supply of bait item

2. modification of holder in due course rule
   a. HDC--good faith purchaser of negotiable instrument for value
   b. FTC holds HDC on consumer transaction will not be paid if consumer has difficulty with goods
   c. does not apply to credit card issuers
3. mail order merchandise
   a. thirty-day rule
   b. unfair to solicit orders unless seller can ship goods within thirty days
   c. if cannot be shipped within thirty days, seller must
      (1) offer buyer a right to cancel
      (2) offer buyer a refund
      (3) offer to let buyer agree to delay
   d. violations
      (1) cease and desist order
      (2) civil penalties of up to $10,000/violation
   e. (3) subscriptions
      (4) seeds and growing plants
      (5) C.O.D.
4. cooling-off period for door-to-door sales
   a. three business day rescission period
   b. must have contract with notice of rescission and a cancellation form
   c. applies to sale, lease, or rental of consumer goods or services with purchase price of $25.00 or more
   d. exemptions
      (1) sales made after visit to showroom
      (2) buyer first contacted seller
      (3) Consumer Credit Protection Act sales
      (4) sale completed by mail or phone
      (5) insurance, realty, or sale of stock by registered broker
      (6) buyer first contacted seller and contract is for repair or maintenance
   e. $10,000 civil penalty

The law attempts to promote product safety by direct regulation of consumer products. The Consumer Product Safety Commission (CPSC) is the main federal agency concerned with product safety. The CPSC has a number of enforcement devices at its disposal.

1. product safety standards
   a. performance requirements
   b. requirements for warnings or instructions
2. banning products
3. suits for seizure of imminently hazardous consumer products
4. notice to commission from manufacturers, distributors, and retailers of hazards from products
   a. when fail to comply with CPSC rule
   b. defect is substantial hazard

5.   action over substantial; product hazard
    a.   public notice of problem from offender
    b.   offender mails notice to each manufacturer, distributor, and retailer
    c.   mail notice to each know purchaser
6.   also force offending party to choose between:
    a.   bringing product into conformity with CPSC rules on repair
    b.   replacing product with equivalent product that com- plies
    c.   refunding the purchase price

The CPSA provides the following remedies:

1. injunctive relief
2. seizure of products
3. civil penalties not to exceed $2,000 per violation
4. criminal penalty for violation after receiving notice on noncompliance from CPSC, fine up to $50,000, imprisonment up to one year, or both
5. civil action by private parties.

See Gulf South Insul v. U.S. Consumer Safety Commission, 701 F.2d 1137 (1983). Ban on urea-formaldehyde foam insulation in residences and schools challenged by industry. The court found that the CPSC regulation did not meet the substantial evidence test. Rule banning UFFI is vacated.

The Truth in Lending Act is a major part of the Consumer Protection Act. The act enables consumers to learn the cost of credit and compare credit costs. The Board of Governors of the Federal Reserve Board has the authority to issue regulations. Basic regs are called Regulation Z. The types of credit covered include:

1.   individuals for personal, family, household, or agricultural purposes not over $25,000
2.   all real estate covered for personal, family, household, or agricultural regardless of amount
3.   exemptions
    a.   loans to business
    b.   loans to federal, state, local governments
    c.   transactions in securities or commodities with registered broker-dealers
    d.   public utility tariffs
4.   creditors covered
    a.   those who extend credit in transactions covered
    b.   bank, etc.
    c.   hospitals, physicians, dentists, etc. must comply if they extend or arrange for credit

Regulation Z requires the disclosure of credit terms, including in most instances the finance charge and the annual percentage rate (APR). Regulation Z also covers the credit card:

1.   credit device used to get money, property, labor or service on credit
2.   may not be issued except in response to request, application, or renewal

3.   liability for accepted credit cards only
    a.   applied for and received
    b.   signed
    c.   used or authorized another to use
4.   lost credit card liability limited to $50.00; see Oclander v. First Nat. Bank of Louisville, 700 S.W.2d 804 (1985)--husband and wife. The credit card charges were made by Bonifacio Aparicio, appellants estranged husband and co-defendant. The court ruled that the wife had misrepresented certain facts to the bank and the bank had then "unblocked" the account. The husband had apparent authority to use the card. The bank wins.

No advertisement for credit is permitted unless the creditor usually arranges terms of that type. Must disclose all credit terms if one credit term is advertised. Penalties include:

1.   criminal--$5,000 and or one year
2.   civil recovery by consumers
    a.   twice the amount of finance charge
    b.   at least $100 but not more than $1,000
    c.   court costs and attorney fees.

Creditors must keep records for at least two years from the transaction date to establish compliance. Enforcers of Truth-in-Lending are private parties and appropriate federal agencies.

The purposes of the Fair Credit Reporting Act is to provide accurate current information about consumers and prevent wrongful disclosure of such information. Consumers have the right:

1. to know credit reporting agency
2. to the information in report that business relies on
3. information must be given free
4. can correct report and notify those that relied on incorrect information for six months before the error--employment two years.

Consumers can sue anyone violating FCRA. Damages, court costs and attorney's fees are recoverable. FTC has authority to enforce the FCRA. See Houghton v. Ins. Crime Prevention Institute, 795 F.2d 322 (1986). The FCRA Act shows Congress' intent to permit the tolling of the statute of limitations (two years) in the case of a material and willful misrepresentation by a defendant. The court refused to read in a discovery exception to the FCRA statute of limitations.

The Equal Credit Reporting Act (ECOA) requires lenders to make credit available to all creditworthy customers without regard to sex, marital status, national origin, race, religion, color or age. The board of governors has the power to promulgate regs under the ECOA. Any person who regularly extends, renews, continues to give credit is covered by the ECOA. Some ECOA applications:

1. may not ask marital status--two exception; (1) unless relying on income from husband, and (2) community property states

2. cannot deny married women asking for credit in their individual names
3. report credit information to third parties in both spouses' names if both use charge account
4. prohibits credit extension based on age
5. may ask whether income includes welfare benefits or government assistance
6. race discrimination prohibited--redlining
7. 30-day notification required on credit applications
8. must be specific in reason for rejection
9. can be verbal if creditor has no more than 50 applications per year.

ECOA enforcement:

1.   private suit by individuals or class
    a.   individual--$10,000 maximum punitive
    b.   class--lesser of $500,000 or one percent of creditor's net worth as punitive damages
    c.   can recover damages, costs, and attorneys' fees in all cases
2.   administrative agency enforcement
    a.   number of agencies have the power to enforce
    b.   consumers can sue under the ECOA--proper administrative enforcer can also sue

ECOA remedies:

1.   private party
    a.   damages--compensatory and punitive
    b.   injunctions
    c.   court costs/attorney fees
2.   statute of limitations--private parties
    a.   within two years of violation or within one year after enforcement agency sues
3.   for an ECOA violation see Miller v. American Express Co., 688 F.2d 1235 (1982). Mrs. Miller's account was terminated in response to her husband's death and without reference to or even inquiry regarding her credit worthiness. The regulations prohibit termination based on a spouse' death in the absence of evidence of inability or unwillingness to pay.

The Fair Credit Billing Act of 1975 establishes a way for consumer to do something about credit card billing errors. Applies only to credit cards.

1. written complain within sixty days of receiving statement
2. creditor must acknowledge within thirty days of receiving complaint
3. explanation or correction within ninety days of receiving complaint.

A retailer who accepts credit cards can offer discounts for cash. Cannot raise prices for credit card customers. Must inform cardholder before delinquencies to third parties.

The general purpose of the Fair Debt Collection Practices Act is to end abusive, deceptive, and unfair debt collection practices by debt collectors. Only personal, family or household debts are covered. The act does <u>not</u> protect business debtors. The act defines debt collectors:

1. anyone other than the creditor who regularly collects debts of others
2. creditor's attorney's collection efforts.

A debt collector may contact a debtor. Contact may not occur at inconvenient or unusual hours, such as before 8:00 a.m. or after 9:00 p.m. A debt collector may not contact a debtor at work if the employer disapproves. A debt collector must stop contacting a debtor if the debtor says so in writing. Debt collectors may contact any person to locate a debtor--skip tracing. The debt collector must not tell anyone that the debtor owes money. The debt collector must give written notice within five days after first contact:

1. amount debtor owes
2. who the creditor is
3. what debtor should do if money not owed.

A debt collector may not harass, oppress or abuse any person. Examples of prohibited practices include:

1. threats of violence
2. publishing lists of debtors
3. using obscene or profane language
4. repeatedly using the telephone to annoy
5. telephoning without identifying caller
6. advertising a debt
7. using false statements to collect
8. giving false credit information
9. sending the debtor fake official documents
10. using a false name
11. being unfair in collecting
    a. greater amount of date
    b. depositing post-dated check before date
    c. using postcards
    d. making debtor pay for collect calls
    e. threatening to take property without justification
    f. stationery with debtor's name

A creditor is not a debt collector. If the debtor owes several debts to a single creditor, any payment made must be applied as the debtor directs. Remedies, debtor suit in state or federal court. The statute of limitations is one year. The debtor can recover damages, attorney fees and court costs. Class actions are allowed with recovery up to $500,000. The debtor can complain to the FTC. See <u>Venes</u> v. <u>Professional Service Bureau, Inc.</u>, 353 N.W.2d 671 (1984). Repeated abusive phone calls by a debt collection agency to recover monies owed to the Mayo Clinic. The court upheld the jury verdict in favor of the debtor. The purpose of the act is to eliminate abusive debt collection practices, to protect consumers and redress their injuries.

The Electronic Fund Transfer Act sets out the liability rules governing EFTs. This includes financial payment systems using computer and electronic technology which increases speed and reduces costs and paperwork in transactions. If a consumer receives EFT services, the financial institution must disclose the following:

1.   customer liability for unauthorized use
2.   instructions for recourse for theft or loss
3.   charges and availability of systems
4.   ways to correct errors and rights concerning records
5.   rights to stop payment
6.   rules on disclosure to third parties
7.   financial institution liability
8.   transactions in writing if requested
9.   what systems are available

Financial institutions must give customers periodic statements and must notify if automatic deposit not made as scheduled. If EFT access device is lost consumer must notify within two business days after discovery, liability limited to $50; after second business day $500 ceiling; after 60 days unlimited liability. Consumers discovering errors in their statements must:

1.   notify within 60 days after receiving statement
2.   can be oral or written, must contain
      a.   account # and name
      b.   error and amount
      c.   reasons for belief
3.   financial institution -- 10 days to investigate and report to consumer, or
4.   can credit consumers account/45 days to investigate
5.   if error discovered, institution has one day to adjust account
6.   if no mistake is discovered, institution must give consumer full report
7.   financial institution that fails to abide by account terms responsible for all errors proximately caused.

The EFTA contains civil and criminal sanctions:

1.   consumer may recover
      a.   actual damages
      b.   punitive damages
            (1)   single--$100-$1,000
            (2)   class action--lesser of $500,000 or one percent of institution's net worth
2.   criminal sanctions
      a.   federal misdemeanor--not exceeding one-year imprisonment plus $5,000 fine are possible
      b.   federal felony to use fraudulent EFT device--ten-year imprisonment plus $10,000 fine.

See <u>Ognibene</u> v. <u>Citibank, N.A.</u>, 446 N.Y.S. 2d 845 (1981). The bank must prove that it disclosed to the consumer his liability for unauthorized transfers... The bank did not establish that it made such disclosures. Accordingly, it is not entitled to avail itself of the benefit of the limited liability for unauthorized transfers imposed upon consumers by the Act.

Bankruptcy is governed by the Bankruptcy Reform Act of 1978. The bankruptcy code provides two general types of relief for consumer debtors: (1) straight bankruptcy, which can be voluntary or involuntary, and (2) adjustment of debts of individuals with a regular income. Straight bankruptcy:

1. property turned over to court
2. debts canceled
3. voluntary--debtor files
4. involuntary
   a. three creditors with unsecured claims of at least $5,000 if twelve or more creditors
   b. one creditor with claim of at least $5,000 if less than twelve creditors
5. all but nonexempt property turned over to court
   a. federal exemptions
   b. states can substitute exemptions
6. priority of claims
   a. secured creditors
   b. bankruptcy administration costs
   c. debts incurred by debtor's business during bankruptcy
   d. employee wages, salary, and commission claims
   e. claims for contributions to employee benefit plans
   f. taxes
   g. general creditors
7. consumer protections of bankruptcy
   a. discharge
   b. voluntary unlimited
   c. reaffirmation of debts is harder
   d. less honest debtors can go bankrupt
   e. utility service cut-off is limited
   f. nullifying of bankruptcy clauses
   g. limits on waiver of exemptions
   h. Perez Doctrine--state law invalid if penalty or punishment for exercise of federal bankruptcy rights; see <u>Perez</u> v. <u>Campbell</u>, 402 U.S. 637 (1970)
8. limitations on bankruptcy
   a. every six years
   b. nondischargeable debts
      (1) taxes
      (2) educational loans
      (3) intentional torts
      (4) child support

(5)   fines.

Debt adjustment:

1. amount owed all creditors is reduced, maturities are extended, or some combination of the two
2. individuals with regular income with less than $100,000 in unsecured debt and $350,000 in secured debt qualifies.

1984 Bankruptcy Code amendments:

1.   those in straight bankruptcy to be advised on chapter 13 alternative
2.   power to dismiss chapter 7 petition if abuse
3.   legally intoxicated liability no longer discharged in bankruptcy
4.   "loading up" on luxury goods and services to maximize use of exemptions severely limited
    a.   consumer debts to single creditor--more than $500 for luxury goods or services within 40 days before filling--presumed non-dischargeable
    b.   also cash advances more than $1,000 on or within 20 days before filing
5.   chapter 13 unsecured creditors have veto over the plan in certain cases

Many state statutes protect consumers to some extent, including:

1.   UCC--Uniform Commercial Code
    a.   contract law
    b.   unconscionability is part of it
2.   UCCC--Uniform Commercial Credit Code
    a.   limitations on garnishment
    b.   cooling-off period for door-to-door sales
3.   Usury laws
    a.   limitations on interest rates
    b.   varies from state to state
4.   Occupational licensing statutes
    a.   regulatory--proficiency test
    b.   revenue raising--not serious offense
5.   State consumer protection agencies

Review Questions

True/False

_____ 1.   Consumers are persons buying goods or services for their personal consumption.

_____ 2.   The FTC modification of the holder in due course rule is applicable to all transactions involving commercial paper.

____ 3.   Regulation Z covers all real estate credit extended to individuals for personal, family, household, or agricultural purposes regardless of the amount.

____ 4.   One of the remedies available to the Consumer Product Safety Commission or the attorney general under the CPSA is actual seizure of products.

____ 5.   The Fair Credit Reporting Act contains protection provisions for businesses denied credit.

____ 6.   The Equal Credit Opportunity Act is applicable only to consumer loans.

____ 7.   Under the FCBA, dealers can raise retail prices for those purchasing with credit cards.

____ 8.   The Fair Debt Collections Practices Act protects business debtors.

____ 9.   Straight bankruptcy is available to businesses but not to consumers.

____ 10.   Under the 1984 Amendments to the Bankruptcy Code, a consumer may not "load up" for luxury goods on his credit card.

Multiple Choice -- Please circle the best answer.

1.   A doctrine that has benefitted consumers in the twentieth century is
   a.   caveat emptor.
   b.   privity rule.
   c.   caveat venditor.
   d.   freedom of contract.

2.   A consumer is a person who
   a.   purchases inventory for resale.
   b.   discounts commercial paper.
   c.   buys machinery for a plant.
   d.   buys a TV to watch the Alabama-Auburn game.

3.   An illegal contract is
   a.   void.
   b.   voidable.
   c.   exculpatory.
   d.   fraudulent.

4.   A retailer who instructs sales personnel not to show a low priced advertised item in favor of a higher priced item is guilty of
   a.   price fixing.
   b.   bait and switch.

     c.   fraud.
     d.   undue influence.

5.   The FTC 30-day mail order merchandise rule exempts
     a.   fly fishing equipment.
     b.   seed orders.
     c.   Mont Blanc pens.
     d.   catalogs.

6.   The Equal Credit Opportunity Act prohibits discrimination based on
     a.   wealth.
     b.   income level.
     c.   a and b.
     d.   marital status.

7.   The Fair Debt Collection Practices Act covers debt incurred for
     a.   redlining.
     b.   equipment.
     c.   household goods.
     d.   business goods.

8.   The Electronic Fund Transfer Act covers
     a.   automated teller machines.
     b.   authorization services.
     c.   electronic processing check systems.
     d.   all of the above.

9.   An individual with a regular income who wants to pay something to his creditors would
     a.   file chapter 7 Bankruptcy.
     b.   load up and pay weekly.
     c.   ask for a waiver of exemptions.
     d.   file chapter 13 Bankruptcy.

10.   A clause in a contract in which one party contracts away liability is
     a.   illegal per se.
     b.   voidable.
     c.   lawful.
     d.   against public policy.

11.   A person who makes a contract with a close relative, lawyer or business associate relying on the trust relationship of the other party as protection and there is a double-cross. This is called
     a.   fraud.
     b.   undue influence.
     c.   duress.

      d.   bad faith.

12.   Harry, a tv salesperson, tells Stewart that the tv Stewart is thinking about buying "is the best tv set on the market." This is called
      a.   fraud.
      b.   misrepresentation of fact.
      c.   puffing.
      d.   misrepresentation of law.

13.   A usual remedy for innocent misrepresentation is
      a.   compensatory damages.
      b.   punitive damages.
      c.   an injunction.
      d.   rescission and restitution.

14.   The FTC reg that modifies the Holder in Due Course Rule applies to
      a.   individual consumers.
      b.   businesses.
      c.   credit card issuers.
      d.   goods.

15.   The Truth-in-Lending Act covers this type of transaction
      a.   credit extended to individuals to purchase business equipment.
      b.   loans to local and state government.
      c.   real estate credit extended to an individual to purchase a personal residence.
      d.   to individuals for personal purposes not over $50,000.

Short Answer

1.   Give two justifications for protecting consumers.

      a.   _____

      b.   _____

2.   List four consumer protections available under common law.

      a.   _____

      b.   _____

      c.   _____

    d. _____

3.   List the six elements of fraud.

    a. _____

    b. _____

    c. _____

    d. _____

    e. _____

    f. _____

4.   State the effect of the FTC modification of the holder in due course rule.

5.   List two types of credit covered under the Truth-In-Lending Act and Regulation A.

    a. _____

    b. _____

6.   Consumers discovering errors in periodic statements under the EFTA must provide notice of the error to the financial institution that includes:

    a. _____

    b. _____

    c. _____

7.   List three forms of remedies available under the Consumer Product Safety Act.

    a. _____

b. _____

c. _____

8. The Equal Credit Opportunity Act prohibits discrimination on what bases?

a. _____

b. _____

9. Furnish the appropriate time limits for each of the following circumstances under the Fair Credit Billing Act.

a. Time within which consumer must send written billing complaint.

_____

b. Time within which creditor must explain or correct complained of error.

_____

10. List three practices prohibited under the Fair Debt Collections Practices Act.

a. _____

b. _____

c. _____

Answers to Review Questions

True/False

1. T	3. T	5. F	7. F	9. F
2. F	4. T	6. F	8. F	10. T

Multiple Choice

1.	c.	4.	b.	7.	c.	10.	d.	13.	d.
2.	d.	5.	b.	8.	a.	11.	b.	14.	a.
3.	a.	6.	d.	9.	c.	12.	c.	15.	c.

Short Answer

1.   a.   Natural law suggests such fairness.
     b.   Businesses are protected by encouraging more buying and eliminating dishonest dealers.

2.   a.   consideration
     b.   undue influence
     c.   duress
     d.   fraud
          or, innocent misrepresentation
          public policy
          illegality
          unconscionability

3.   a.   misrepresentation
     b.   of a material fact
     c.   knowledge
     d.   intent
     e.   damages
     f.   reasonable reliance

4.   Those who buy consumer installment contracts with defense waiver clause or commercial paper and who would otherwise have been holders in due course take subject to consumer claims and defenses against the seller.

5.   a.   credit extended to individuals for personal, family, household or agricultural purposes not over $25,000
     b.   all real estate credit extended to individuals for personal, family, household, or agricultural purposes regardless of amount.

6.   (it can be oral or written)
     a.   account number and name
     b.   statement that an error has been made, along with indication of amount of alleged error
     c.   the reasons the consumer believes an error has been made

7.   a.   injunction or seizure of products through commission or the attorney general
     b.   civil penalties (possible money penalty)
     c.   criminal penalties (possible fine and imprisonment)
     d.   private parties (injunction or damages if exceeding $10,000)

8.   a.   sex
     b.   marital status
     c.   national origin
     d.   race

e.   religion
f.   color
g.   age

9. a.   sixty days of receipt of bill
    b.   ninety days of receipt of complaint

10. a.   threats of violence
    b.   publishing lists of consumer names
    c.   using obscene or profane language
          or, any of the eleven tactics listed in text

Key Terms

caveat emptor: let the buyer beware; former standard of liability.

caveat venditor: let the seller beware; current standard of liability.

common law: judge-made law.

laissez faire: freedom from government restraints.

freedom of contract: making one's agreements unhampered by government.

privity rule: consumer may sue only the person who sold them the defective goods--immediate seller is ultimately responsible.

consideration: voluntary, bargained-for giving up of a right in exchange for someone else's right.

undue influence: person taking contractual advantage of a trust relationship.

duress: person committing wrongful act to obtain a contractual promise.

fraud: intentional misleading of another to obtain a contractual promise.

innocent misrepresentation: accidental misleading of another to obtain a contractual promise.

in pari delicto: equally guilty.

public policy: desirable social goals and conduct.

damnum absque injuria: a harm without legal remedy.

void contracts (illegal contracts): contracts with illegal subject matter.

exculpatory clauses: portions of contracts where a part attempts to hold itself not responsible for its own negligence.

unconscionability: extreme favorability and unfavorability on either side of a contract.

voidable: a contract that one party has the right to disaffirm.

puffing: sales talk; opinion on a product or service.

bait and switch: deceptive method of advertising to induce purchases.

promissory notes: form of commercial paper which is a promise to pay money.

commercial paper: checks, notes, and draft.

waiver of defenses clause: (in installment contracts)--clause in which purchaser waives right to assert defenses.

negotiable note: commercial paper meeting certain standards that is easily transferred.

holder in due course: good faith purchaser of negotiable instrument for value.

cooling-off period: three day rescission rights on door-to-door sales.

rescission: process of holding that a contract no longer exists.

restitution: awarding of damages so as to restore parties to their original position.

thirty-day mail order regulation: rule requiring sellers soliciting mail orders to be able to ship within thirty days.

Consumer Product Safety Act (CPSA): most important federal measure aimed at achieving product safety by direct regulation of consumer products.

Consumer Product Safety Commission (CPSC): the five-member federal agency appointed by the president to regulate consumer products.

consumer products: articles customarily produced or distributed for a consumer's personal use, consumption, or enjoyment.

product safety standards: standards issued by the CPSC that are reasonably necessary to prevent or reduce an unreasonable risk associated with a product.

imminently hazardous products: products that present an imminent and unreasonable risk of death, serious illness, or severe personal injury.

substantial product hazard: substantial risk of injury to the public.

Truth-In-Lending Act: federal law governing disclosure of cost of credit.

Regulation Z: basic regulations passed to accompany the Truth-In-Lending Act.

finance charge: charge for credit in dollars.

APR: charge for credit as a percentage of the loan.

credit card: single credit device used to get money, property, labor, or services.

accepted credit card: card requested, applied for or received and signed by a person.

redlining: loaning of money on the basis of property location rather than credit worthiness.

Fair Credit Reporting Act: federal law requiring consumer credit information.

Equal Credit Opportunity Act: federal law requiring equal opportunity for credit and prohibiting credit discrimination on basis of sex, national origin, race, religion, color, age, or marital status.

Fair Credit Billing Act: federal law requiring procedures for correcting credit card errors.

Fair Debt Collection Practices Act: federal law prohibiting abusive, deceptive, and unfair debt collection tactics.

debt collectors: those parties (not original creditors) who collect bills for others.

skip tracing: the practice of trying to locate debtors.

Electronic Fund Transfer Act (EFTA): the 1978 federal act, which in conjunction with the Federal Reserve System regulations promulgated under it, sets out liability rules under electronic fund transfers (EFTs).

EFT: abbreviation given to electronic fund transfer devices used to transmit money and may include automatic tellers, pay-by-phone services, computers, and other electronic technology.

bankruptcy: turning over of assets to court for distribution and liability discharge.

straight bankruptcy: process in which all property is returned to bankruptcy court for cancellation of debts.

voluntary/involuntary bankruptcy: voluntary is bankruptcy initiated by a debtor; involuntary is that initiated by creditors.

nonexempt property: property of debtor which must be turned over to bankruptcy court.

exempt property: property which the debtor is allowed to keep when declaring straight bankruptcy.

federal exemptions: exempt property as listed in the federal bankruptcy code.

state exemptions: exempt property as provided by state statutes.

discharge in bankruptcy: cancellation of debtor's debts.

Perez Doctrine: state law is invalid if it penalizes or punishes persons for exercising their federal bankruptcy rights.

debt adjustment: amount owed creditors is reduced or time for payment is extended or both.

UCC: Uniform Commercial Code governing law of contracts for sale of goods.

UCCC: Uniform Commercial Credit Code governing rights of consumer creditors.

usury laws: laws regulating maximum interest rates.

occupational licensing statutes: state statutes requiring licensing to act in an occupation.

CHAPTER 23

PRODUCT LIABILITY

Chapter Summary

Suits for defective goods in the nineteenth century generally favored sellers and manufacturers. The doctrine of "caveat emptor" was widely followed. Three social factors stand out: laissez-faire and freedom of contract; promotion of industrialization and buyer self-protection. Since around the turn of the century, there has been a continuing expansion of seller and manufacturer liability for defective products. Today, the rule of thumb is "caveat venditor": "Let the seller beware." Modern product liability law has come to possess at least three general features: increased government intervention/ reduction of freedom to contract; greater liability; and socialization of risk. In recent years, product liability law has come under criticism.

1. Excessive damages plaintiffs receive.
2. Increased financial burdens on sellers and manufacturers.
3. Some business unable to obtain insurance--higher insurance prices.
4. Product innovation is deterred.

Due to these concerns, a tort reform movement has emerged. To date, it has not had a major impact on product liability law. There has been no government legislation, yet.

The five major theories of product liability will be discussed. The plaintiff may employ several of these theories simultaneously. The first three theories are contract based and are created by Article 2 of the UCC. Article 2 governs the sale of goods, movable things. Services and real estate do not qualify. The last two theories are tort based.

Express warranty (2-313)--contractual promise regarding nature of goods sold.

1.   no intent is required to establish that warranty was made
    a.   promise can be made unintentionally
2.   methods of creation
    a.   affirmation of fact or promise relating to goods sold
    b.   description of goods
    c.   providing sample or model where intent is to represent quality of goods sold.
3.   value, opinion and sales talk
    a.   statements do not create warranties
    b.   some cases unclear
4.   language used must be part of the basis of the bargain
    a.   courts differ as to meaning of this phrase
5.   statements in advertisements can be express warranties; see Keith v. Buchanan, 220 Cal. Rptr. 392 1985).   Statements made by a seller in an advertising brochure can create express warranties. The statements in the brochure are specific and unequivocal in asserting that the vessel is seaworthy. The representations regarding seaworthiness were affirmations of fact relating to the quality or condition of the vessel. A warranty statement is presumptively part of the basis of the bargain.

Implied warranty of merchantability (2-314)--a warranty that the goods are of merchantable quality.

1.   promise arising by operation of law
2.   must have seller who is a "merchant"
    a.   one who deals in goods of the kind
    b.   one who by his occupation holds himself out as having knowledge or skill peculiar to the practices or goods involved in the transaction
3.   coverage
    a.   sale of goods
    b.   sale of goods with installation (sometimes)
    c.   food or drink in restaurants
    d.   must be merchant in goods of kind sold
    e.   business professional--2-104 (1)
4.   standard of merchantability
    a.   fit for ordinary purposes for which goods are used
    b.   must meet reasonable expectations of average consumer

Implied warranty of fitness.
1.   seller need not be a merchant
2.   fit for buyer's particular purpose
3.   where buyer puts himself or herself in the seller's hands and requests selection of suitable goods.
4.   less common than merchantability
5.   see Taterka v. Ford Motor Co., 271 N.W.2d 653 (1978). Rust problems do not render a car unfit for the purposes of driving and therefore unmerchantable. Where automobiles are concerned, the term "unmerchantable" has only been applied where a single defect poses a substantial hazard or numerous defects classify the car as a "lemon."

Negligence--main problem for plaintiff is proving a breach of duty on the defendant's part. To do so, plaintiffs argue that the defendant failed to act as a reasonable person would have acted under the circumstances. In product liability cases

1.   improper manufacture, packaging, handling or inspection
    a.   res ipsa loquiter may help plaintiff
    b.   wholesaler/retailer--no duty to inspect where unduly difficult, unless defect obvious
2.   duty to warn
    a.   under a duty to warn if had reason to know
        (1)   product likely to cause harm if used in a foreseeable way
        (2)   user unlikely to realize danger
3.   design defects
    a.   product should be designed so it is safe
    b.   risk benefit analysis
    c.   product safety standards
    d.   similar products
    e.   state of the art
    f.   social utility

Strict liability is liability irrespective of fault.

1.   Section 402A of Restatement of Torts is common product liability recovery theory
    a.   if elements are met there is liability regardless of care used
    b.   limited forms of defense
2.   elements
    a.   defendant must be engaged in business of selling the product whose defect is at issue
        (1)   similar to UCC merchant requirement
        (2)   manufacturers, wholesalers and retailers included
        (3)   not occasional sales by those not regularly selling it
    b.   no substantial change
        (1)   product must reach consumer without substantial change in the condition in which it was sold
        (2)   protects seller from suits on substantially modified products
    c.   defective condition unreasonably dangerous
        (1)   prove product is defective--similar standard to merchantability
        (2)   show it is unreasonably dangerous to person or property
            (a)   product must have some significant and unexpected capacity to cause personal injury or property damage
            (b)   narrower than Implied Warranty of Merchantability
3.   design defects-failure to warn
    a.   can be brought under 402A
    b.   resemble negligence cases; see Hagans v. Oliver Machinery Co., 576 F.2d 97 (1978). By designing with a removable blade guard, defendant struck a compromise that maximized the product's utility and safety. The plaintiff knew the danger of cutting

knotted wood. Oliver Machinery was not negligent in designing the saw.

Other theories of recovery:

Magnuson-Mass Act--

1.   passed in 1975
2.   applicability
    a.   consumer products
        (1) normally used for personal, family or household purposes
    b.   does not cover wholesale sales
3.   type of warranties
    a.   if giving written warranty on product costing more than $10, must designate as full or limited
    b.   full warranty--repair, remedy or replacement
        (1) seller obligated to remedy or repair the product in case of defect
        (2) enable consumer to obtain a replacement product or a refund after a reasonable number of remedy attempts
    c.   limited warranty--one not qualifying as full; seller bound to do whatever he promises

Misrepresentation--402B

1.   applies where seller makes representations about goods and then fails to conform
2.   similar to express warranty liability
3.   applies only to those in business of selling that product
4.   must be a misrepresentation of a material fact
5.   must be made to public and not individual--advertising, leaflets, etc.
6.   consumer must actually and justifiably rely on representation
7.   applies to personal injury

Industry-wide liability--

1.   some courts have dispensed with specific causation proof
    a.   defendants liable where cause unclear
        (1) standardized product
        (2) injury suffered
        (3) apportion liability among firms in industry
            (a) based on market share
            (b) examples--DES and asbestos cases

The damages a plaintiff might recover in a product liability case break down into three general categories. It is possible for a single product liability suit to involve all three types of damages. The general categories are:

1.   "basis of the bargain" damages
    a.   direct economic loss
    b.   recover value of defective goods
    c.   difference between value of the goods as contracted for and value of goods received
2.   consequential damages
    a.   personal injury--bodily harm, pain, suffering
    b.   property damage
    c.   indirect economic loss--lost profits, lost business, lost goodwill
3.   punitive or exemplary damage
    a.   punishment
    b.   awarded where conduct is reckless

Punitive damages are usually unavailable in express and implied warranty suits under the UCC. Determining the other damages can be a complex matter. An important factor is whether there was privity of contract between the plaintiff and the defendant.

1. plaintiff deals directly with the defendant--basis of the bargain damages.
2. can also various consequential damages.

Outside privity:

1. sometimes cannot recover under the UCC
2. if plaintiff can recover, types of damages are limited. Quite likely to recover personal injury; fairly likely to recover for property damage; unlikely to recover basis of the bargain damages; and quite unlikely to recover indirect economic loss.

Negligence and section 402A are best suited for obtaining personal injury, property damage and punitive damages. See Spindler v. North Central Harvestore, 656 F. Supp. 653 (1987). Under strict liability, economic losses (lost profits) are not recoverable in tort. Plaintiffs remedy lies in the UCC.

Privity of contract is the existence of a direct contractual relationship between two parties. In the nineteenth century, the absence of privity was an important defense for sellers and manufacturers of defective goods since buyers could only recover from their immediate seller (retailer). Remote parties (manufacturer, wholesaler) "outside Privity" were not subject to suit. Over the past 100 years, the old no-privity has lost a great deal of its vitality. It still may pose some problems under the UCC. Privity under the UCC is governed by Sec. 2-318 and gives the states three alternatives:

1. Alternative A--warranty extends to any person who is in the household of the buyer or is a guest in the buyer's home who suffers personal injury (majority of states).
2. Alternative B--warranty extends to any natural person who may reasonably be expected to use, consume or be affected by the goods.
3. Alternative C--much the same, allows recovery by an "person" (not just natural person) and that party must be injured.

Considerable confusion exists among the states today, although a majority adhere to Alternative A. The no-privity defense usually is ineffective in a 402A action.

Provisions are routinely included in sales contracts that disclaim the seller's liability for product defects. The main argument for enforcement is freedom of contract. Disclaimers are sometimes not enforced by the courts. Some theories of recovery are easier to disclaim than others.

Express warranty:

1.   attempt to disclaim is almost always unreasonable--why make one in the first place?

Negligence and 402A disclaimers:

1.   disclaimer is really a contractual assumption of risk
2.   disclaimers is valid only if plaintiff's assumption is knowing and voluntary--rarely effective in consumer cases
    a.   disparity in bargaining power--not voluntary
    b.   inconspicuous disclaimer--not knowing
    c.   if clear reference to negligence liability and actual negotiation--often effective in commercial cases
        (1) sophisticated parties
        (2) relatively equal bargaining power.

Disclaimers of implied warranties:

1.   merchantability
    a.   must use the term "merchantability"
    b.   if written, must be conspicuous
        (1) large or bold-faced type
        (2) different color
        (3) on back presents problems
    c.   written or oral is effective
2.   fitness
    a.   must be in writing
    b.   must be conspicuous
    c.   no particular language is required
3.   additional methods to disclaim both
    a.   "as is," "with all faults," "as they stand"
        (1) probably must be conspicuous
        (2) may not apply to new goods
    b.   actual inspection of goods by buyer or failure to inspect when seller requests
        (1) reasonably apparent defects
        (2) if obvious, disclaimer
    c.   can disclaim by

      (1) course of dealing--previous conduct between parties

      (2) course of performance--past performance by one contracting party not objected to

by   the other

      (3) usage of trade--commercial practice having wide acceptance.

Unconscionability:

1.   disclaimer may be invalid as unconscionable--grossly unfair
2.   substantive unconscionability--terms of contract
3.   procedural unconscionability--various factors which resulted in the contract terms
     a.   sales hype
     b.   difference in bargaining power
     c.   disparity of education or intelligence
     d.   high pressure sales tactics
     e.   fine print clauses
4.   courts frequently find warranty disclaimers unconscionable in consumer cases
5.   some courts will enforce the disclaimer where plaintiff is a business actor.

Maguson-Moss:

1.   if full warranty given, cannot disclaim, modify or limit
2.   if limited warranty given, can limit only its duration
3.   seller can avoid by refusing to give written warranty

See <u>Myers</u> v. <u>A. O. Smith Harvestore Products, Inc.</u>, 757 P.2d 695 (1988). The disclaimer was not part of the small print. Little in the testimony to suggest that Dale Myers was directed to ignore the disclaimer. He apparently was allowed to read it. We hold that the implied warranty claims were barred by the disclaimer.

      Remedy limitations do not attack the underlying theory of recovery but prevents plaintiffs from recovering certain damages. Most remedy limitations attempt to exclude consequential damages. In negligence and 402-A cases, remedy limitations are unlikely to be enforced in consumer cases. Under the UCC, remedy limitations are treated differently from disclaimers. UCC section 2-719(1) and 2-719(3) allow the seller to limit the buyer's remedies in express and implied warranty cases. Limitation of consequential damages may be unconscionable where plaintiff's loss is commercial (case-by-case determination). Limitation of consequential damages is presumed to be unconscionable where plaintiff has suffered personal injury resulting from the sale of consumer goods. See <u>Construction Associates, Inc.</u> v. <u>Fargo Water Equipment Co.</u>, 446 N.W.2d 237 (1989). Numerous courts have held remedy limitations unconscionable. This is particularly true where the defect is latent so that the buyer is unable to discover the defect until additional damages are incurred. Construction did not discover the defect (leaks) until the pipe was placed underground. The clause limiting remedies and excluding consequential damages was unconscionable.

      Product liability law puts a number of limitations on the time period within which suit may be brought. Most important of these are limits in statute of limitations:

1.   under UCC--four years from time the breach occurs for express or implied warranties
2.   negligence 402A and 402B--often shorter period
    a.   dated from time of injury
    b.   or dated from time defect should have been discovered.

Some states have enacted various other limitations on the time within which certain product liability suits must be brought. These rules override the state's basic tort and UCC statute of limitations. The most important of these are:

1. special statutes of limitations for delayed manifestation injuries
2. special statute of limitations involving death, personal injury and property damage
3. statutes of repose and useful-safe-life defenses.

    Defenses involving plaintiffs behavior:

1. product misuse
2. contributory negligence
3. assumption of risk
4. recent years--system of comparative fault.

Review Questions

True/False

_____ 1.   The implied warranty of merchantability is given even when there is no intent to make a warranty.

_____ 2.   The implied warranty of fitness for a particular purpose can only be given by a merchant.

_____ 3.   The seller can avoid the Magnuson-Moss Act's restrictions by refusing to give a written warranty.

_____ 4.   Consequential damages include personal injury, property damage and indirect economic loss.

_____ 5.   Section 402A damages are limited to personal injury and property damages.

_____ 6.   A disclaimer for the warranty of merchantability must be in writing.

_____ 7.   A limitation of remedies is the same thing as a warranty disclaimer.

____ 8.   It is prima facie unconscionable for a seller to exclude consequential damages where a plaintiff has suffered personal injury.

____ 9.   The 402A statute of limitations is dated from the time of the product purchase.

____ 10.   Statutes of repose run from the time the product is sold to the last person in the chain of distribution who is not buying for resale.

Multiple Choice -- Please circle the best answer

1.   Article 2 of the Uniform Commercial Code governs
      a.   the sale of goods and services.
      b.   the sale of goods.
      c.   real estate transactions.
      d.   mixed transactions.

2.   The statement, "This car has a brand new engine," is a(an)
      a.   statement of opinion.
      b.   advertisement.
      c.   affirmation of fact.
      d.   puffing.

3.   The implied warranty of fitness would not apply if the buyer
      a.   relied on the seller's skill.
      b.   informed the seller of special needs.
      c.   informed the seller that he was not familiar with goods of this type.
      d.   provided the seller with plans and specifications.

4.   An individual who sells an item at a weekend garage sale makes
      a.   an implied warranty of merchantability.
      b.   an express warranty.
      c.   no warranties.
      d.   a 402A claim.

5.   In a product liability case based on negligence, the main problem the plaintiff faces is establishing
      a.   a breach of duty.
      b.   proximate cause.
      c.   damages.
      d.   the reasonable prudent man test.

6.   Section 402A of the Restatement (second) of Torts would apply to
      a.   all sellers.

    b.   merchants.

    c.   non-merchants.

    d.   the Uniform Commercial Code.

7.   Section 402A covers a narrower range of product defects because

    a.   it does not cover goods.

    b.   it sounds in tort.

    c.   of the unreasonably dangerous requirement.

    d.   of the reliance requirement.

8.   The Magnuson-Moss Act applies to

    a.   inventory.

    b.   equipment.

    c.   consumer goods.

    d.   insurance policies.

9.   "Basis of the bargain" damages include

    a.   indirect economic loss.

    b.   direct economic loss.

    c.   property damage.

    d.   personal injury.

10.   Privity is rarely a defense in

    a.   negligence actions.

    b.   402A actions.

    c.   warranty actions.

    d.   a. and b.

11.   A remedy limitation effects

    a.   certain kinds of damages.

    b.   the plaintiff's theory of recovery.

    c.   the plaintiff's evidence.

    d.   how a plaintiff will prove a case.

12.   The use of the phrases "as is," and "with all faults," disclaim

    a.   express warranties.

    b.   strict liability.

    c.   implied warranties.

    d.   402B actions.

13.   The Statute of Limitations under the UCC is

    a.   three years.

    b.   six months.

    c.   seven years.

 d.   four years.

14.   _____ is a defense in negligence, warranty and 402A cases.
 a.   Contributory negligence
 b.   Section 25125(1)
 c.   Assumption of risk
 d.   Lack of notice

15.   The general test for merchantability is
 a.   that the good must be like all other goods.
 b.   that the good must meet the reasonable expectations of the average consumer.
 c.   that the good must meet the reasonable expectations of goods in the trade.
 d.   that the good must meet general government specifications.

Short Answer

1.   List the three features of twentieth century product liability law.

 a.   _____

 b.   _____

 c.   _____

2.   List the four contract-based theories of product liability recovery.

 a.   _____

 b.   _____

 c.   _____

 d.   _____

3.   List three ways in which an express warranty can be made.

 a.   _____

 · b.   _____

 c.   _____

4.   Briefly explain the concept of "Industry-Wide Liability" and the factors in its utilization.

_____

_____

_____

5.   List the four elements that must be established to recover under 402A.

a.   _____

b.   _____

c.   _____

d.   _____

6.   List five categories of damage in product liability cases.

a.   _____

b.   _____

c.   _____

d.   _____

e.   _____

7.   List the three types of liability limitations sellers have used.

a.   _____

b.   _____

c.   _____

8.   List three factors included as part of procedural unconscionability.

a.   _____

b.   _____

c. _____

9.   List the three major timing problems in product liability cases.

a. _____

b. _____

c. _____

10.   List four defenses available in product liability actions.

a. _____

b. _____

c. _____

d. _____

Answers to Review Questions

True/False

1. T	3. T	5. T	7. F	9. F
2. F	4. T	6. F	8. T	10. T

Multiple Choice

1. b	4. c	7. c	10. d	13. d
2. c	5. a	8. c	11. a	14. c
3. d	6. b	9. b	12. c	15. b

Short Answer

1. a. increased government intervention in economy and reduced freedom of contract
    b. greater liability for sellers and manufacturers
    c. socialization of risk--product prices increase to cover insurance

2. a. express warranty
    b. implied warranty of merchantability
    c. implied warranty of fitness for a particular purpose

        d.   Magnuson-Moss Warranty Act

3.   a.   affirmation of fact of promise relating to goods
        b.   description of goods
        c.   sample or model intended to represent quality of goods

4.   --used by few courts--lack of clarity of causation--liability regardless of whether defendants caused specific injury to plaintiff

5.   a.   defendant is seller or manufacturer of product
        b.   product reached consumer without substantial change in condition in which it was sold
        c.   product is defective
        d.   unreasonably dangerous

6.   a.   basis of the bargain damages/direct economic loss
        b.   consequential damages--personal injury
        c.   consequential damages--property damage
        d.   consequential damages--indirect economic loss (lost profits)
        e.   punitive or exemplary damages

7.   a.   warranty disclaimers
        b.   limits on warranty's duration
        c.   limits on remedies or exclusion of certain losses

8.   a.   difference in bargaining power
        b.   disparity of education, intelligence or experience
        c.   high pressure sales tactics
        d.   sales hype
        e.   fine print clauses

9.   a.   statutes of limitations
        b.   statutes of repose
        c.   notice

10.   a.   product misuse or abnormal use
        b.   contributory negligence/comparative negligence
        c.   assumption of risk
        d.   comparative fault

Key Terms

product liability: civil liability of a seller or manufacturer of defective good to purchasing or injured parties.

theories of product liability recovery: rules of law stating the things a plaintiff needs to prove in order to recover damages from a seller or manufacturer of defective goods.

caveat emptor: let the buyer beware.

laissez faire: freedom from governmental restraints.

UCC: the Uniform Commercial Code governing the law of contracts for sales of goods.

socialization of risk: economic losses caused by defective goods are effectively spread throughout society.

goods: moveable things.

express warranty: contractual promise as to the nature of the goods sold which is expressly made.

implied warranty of merchantability: contractual promise as to the nature of the goods sold which arises by operation of law.

merchant: seller who deals in goods of the kind or holds himself out as having knowledge or skills peculiar to the goods involved in the transaction.

implied warranty of fitness for a particular purpose: implied contractual promise made by seller to buyer that goods are appropriate for the buyer's needs.

negligence: tort imposing liability for unreasonable conduct.

proximate cause: involves question of necessary proximity or closeness between breach and injury in negligence.

res ipsa loquitur: "the thing speaks for itself" --method of proving breach of duty where cause of injury cannot be proven.

strict liability: liability without fault.

second restatement of torts: statement of the law of torts by the American Law Institute.

design defects: unacceptable risks of harm in a product due to faulty design.

product safety standards: standards set by the government designed to prevent or reduce unreasonable risks associated with use of a product.

state of the art: state of existing scientific and technical knowledge.

social utility: measuring the value of a product based on the demands of society and the lack of feasible alternatives to improve it.

Sec. 402A: restatement that states rule of strict liability based upon defects, failure to warn, and type of the seller.

Sec. 402B: restatement that states rule of strict liability based upon misrepresentation.

Magnuson-Moss Warranty Act: federal statute regulating warranties given on consumer products.

basis of the bargain damages: direct economic loss suffered from defective product.

consequential damages: personal injury damage, property damage, and indirect economic loss caused by defective goods.

indirect economic loss: lost profits or loss of business goodwill.

punitive damages: damages for punishment for recklessness.

incidental damages: costs of inspection, storage and transportation of defective goods.

privity: direct contractual relationship between two people.

disclaimer: contract provision whereby the seller and the buyer agree that the seller's liability for defective goods will be eliminated or limited.

remedy limitation: clause in the sales contract attempting to prevent the recovery of certain kinds of damages.

course of dealing: previous conduct between contracting parties.

course of performance: past performance by one party to a contract not objected to by the other party.

usage of trade: a commercial practice having wide acceptance in the locality or trade involved.

consumer goods: goods used for personal, family or household purposes.

statute of limitations: time within which suit on a legal matter must be brought.

statutes of repose: statutes preventing seller or manufacturer liability for goods which have been in use for extended periods of time.

safe life statute: loss must occur during the safe life of the product.

product misuse: defense where product is used in some unusual unforeseeable way and such use causes injury or loss.

contributory negligence: failure by plaintiff to act reasonably; a complete defense to negligence.

comparative negligence: defense allocating fault between plaintiff and defendant on a percentage basis.

assumption of risk: voluntary acceptance of a known risk or harm.

comparative fault: a defense available in some states which combines the above defenses and allocates liability on the basis of fault.

Federal Product Liability Act: proposed federal act not yet adopted by Congress.

24 ENVIRONMENTAL LAW: PARTICULAR FEDERAL STATUTES

Chapter Summary

Environmental law has been criticized for the following reasons: cost, benefits difficult to measure, prevents economic expansion and being elitist. GNP cannot measure all positive environmental benefits such as cleaner air and water, fewer health problems and less property damage. The following list includes some important environmental laws:

1. National Environmental Policy Act of 1969
2. Clean Water Act
3. Clean Air Act
4. Federal Noise Control Act of 1972
5. Resource Conservation and Recovery Act of 1967
6. Federal Insecticide, Fungicide and Rodenticide Act
7. Toxic Substances Control Act
8. Marine Protection, Research and Sanctuaries Act of 1972
9. Energy Supply and Environmental Coordination Act of 1974
10. Endangered Species Act
11. Safe Drinking Water Act of 1974
12. Nuclear Waste Policy Act
13. The Comprehensive Environmental Response Compensation and Liability Act.

International environmental includes treaties such as:

1. Antarctic Treaty
2. International Convention for the Regulation of Whaling

3.   Agreement on the Conservation of Polar Bears

There are many environmental protection statutes on the state and municipal level.

The National Environmental Policy Act (NEPA) of 1969 does three things:

1. establishes Council on Environmental Quality
2. requires federal agencies to take the environment into account when they act
3. requires federal agencies to prepare detailed statements of environmental effects of projects called environmental impact statements (EISs) in certain situations.

To put a national environmental policy into operation, NEPA recognizes these specific responsibilities:

1. fulfill responsibility as trustee of environment for future generations
2. assure for all Americans a healthy, productive and culturally pleasing surrounding
3. attain widest use of beneficial use of resources without degradation or risk to health
4. preserve historic, cultural and natural aspects of heritage
5. achieve balance between population and resources for high standard of living
6. enhance quality of renewable resources and recycling depletable resources.

NEPA says that each person should enjoy (not will or has a right to) a healthful environment. NEPA requires federal administrative agencies to prepare environmental impact statements (EISs) in two cases:

1. when the agency sends a proposed law to Congress
2.   also prepared when agency proposes action significantly affecting the quality of the human environment.

EIS must contain:

1. environmental impact of proposed action
2. any adverse environmental effects of the action
3. alternatives to the proposed action
4. relation between short-term uses of the environment and the maintenance and enhancement of long-term productivity
5. any irreversible and irretrievable resource commitments.

Nothing happens if a federal agency fails to prepare an EIS unless someone sues the agency. A court can enjoin (stop) a project until an EIS is prepared. EISs are to be no longer than 150 pages under ordinary circumstances. A federal agency can be sued if the EIS is inadequate--project can be stopped. A member of the public can obtain an EIS. Public also has a right to participate in writing an EIS. Unless an agency prepares an EIS, the agency's conferral of a permit to a business could be invalid. See Sierra Club v. U.S. Forest Service, 842 F.2d 1990 (1988). Because substantial questions have been raised concerning the potential adverse effects of harvesting timber sale, an EIS should have been prepared. The Forest Service failed to account for factors necessary to determine whether significant impacts would occur. The court issued an injunction halting further logging.

The EPA tries to control water pollution. The Clean Water Act set goals in stages: 1983--swimmable, fishable waters, 1985--zero discharge of pollutants. The act tries to stop water pollution by making it illegal to discharge pollutants from point sources into waters of the U.S. without an NPDES permit.

Definition of water pollution:

1.   pollutant--anything foreign to water in its natural state
2.   waters
    a.   any water--all effect interstate commerce
    b.   require National Pollutant Discharge Elimination System permit to release in any water
        (1) obtained by EPA
        (2) limit set in permit of what can be put in water.

The EPA is directed to conduct studies that tell which pollutants are harmful and how harmful they are. The Clean Water Act set out phases of pollution control for point source dischargers to meet:

1.   municipalities--treatment BPT 1983
2.   Industrial dischargers BAT 1983--stricter
    a.   have limitations on waste--"effluent limitations"
    b.   pretreatment required
3.   natural runoffs not regulated.

Understanding EPA's water pollution regulations requires knowledge of two other ideas:

1. effluent guidelines--EPA sets ranges of discharge for each of 27 industrial groups
2. effluent limitations--within an industrial group, a particular plant dumping waste directly into a stream would have an effluent limitation set for it.

Midcourse corrections tried to toughen treatment of extremely dangerous water pollutants (toxins) and loosen up on less harmful pollutants. Three broad groups of pollutants established:

1. convention pollutants--best conventional treatment
2. toxins--best available treatment--BAT (strict)
3. nonconventional--BAT.

Amendments in 1977 authorized EPA to issue best management practices regulations to control plant operations to restrict toxic runoff and hazardous materials. Either private parties or governmental bodies can enforce the act. Governmental units may bring either civil suits (stop dumping) or criminal suits. Violators are liable for damages, civil penalties, cleanup costs, fines (up to $25,000 per day), and prison terms of up to one year. See U.S. v. Frezzo Bros., Inc., 602 F.2d 1123 (1979). Courts will put business people in jail and impose stiff fines if they dump pollutants into streams without having

NPDES permits.

In 1987, Congress passed the Water Quality Act of 1987--amends the Clean Water Act--fine tunes CWA.

1. Negligent violations of NPDES permits or negligently dumping pollutant into a sewer system--fines of at least $2,500 to a maximum of $25,000 per day or one year in prison or both. Repeat offenders--double maximum for first violations.
2. Knowing violations--fines of no less than $5,000 per day and not more than $50,000 per day or imprisonment of three years, or both.
3. Knowing endangerment--up to $250,000 or imprisonment up to 15 years or both. Organizations--up to $1 million. (Places another imminent danger of death or serious bodily injury.)
4. Knowingly making a material false statement in a report, record or document filed under the act-- fine of not more than $10,000, imprisoned up to two years, or both.
5. Civil penalties increased to a maximum of $25,000 per day. Good faith compliance may be a defense.
6. Administrative penalties can be assessed by EPA.
7. Introduces concept of anti-backsliding.

Congress passed the Clean Air Act in 1963. Original act did not define air pollution and weak enforcement procedures.

Amendments 1965:

1.   set emission standards for mobile sources
2.   economic and technical feasibility defenses still available.

Amendments 1967:

1.   states required to establish ambient air quality standards
2.   states required to establish implementation standards to achieve standards
3.   defenses still available.

Amendments 1970:

1.   defined air pollution
2.   eliminated economic and technical feasibility loophole
3.   established primary air quality standards
      a.   protection of public health
      b.   1975--compliance
4.   established secondary standards
      a.   protect public welfare
      b.   goal of sometime after 1975
5.   pollutants covered

    a.   hydrocarbons
    b.   carbon dioxide
    c.   sulfur dioxide
    d.   nitrogen dioxide
    e.   particulates
    f.   photochemical oxidants
    g.   expansion of pollutants covered is permitted
    h.   new standards can be set for products.

Basic air pollution concepts under the Clean Air Act:

1. Air Quality Control Region (AQCR)
    a.   U.S. divided into 247 regions
    b.   similar topography, climates, etc.
2. criteria
    a.   scientific studies setting forth parameters for primary and secondary standards
    b.   provide support for decisions on what standards will be--ambient air quality standards.
3. State implementation plans (SIP)
    a.   plan each state submits for compliance with standards
    b.   includes state and local statutes and compliance schedules

Enforcement

1.   EPA can require installation of equipment
2.   EPA has right of entry and inspection
3.   civil sanctions--citizen rights
4.   criminal penalties of up to $25,000 per day and one year in prison
5.   regulates vehicle construction and fuel.

In August 1977, Clean Air Amendments became law. Some standards were relaxed.

1.   extended auto emissions deadline
2.   catalytic converter regulations
3.   regulations preventing deterioration of significantly clean air
    a.   Class I--parks--little deterioration permitted
    b.   Class II--moderate deterioration permitted
    c.   Class III--significant deterioration permitted
4.   non-attainment areas
    a.   areas not meeting air quality requirements
    b.   preconstruction review to assure no future pollution
    c.   proposal of emission offset
5.   sets penalty for industry noncompliance
    a.   economic impact statements for new regulations under the Clean Air Act.

See <u>Chevron</u> v. <u>National Resources Defense Council</u>, 467 U.S. 837 (1984). A state may treat all of the pollution-emitting devices within the same industrial grouping as though they were encased within a single "bubble." The Supreme Court upheld the bubble policy.

See <u>United States</u> v. <u>Haney Chevrolet, Inc.</u>, 371 F. Supp. 381 (1974). Haney Chevrolet tampered with a Corvette's pollution control equipment. The court upheld a civil penalty of $500 against Haney.

In November, the 1990 Amendments to the Clean Air Act were signed into law. Most of the Clean Air Acts structure--such as SIPs and primary and secondary air quality standards remain.

1. stricter emission limits for cars
2. provisions to slow destruction of the earth's ozone layer
3. sections to control acid rain and toxic pollutants
4. compensation to workers displaced under the act.

In 1965, Congress passed the Solid Waste Disposal Act. First federal statute to deal with dumping's effect on the environment. Gave money for state and local disposal research. Congress amended this act when it passed the Resource Recovery Act of 1970.

1. recognized economic benefits of recycling
2. gave federal funds to urban areas with severe solid waste problems.

The Resource Conservation and Recovery Act of 1976 (RCRA).

1.   regulates hazardous and nonhazardous waste
2.   defines solid wastes to include waste solids, sludges, liquids and contained gases
3.   defines hazardous wastes
4.   creates a manifest system which is similar to a permit system--applies only to hazardous waste
5.   sanctions
      a.   civil--up to $25,000 per day per violation
      b.   criminal--one year and/or $25,00 per day per violation
            (1)   corporations and responsible employees can be criminally liable; see <u>U.S.</u> v. <u>Johnston & Towers, Inc.</u>, 741 F.2d 662 (1984). We hold that the Act covers employees as well as owners and operators of the facility who knowingly treat, store, or dispose of any hazardous waste.

The Toxic Substance Control Act (TOSCA) does the following:

1. EPA given task of regulating toxic substances
2. can regulate chemicals over their entire life cycle
3. EPA requires inventory and notification by manufacturers and imposes recordkeeping requirements
4. EPA can stop manufacture of chemicals
5. EPA has burden of establishing if new chemical causes an unreasonable risk
6. complaints about costs and enforcement.

The Nuclear Waste Policy Act (NWPA) (1982) mandates that the federal government construct and operate nationally at least two high-level waste dumps. The NWPA has an elaborate process to decide which state will receive the dump. President can approve or disapprove but must recommend one site to Congress. Congress ultimately decides. EPA has authority to issue regs to protect the general environment from off-site nuclear releases from the dump site. See Natural Resources Defense Council v. U.S.E.P.A., 842 F.2d 1258 (1987). Several states and several environmental groups argued that the EPA should use its authority under the Safe Drinking Water Act to stop on-site nuclear contamination. Court held that because EPA did not consider the interrelationship of high level waste rules and the Safe Drinking Water Act and thus either failed to reconcile the two standards or to adequately explain divergence--act of agency was arbitrary and capricious.

The Comprehensive Environmental Response Compensation and Liability Act (CERCLA) was passed by Congress to clean up waste dumps and created the "superfund" to assist the federal government with the task. After the cleanup, the government bills the dump's present owners as well as transporters of hazardous wastes to the dump. See U.S. v. Fleet Factors Corp., 901 F.2d 1550 (1990). The court adopts the rule that a secured creditor may incur Sec. 9607(a)(2) CERCLA liability by participating in the financial management of a facility to a degree indicating a capacity to influence the corporation's treatment of hazardous waste. Secured creditor need not involve itself in the day-to-day operations of the facility. Nor is it necessary for the secured creditor to participate in management decisions relating to hazardous waste. Fleet's involvement with the facility was within the parameters of the secured creditor exemption to liability.

The Endangered Species Act of 1973 prohibits federal money from being spent on any federal agency project that would wipe out a fish, plant, or wild animal species off the face of the earth. The act authorizes the U.S. Secretary of the Interior to designate those species that were endangered. Act imposes fines on private parties caught transporting, buying, selling, importing, or exporting endangered species. A second-tier review committee has the power to exempt a project from the act.

Three discernable stages in U.S. environmental law have taken place in the last 40 years.

1. Window dressing stage--1948 to the mid-1950s. Recognition of problems, but no solutions.
2. Hue and cry--1965 until about 1977. Public outcry caused passage of enabling acts, authorized federal agencies to make regulations.
3. Hard look stage--flood of federal regulations led to this present stage. Businesses faced with incredible pollution control costs question environmental control. Demand cost-benefit analysis and data on which studies are based. Business seldom had the right to cross-examine federal agency experts. Agency must answer reviewing court's questions.

As a result of stage 3, changes have occurred in environmental laws:

1. loosening of regs of less harmful pollutants--greater control on toxins
2. development of bubble policy
3. emission offsets
4. marketable pollution rights.

Review Questions

True/False

_____ 1.   State governmental agencies are required to file EIS under federal regulations.

_____ 2.   Failure to file an EIS will result in sanctions only if private suit is brought.

_____ 3.   GNP generally does recognize environmental improvements.

_____ 4.   NEPA has broad powers to correct many kinds of environmental harm.

_____ 5.   Any member of the public can obtain an EIS.

_____ 6.   Every point source discharger is required to have and NPDES permit.

_____ 7.   Effluent limitations refer only to solid wastes.

_____ 8.   Best management practices are under the control of the EPA.

_____ 9.   Air quality control regions are set by the EPA.

_____ 10.   States are responsible for implementation of clean air standards.

Multiple Choice -- Please circle the best answer

1.   The National Environmental Policy Act (NEPA) gives people
      a.   a right to a healthy environment.
      b.   an opportunity to enjoy a healthy environment.
      c.   a cause of action for lung cancer.
      d.   a right not to live by a nuclear waste dump.

2.   The NEPA requires a federal agency environmental impact statement (EIS) when
      a.   required to do so by Congress.
      b.   adverse environmental effects may not occur.
      c.   there are alternatives to a proposed action.
      d.   the agency sends a proposed law to Congress.

3.   The Clean Water Act tries to stop water pollution by making it illegal
      a.   to discharge waste without an NPDES permit.
      b.   to discharge pollutants from point sources into the waters of the U.S.
      c.   to discharge pollutants from all sources into the rivers of the U.S.
      d.   not to use the best practicable treatment control by 1980.

4.   The 1977 amendments to the Clean Air Act extended the auto emission reduction deadline for
      a.   unburned hydrocarbons to 1980.
      b.   nitrogen oxide to 1990.
      c.   carbon monoxide to 1991.
      d.   all pollutants to 1995.

5.   The Resource Conservation and Recovery Act of 1976 does not cover
      a.   waste solids.
      b.   sludges.
      c.   contained gases.
      d.   industrial discharge.

6.   The Toxic Substances Control Act (TOSCA) requires
      a.   the EPA to regulate the disposal of all chemicals.
      b.   the EPA to be notified of all new chemical substances.
      c.   the EPA to issue an inflation impact statement.
      d.   chemical companies to prove that chemicals are safe.

7.   Under the Nuclear Waste Policy Act, the _____ has the final authority in determining the location of a nuclear waste dump.
      a.   president
      b.   Congress
      c.   EPA
      d.   states

8.   The decision of the Secretary of the Interior declaring a species to be endangered
      a.   is final within the agency.
      b.   may be reviewed within the agency.
      c.   may not be reversed by Congress.
      d.   is final period.

9.   The "bubble policy" is an example of
      a.   strict enforcement.
      b.   the emission offset policy.
      c.   the hard look policy.
      d.   marketable pollution rights.

10.   The NEPA requires the environmental impact statement (EIS) to include the following:
      a.   environmental impact.
      b.   alternatives to proposed action.
      c.   adverse environmental effects.
      d.   all of the above.

11.   Failure to prepare an EIS has the following effect on the agency:
    a.   Congressional reprimand.
    b.   nothing happens.
    c.   court will issue an injunction.
    d.   none of the above.

12.   The Clean Water Act adopts a(an) _____ definition of water.
    a.   EPA.
    b.   limited.
    c.   commerce clause.
    d.   point source.

13.   What type of treatment is required for toxins under the 1977 Amendments to the Clean Water Act?
    a.   best available treatment.
    b.   best conventional treatment.
    c.   best management practices.
    d.   bubble policy.

14.   The 1987 Amendments to the Clean Water Act
    a.   make structural changes in the CWA.
    b.   retains the NPDES permit system.
    c.   rejects the concept of point source discharger.
    d.   does away with criminal penalties.

15.   The 1967 Amendments to the Clean Air Act
    a.   gave primary authority to the federal government.
    b.   gave primary authority to the states.
    c.   defined air pollution.
    d.   established private suit divisions.

Short Answer

1.   List five environmental laws.

    a.   _____

    b.   _____

    c.   _____

    d.   _____

e. _____

2. List the three purposes of NEPA.

a. _____

b. _____

c. _____

3. List the five content requirements for an EIS.

a. _____

b. _____

c. _____

d. _____

e. _____

4. What are point source dischargers?

_____

_____

5. What are the three types of water pollutants established under the 1977 Amendments to the Clean Water Act?

a. _____

b. _____

c. _____

6. What penalties exist under the Clean Air Act?

_____

7. What are major noise sources under the Noise Control Act?

a. _____

b. _____

c. _____

8.   List the five prohibited acts under the Noise Control Act.

a. _____

b. _____

c. _____

d. _____

e. _____

9.   What are the two goals of the Resource Conservation and Recovery Act of 1976?

a. _____

b. _____

10.   What is the purpose of the Endangered Species Act?

_____

_____

_____

_____

Answers to Review Questions

True/False

1.	F	3.	F	5.	T	7.	F	9.	T
2.	T	4.	F	6.	T	8.	T	10.	T

Multiple Choice

1.	b.	4.	a.	7.	b.	10.	d.	13.	a.
2.	d.	5.	d.	8.	b.	11.	b.	14.	b.
3.	b.	6.	b.	9.	c.	12.	c.	15.	b.

Short Answer

1.   a.   National Environmental Policy Act
        b.   Clean Water Act
        c.   Clean Air Act
        d.   Federal Noise Control Act
        e.   Resource Conservation and Recovery Act or, any other of the statutes listed in the text

2.   a.   established CEQ
        b.   requires federal agencies to take environmental factors into account when proposing projects
        c.   requires federal agencies to prepare and EIS when proposing major action.

3.   a.   environmental impact of the proposed action
        b.   adverse environmental effects of the proposed action
        c.   alternatives to proposed action
        d.   relation between short-term uses and maintenance or enhancement of long-term productivity

4.   Municipalities, farms, businesses discharging directly from pipe or outlet into U.S. waters

5.   a.   conventional
        b.   non-conventional
        c.   toxic

6.   criminal--$25,000 per day and /or one year
        citizen suits for civil damages and penalties

7.   a.   appliances
        b.   vehicles and transportation equipment
        c.   machinery

8.   a.   manufacturers selling nonconforming new products in interstate commerce
        b.   defeating noise control devices by removing or rendering them inoperative.
        c.   distributing noisy products without labels
        d.   removing noise labels
        e.   importing foreign products in violation of noise standards

9.   a.   control management of solid waste
        b.   encourage resource conservation and recovery

10.   disallow spending of money on any federal agency project which would wipe a fish, plant or wild animal species from existence

Key Terms

environmental ethic: school of thought seeking to strike a balance between present consumption and future maintenance.

pollution: any unwanted substance.

nondiscretionary duty: function of an agency that is mandatory.

Clean Water Act (FWPCA): environmental law regulating water pollution.

RCRA: Resource Conservation and Recovery Act of 1976.

Clean Air Act: environmental law regulating air pollution.

FIFRA: Federal Insecticide, Fungicide and Rodenticide Act.

Ocean Dumping Act: Marine Protection and Sanctuaries Act.

ESECA: Energy Supply and Coordination Act of 1974.

Endangered Species Act: environmental preservation act.

Surface Mining Control and Reclamation Act: act regulating surface mining.

Safe Drinking Water Act of 1974: act regulating standards for drinking water.

Wild and Scenic Rivers Act: preservation act.

Alaska Lands Act of 1980: preservation act.

EPA (Environmental Protection Agency): federal agency concerned with pollution control.

CEQ (Council on Environmental Quality): council appointed by the president to publish information on the environment and oversee other agencies in their environmental roles.

Department of the Interior: federal agency enforcing environmental laws.

National Resources Defense Council: private environmental group.

National Environmental Policy Act: federal law establishing the CEQ, requiring federal agencies to consider environmental impact in their actions and prepare EISEs.

point sources: pipe or outlet.

NPSES permits: National Pollutant Discharge Elimination System--system for discharge.

effluent limitations: limit on waste dumped into water.

effluent guidelines: guidelines on water waste dumping.

best conventional treatment (BCT): control required for conventional pollutants.

best available treatment (BAT): strictest standards of control required for toxics and nonconventional pollutants.

pretreatment: treatment of sewage prior to its discharge.

BCT control: best conventional treatment.

conventional pollutants: pollutant classification under Clean Water Act of 1977.

nonconventional pollutants: pollutant classification under Clean Water Act of 1977.

toxic pollutants: pollutant classification under Clean Water Act of 1977.

best management practices: standard of control permitting management of waste.

anti-backsliding: prevents reissuance of an NPDES permit with less stringent limits than the permit it replaces.

Clean Air Act: federal legislation regulating air pollution.

ambient air quality standards: air quality standards established by states.

state implementation plans: plans by states to achieve ambient air quality.

primary air quality standards: ambient or general environmental standards.

secondary standards: air standards for public welfare protection.

direct emission standards: standards regulating release of pollutants.

standards of performance: standards for equipment for new pollutant sources.

air quality control region: twenty-seven areas designated as areas of control on the basis of common topography and climates.

air quality control region (AQCR) criteria: scientific standards for parameters on primary and secondary ambient air quality.

nondeterioration standards: standards preventing further pollution.

mobile sources: autos and moving sources of air pollution.

prevention of significant deterioration: regulations preventing pollution of air above ambient standards.

preconstruction review mechanism: review of plants before construction for environmental effects.

emission offset policy: policy of limiting emissions or controlling.

economic impact statement: impact and cost of pollution control.

noncriteria pollutants: pollutants not regulated.

greenhouse effect: effect of carbon dioxide pollution.

SIP: state implementation plan for achieving air quality.

Noise Control Act: federal legislation regulating noise pollution.

noise emission limits: limitations on noise pollution.

major noise sources: sources identified as major noise pollutants (appliances, vehicles, etc.)

retrofit requirements: products manufactured before noise standards don't have to meet requirements.

Solid Waste Disposal Act: federal legislation controlling garbage disposal.

open dumping: trash disposal in dumps.

Resource Recovery Act: federal legislation providing funds for recycling and curing of urban areas.

RCRA's manifest system: dumping permit system.

Toxic Substances Control Act (TSCA): federal legislation giving the EPA authority to regulate the manufacture, use and disposal of toxic substances.

PMN (premanufacture notice): notice prior to manufacture of toxic substance.

Endangered Species Act: federal legislation prohibiting spending of money or federal funds which would destroy a species.

bubble policy: examination of pollution by factory rather than smokestack.

emission offsets: allow new pollution for reduction in old pollution.

marketable pollution rights: selling of right to pollute.